TICKET TO TOLTEC

The first excursion on the San Juan Extension reached Toltec Gorge October 4, 1880 with famous western photographer William H. Jackson on board. A newspaper article described the trip: "Mr. Jackson is busy, for the scenes about him call forth the highest exercise of his art, and his camera is perched now here, and now there upon every point or overhanging cliff." This Jackson photograph is not dated, but it is easy to imagine that those passengers on the first excursion posed for a similar photograph. This scene must have been taken after the one on p. 19, because the telegraph poles are in place and are notched for cross-arms.

(Colorado Historical Society)

TICKET TO TOLTEC

A MILE BY MILE GUIDE®
for the
CUMBRES & TOLTEC SCENIC
RAILROAD

by
Doris B. Osterwald

Western Guideways, Ltd.

Publisher – Guidebooks · Railroad and Western History
PO Box 343 · Hugo, Colorado 80821 · 719/743-6818

Second Printing, 1993
Third Printing, 1994
Fourth Printing, 1996
Fifth Printing, 1998
Sixth Printing, 2000
Seventh Printing, 2001
Eighth Printing, 2002
Ninth Printing, 2004

International Standard Book Number 0-931788-27-7

Color Separations by
LithoColor
Denver, Colorado

Electronic imagesetting by
National Teleprinting, Inc.
Denver, Colorado

Printed by
Golden Bell Press

Set in Monotype Abadi Light, Abadi Extra Bold, & Calisto PostScript typefaces

For

Ray, Carl, and Becky

with love

ON A PERSONAL NOTE

In the 36 years since my family and I first started watching and riding trains across Cumbres Pass, many changes have taken place and a new generation is discovering the pleasure of a leisurely ride on the C&TS narrow gauge. I hope this new edition and subsequent printings continue to document the growth of the railroad since its beginning in 1970 when volunteers (including my family) helped move equipment from Antonito to Chama Through the years, volunteers have continued to be a vital part in keeping this railroad operating.

I particularly wish to acknowledge and thank the staff of the C&TS Railroad, General Manager Joe C. Vigil, Safety & Compliance Officer Earl G. Knoob, Trainmaster Gerald M. Blea, Chief Mechanical Officer John Bush, and Executive Director of the Cumbres & Toltec Scenic Railroad Commission, Leo Schmitz, for their interest and support. Each was always willing to answer questions and was most helpful. I spent two delightful evenings with Gerald Blea and his family looking at his large collection of photographs taken during his years of service on the C&TS. His photographs are an important addition to the book. Earl Knoob offered a number of old, historic photos from his collection, which fill several gaps in the photographic record of the line, and he graciously reviewed the manuscript for accuracy.

Jackson C. Thode offered me old photographs from his extensive collection and we spent a wonderful afternoon going through old D&RGW records to document the wreck of engine 489 in May 1926. Jim Ozment graciously projected slides of his recent excursions on the C&TS and I am pleased to include several of his photographs. Margaret and Clif Palmer shared their photographs of movies made in the Chama area and of the Gramps oil field. Les Jarrett, of Railway Productions, provided his videos and offered suggestions for this edition.

Bill Lock, of the <u>Friends of the C&TS Railroad</u>, prodded me into undertaking this revision, and I am most appreciative of his interest and help in many ways, including editing the chapters on the accomplishments of the <u>Friends</u> and on the tank cars. He too offered photographs of the volunteers at work restoring and preserving the C&TS. To Charles Albi and the staff of the Colorado Railroad Museum, my thanks for searching out answers to a number of questions. The cover was designed by artist Stuart Leuthner. The cover photographs at Toltec Gorge are mine; the photograph of the doubleheaded train entering "The Narrows" was taken by my daughter, Becky. My thanks to Tom Cardin and Earl Knoob who contributed photographs for the 2001 printing.

As always, each of my family helped in ways too numerous to list. Ray helped immeasurably with rewriting and updating the railroading history, while Carl redrafted the guide maps and ably handled the layout using a Macintosh computer. My heartfelt thanks to all.

TABLE OF CONTENTS

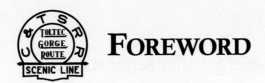

FOREWORD

This new edition of *Ticket to Toltec* gives a greatly expanded view of the history and operation of the Cumbres & Toltec Scenic Railroad since 1970. It offers a window for the reader to enjoy a ride on what has been described as one of "America's best working museums."

To make the text easier to read, guides for both direction of travel are included. Many newly acquired photographs have been added to this edition.

The author has dedicated innumerable hours of research to present accurate and informative material to better acquaint the reader with how the railroad became a reality and how it has continued to be a project that affects the lives of many individuals. *Ticket to Toltec* recognizes the tremendous effort and time given by volunteers who were, and still are, involved in the restoration, operation, and interpretation of this unique project.

Working with Doris was exciting. We knew her work would entail much dedicated effort which now allows the reader to more fully enjoy our special narrow gauge railroad.

We hope you will enjoy and appreciate this wonderful interpretation by a beautiful friend, Doris Osterwald.

Joe C. Vigil
General Manager,
Cumbres & Toltec Scenic Railroad

10

Index Map of
The Cumbres & Toltec Scenic Railroad
Between
Antonito, Colorado & Chama, New Mexico
With Outlines of Individual Guide Maps

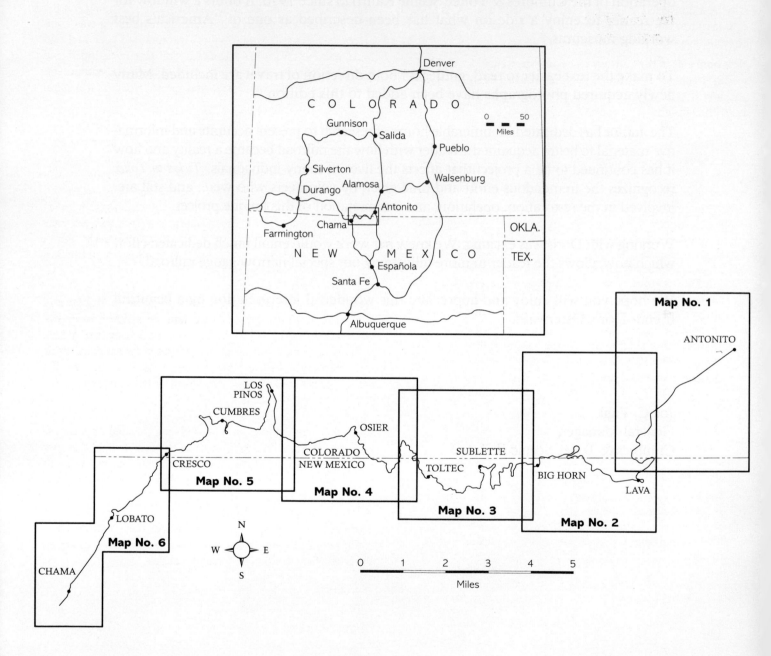

INTRODUCTION

Welcome aboard the Cumbres & Toltec Scenic Railroad. You are about to embark on an unforgettable trip on America's longest and highest narrow gauge steam railroad. The car in which you ride may have been built as recently as 1987 or it may be a converted freight car that once hauled supplies and equipment to the mines in the San Juan Mountains and ore concentrates from the mines to the smelters.

Nowhere else in the country can you experience the thrill of seeing a secluded, virtually unspoiled area from an open gondola that once carried coal, ore, gravel, crushed rock, and other freight.

So let's step back into the late nineteenth century for a day, and enjoy the scenery and train trip as earlier tourists did, even though we are not on a fancy passenger train operated by the Denver and Rio Grande Railway Company (D&RG). One such train was described in the March 31, 1881 issue of the Pueblo, Colorado *Weekly Colorado Chieftan:*

> **A complete passenger train consisting of an express, baggage, mail car, two coaches, and two pullman sleepers passed through this city yesterday afternoon for the San Juan Division, and will be put into service on that division when the new timetable takes effect.**

One question frequently asked is why in the world was this remote, meandering route chosen by the Denver & Rio Grande Railway to reach the booming mining camps in the San Juan Mountains? Why did the D&RG locating engineers choose the Cumbres Pass route instead of other routes they surveyed?

To quote from the Annual Report of the railroad for 1880:

> **...Our engineering parties had been examining the mountain range dividing the waters of the Rio Grande from the waters of the San Juan, with a view of securing the best line to the town of Silverton, in the heart of the San Juan mining country.**

> **Lines were run over Cunningham Pass, South Fork Pass, and Alamosa Pass, and barometric examinations made of other parts of the range, and late in the summer of 1879 the route along which we are now constructing was adopted.**

The Cumbres Pass route appears to have been a compromise, at it was not nearly as high as Cunningham Pass, and thus less difficult to build and maintain, but it was much longer. (Probably no records were available as to the huge amounts of snow that Cumbres Pass received most winters!) Grading for the New Mexico Extension southward from Alamosa was completed and the company town of Antonito had been laid out. Also, the Park View and Conejos Toll Road was open and offered an easy way to transport grading crews and equipment, as the projected railroad followed the toll road in a general way.

The accessible coal deposits west of Chama may have been another reason that this route was selected. Handling coal shipments was one more source of revenue for the struggling railroad. In addition, there was the distinct possibility that the AT&SF might build a line to the San Juans from the south and compete with the Rio Grande for the lucrative mining business. It was thought that the Cumbres Pass route would forestall any such construction by the Santa Fe. More details on the construction and history of the San Juan Extension are on p. 18.

Before we leave the station this morning, the conductor will explain safety regulations that will be strictly enforced. Please listen; do not let an accident spoil your trip. When moving around in your car or walking between coaches or to the open gondola car, brace yourself against any sudden jostling. Do not throw anything out of the cars; trash cans are provided for your use.

So sit back, relax and enjoy a leisurely trip through the vastness of the southern San Juan Mountains. Be grateful that this very special 64-miles of narrow gauge track, buildings and assorted rolling stock have been preserved as a living museum for future generations to enjoy.

The train travels about 12 to 22 miles per hour, which allows plenty of time to enjoy each new viewpoint and photograph all the magnificent scenery. Have a great day.

HISTORY

EARLY MAN IN THE SAN LUIS VALLEY

At least 15,000 years ago, the Rio Grande Valley of New Mexico and Colorado was home to Paleoindians who hunted mastodons and mammoths along the fertile watercourse. Archeological evidence indicates that nomadic tribes of hunters wandered back and forth along the Rio Grande Valley where there was a great diversity of plants and animals. For centuries, these early Indians followed animal migrations in their never-ending search for food; a successful hunt brought food, clothing and necessary tools and implements needed for survival. They also collected obsidian from San Antonio Peak to make weapon points and mined turquoise in the San Luis Valley.

Sometime between 1 A.D. and 900 A.D. descendents of those earliest Paleoindians still lived along the Rio Grande, as well as in the warmer valleys of southwestern Colorado and the San Juan Basin. They first lived in caves, later in crude pit houses, and when the Indians became more sedentary and began farming, they built distinctive pueblo-style houses and cliff dwellings. From 1276 A.D. to 1299 A.D. a great drought in the southwest forced the Indians to abandon their homes and the the golden age of the Anasazi culture ended. When Indians of the Colorado Plateau left their homes, it is believed, they migrated southward to the rich bottomlands of the lower Rio Grande and its tributaries.

Early European explorers, who ventured into the Great Plains and Rocky Mountains, found nomadic Indian tribes living in small villages. The explorers mistakenly assumed that each tribe had lived for hundreds or thousands of years in the same area in which they were first found. Indians moved from place to place following animal migrations. Many tribes had lived in one place less than 100 years. These nomadic tribes had no real sense of land ownership, believing instead that they should cherish and care for the land for the benefit of all.

Indian migrations from other parts of the West brought many different Indian tribes into the region. Sometimes these tribes lived together peacefully; sometimes there were violent wars. Early Spanish documents reveal that different bands of the Ute nation were scattered throughout Colorado.

Formal Spanish expeditions (Entradas) into northern New Mexico began in 1540 and for the next 140 years the Spanish attempted to colonize the area. The Spanish felt it was entirely proper to take the land from the "heathens" in the name of Christianity and the Spanish crown. There were five formal expeditions into New Mexico and the southwest.

The first recorded entry of the Spanish into the San Luis Valley was in 1694 when De Vargas explored the land north of Santa Fe while searching for a band of Utes who had raided the Taos Pueblo. His soldiers and Indian allies ran out of food and were attacked by the Utes near what is now Antonito. Throughout the 1700s, the Utes, Comanches, Navajos, and Prairie Apaches living in northern New Mexico and southern Colorado fought many battles—mostly over favorite hunting grounds or to raid each other for horses and/or Indians to serve their new owners as slaves.

Trappers, hunters, and scouts came into the San Luis Valley from time to time, but after 1821, when Mexico declared its independence from Spain, the valley became the northern frontier of the Mexican state of Nuevo Mejico. In order to colonize the area and to reinforce Mexican claims to this land, the Mexican government began to give large grants of land to Mexican citizens who would promise to settle in the region. The first attempt by the Mexicans to settle in the San Luis Valley was along the Conejos River in 1833. It did not take the Utes long to attack and drive those settlers away.

War between Mexico and the United States erupted in 1846 and U.S. Gen. Stephen W. Kearney marched into Santa Fe to claim possession of New Mexico for the United States. Two years later the war ended when both countries signed the Treaty of Guadalupe-Hildalgo. The United States paid Mexico $15,000,000 for land that is now New Mexico, Arizona, California, and a portion of the southern San Luis Valley. Under terms of the treaty, the United States agreed to honor the land grants given Mexican families by the Mexican government, if they could prove a clear title. The Conejos Land Grant in the San Luis Valley was rejected by the United States because of non-compliance with the terms for settlement by the Mexicans.

Indian troubles did not end in the San Luis Valley after the United States assumed control of the area following the Mexican war, however. Many more battles were fought before the proud Utes signed the Treaty of Conejos in 1863. As a result of that treaty, the Utes were moved from their beautiful valley to land beyond Cochetopa Pass northwest of present-day Saguache, Colorado.

With the "Indian Wars" finally over, Spaniards, Mexicans, and Americans once more started coming to the San Luis Valley to farm and ranch. The oldest church in Colorado, Our Lady of Guadalupe, is at Conejos, a mile north of Antonito. The Spanish-Mexican culture and architecture are closely interwoven in the history of this lovely valley. The small settlements, ranches and farms were remote from the rest of Colorado and would probably have remained isolated if rich miner-

This photograph was probably taken in the 1880s, judging from the old-style lettering on the tender at the right rear of the beautiful stone Antonito depot. The tall man with a cap at the right corner of the building is D&RG agent Ammerman. The man at his left between two ladies is Frank Killala, foreman of water service for the railroad. Others are local townspeople.

(Colorado Historical Society)

By 1913, or 1914, Antonito, Colorado was a well-established town with many substantial buildings, many of which are still standing. Judging from the number of flags flying, this may have been the 4th of July.   *(W.D. Joyce collection)*

al deposits had not been discovered in the San Juan Mountains in the early 1870s. With the influx of miners and adventurers on their way the the latest Eldorado, new trails, primitive roads, and finally the railroad led westward.

The early settlers came to farm and ranch. They built extensive irrigation ditches to bring water from the mountains to the valley. Throughout droughts, depressions, and fluctuating livestock prices, the population has remained quite stable.

In addition to the economic impact the railroads have on the valley, the perlite processing plant south of Antonito is an important industry for the area. Perlite is a special type of silicic volcanic rock (rhyolite), similar in composition to granite, but contains an additional 2 to 5 percent water. When perlite is heated to 1,500°F (820°C), the water becomes volatile and the rock literally explodes. A nickname is "volcanic popcorn." Open-pit mines are near No Agua, New Mexico. The rock is trucked to the plant where it is heated, crushed, sized, and blended for shipment all over the United States. The resulting material is used as a lightweight aggregate in cement, as a substitute for sand in plaster, and in oil well drilling. It can also be used as a filtering agent in the manufacture of drugs, chemicals, and as a sterile material in which plants can be grown.

SETTLEMENTS IN THE UPPER RIO CHAMA VALLEY

Long before the D&RG Railway arrived along the cottonwood-lined Rio Chama, the area was known to many different Indian tribes, to the Spaniards, the Mexicans, and finally to the American explorers. Like the San Luis Valley, the Chama Valley has a long and fascinating history, much of which is similar to that of the San Luis Valley. Many different Indian tribes traveled along the Rio Chama Valley on hunting, trading, and bartering expeditions with the pueblo Indians of New Mexico. The Chama Valley was an important route from New Mexico to the mountains of northern New Mexico and southwestern Colorado.

In 1765, Don Juan Rivera led a major expedition up the Rio Chama. He crossed the Continental Divide and continued into the area around Gunnison, Colorado. Members of this expedition named many of the rivers and mountains in southwestern Colorado and northwestern New Mexico. They also may have mined some silver in the San Juan Mountains. The Rivera expedition returned to Santa Fe through the San Luis Valley, via Cochetopa Pass.

The year 1776, so important in the history of the eastern United States, is an equally important date in the history of the southwestern part of the country. Two brave Franciscan friars set out from Santa Fe to find a new route to Monterey, California. Fathers Francisco Dominguez and Silvestre Escalante, with only eight companions, followed portions of the Rivera route up the Rio Chama, past Abiquiu before turning northwest.

The Old Spanish Trail, a main artery of travel between Santa Fe and California, crossed part of what is now Rio Arriba County, New Mexico. Between 1829 and 1848 this trail passed Abiquiu and followed the Rio Chama to the vicinity of present-day El Vado and Horse Lake before crossing the Continental Divide to the San Juan River.

After Mexico secured its independence from Spain, the custom of granting large blocks of land to Mexicans for settlement became very common in the northern state of Nuevo Mejico. More than 1,700 such grants may have been confirmed by the Mexican government. This procedure helped Mexico reinforce its claim to the vast area. After the Mexican War ended in 1848, the United States was obligated to reconfirm those land grants for which a clear Mexican title could be demonstrated.

Through the years, many grants were sold by the original owners or their descendants. Some grants were lost through ignorance of Mexican laws, and others through the activities of fast-talking land speculators. The Tierra Amarilla Grant, one of the largest in New Mexico, included the Chama Valley and a small portion of present-day Colorado. There were more than ½ million acres in the original grant which was awarded to Manuel Martinez of Abiquiu in 1832. This grant was confirmed by the United States government in 1860. Headquarters for this grant was at the junction of the Rio Chama and the Rio Brazos at Las Nutrias. The name was later changed to Tierra Amarilla ("yellow earth" in Spanish).

The latter half of the 1870s saw the first influx of American settlers in the upper Chama Valley. By that time, miners were passing through on their way to the San Juans, and rumors of a railroad to be built to the mining camps stimulated development even more. An English settlement called Los Ojos (from the Tewa Indian word which means "town" or "springs") was laid out 14 miles south of present-day Chama by a group of Chicago and English land speculators. The name was soon changed to Park View. Many who purchased land in Park View found out later that they could not get a clear title, as the land was on the Tierra Amarilla Grant for which the Mexican title had been confirmed.

The first United States treaty with the Ute Indians was signed in 1849 at Abiquiu. Another treaty with the Jicarilla Apaches was formalized in 1851. The Ute agency, first located at Abiquiu in 1853, was moved to Tierra Amarilla in 1872. The Utes had left the lush Chama Valley by 1878.

The town of Chama is named for the Rio Chama. The word comes from the Tewa pueblo word *tzama,* which is believed to mean, "here they have wrestled." However, another reference states the word means "red" to describe the color of the river water. If there was any settlement before the D&RG track arrived, it probably consisted of only a few summer shacks for sheepherders or cowboys on cattle drives. Chama was granted a post office in 1881.

The main street of Chama, Terrace Avenue, August 13, 1891. The citizens standing on the boardwalk are waiting for the circus to pass. In the background an elephant is leading the parade. Undoubtedly, the circus arrived in Chama on the narrow gauge.

(Collection Earl G. Knoob)

Chama, New Mexico in 1924. This was one year before another fire destroyed much of the main part of town. At this time, a spur track west of the main track was used for extra gang workers living in outfit cars. Some of the cars are still lettered D&RG, but a few have been relettered D&RGW. Ex-coach 0506 (second from right) is still used on the D&SNG's Silverton Branch.

(Edna Sanborn collection)

By the mid to late 1880s, the lumber industry was in full swing. After the timber near the towns was logged off, small branch logging railroads were built to bring timber to mills and to railheads. Some of these logging companies were operated by the D&RG; others were run by private companies. At least five lumber companies built narrow gauge spurs from the D&RG track near Chama to large stands of virgin timber. Some of these companies continued operation until the early 1930s. One mill, near the tail of the Chama wye, operated until 1988. A sheep-dipping plant was located northeast of the present roundhouse at one time.

Fire, always a hazard for early-day western towns, devastated Chama not once or twice, but at least four times. On June 12, 1899, a fire started in the rear of the Broad block about 4:30 PM. Strong north winds fanned the flames that roared through the business portion of town destroying many stores, the post office, T.D. Burns' business block and warehouse on Terrace Avenue. The wind changed to the west and the buildings on the east side of the block burned, including the depot, the roundhouse and 550 tons of coal. The railroad was completely shut down because ties in the yards caught fire and the heat warped the rails. The telegraph line was knocked out for about 24 hours. The present depot was built soon after this fire.

In September 1908, another fire hit Chama, destroying a team of horses and the new ice house owned by Burns-Hall Company. The following year another fire hit the town. Things were rather quiet until July 8, 1925, when yet another fire burned an entire block of businesses. This fire started at Foster's rooming house and spread rapidly to engulf the Chama Mercantile Co., and the McFadden building, Water's pool hall, Broad's dance hall, and several warehouses. That was not the last time Chama suffered the indignity of fire. Jones mercantile store, across the street from the Rio Chama drug store, burned in early spring of 1988.

Today, Chama's economy still depends upon the railroad, but also on ranching, and on the excellent hunting fishing, camping, and snowmobiling available nearby. Chama, like Antonito, has survived many economic reverses, but today is proud to be the headquarters for the Cumbres & Toltec Scenic Railroad. This railroad is a vital part of the town's heritage, as was its predecessor, the Denver & Rio Grande Western Railroad (D&RGW).

TRAILS AND ROADS ACROSS CUMBRES PASS

Animals blazed the original, meandering, indistinct trails across Cumbres Pass as they migrated back and forth between the San Luis and Chama Valleys. Naturally, the Indians followed the migrating animals when they went forth on hunting expeditions. By the time American trappers and traders entered the region, the general route was fairly well-known.

Cumbres Pass was the site of a running Indian battle in July 1848 between a group of Indians (Jicarilla Apaches and Muache Utes) and the 2nd Regiment, Missouri Volunteers. Two soldiers and 36 Indians were killed. The scout for the Missourians, a noted fur trapper and mountain man known as "Old Bill" Williams, was wounded. Poetic justice perhaps—he is reported to have absconded with money for a shipment of furs belonging to his in-laws, the Utes!

No well-marked trail was found by Lt. George S. Anderson of the Sixth Cavalry, when he first surveyed a route across the pass in 1874. His mission was to find a suitable route from Ft. Garland, Colorado, to Ft. Wingate, New Mexico, a military outpost built in 1868 after the Navajo Indians were moved from a temporary reservation on the Pecos River to their new reservation.

In an Army Engineers report published in 1876, Lt. Anderson described in vivid detail his trip with ten men across Cumbres Pass in May 1874. He returned to Ft. Garland in July along a well-known Indian trail south of Cumbres Pass. The map, published with the report in 1876, commonly referred to as the "Ruffner Report," shows both routes in considerable detail. Anderson recommended that a military road be built following the old Indian trail, rather than a route across Cumbres Pass.

In the spring of 1876, a settlement called Park View, located a few miles south of present-day Chama, was laid out by a Chicago and Santa Fe company interested in promoting a new settlement. The same company also applied for a charter to build the Park View and Ft. Garland Freight Road and Telegraph Co. (commonly called the Park View and Ft. Garland Toll Road). This toll road was to go from Park View, up the Rio Chama "to the most practical crossing of the mountains, thence by the most feasible route to Ft. Garland in the State of Colorado."

Perhaps when this Certificate of Incorporation was issued by the State of Colorado on January 26, 1877, the Ruffner Report of 1876 was available, because the projected toll road generally followed Lt. Anderson's 1874 route over Cumbres on his journey to Ft. Wingate.

The earliest reference to actual travel over the Cumbres Pass route by miners and emigrants was in October and November 1876, when the R.W. Belmear family managed to get over the pass by making drags of trees to keep the wagons from going too fast and tipping over. They settled in Animas City, Colorado, just north of Durango.

Undoubtedly, as more families and miners immigrated to the San Juans, they literally built the "road" as they laboriously moved their cattle, wagons, and horses across the mountain. During 1877 a very crude road was started by the toll road company to the top of the pass, but down the steep western side only an indistinct trail was available for those early, adventurous pioneers.

Many hardships were encountered by early travelers crossing Cumbres Pass. The Pargin family started west from Missouri in 1876. They spent the winter in the San Luis Valley and heard glowing reports of the rich land in the San Juan Basin and of the fabulous mines in the San Juan mountains. So in the spring of 1877, they started toward this "veritable Garden of Eden." In *Pioneers of the San Juan Country,* vol. 3, p. 152, the following quote describes this trip:

> **A trail had been blazed over the Cumbres Range, and in the spring of 1877 the Pargins and Quick brothers and a few others started for the San Juan Basin. They loaded all the provisions they could haul in their wagons and began the climb over the range. This part of the journey proved to be very difficult. There was practically no trail and in many places it required six horses to pull one wagon up the slope. As there were three wagons in the party, it frequently took three separate trips to get over the steep places. The descent of the range was more difficult than than the ascent. The men often had to let the wagons down the side of the mountains by means of ropes.**

In the 1878 Annual Report of the Chief of Army Engineers, Cumbres Pass was shown on the map included with the report as a "toll or county road in traveling condition," between Conejos and Cumbres Pass. Dotted lines follow Wolf Creek and the Rio Chama southward from the top of the pass. Apparently the Army did no actual construction on either route.

Also in 1878, two years before the D&RG began construction across Cumbres Pass, a small settlement and tollgate were located at Osier. The October 16, 1880, issue of the *La Plata Miner* stated that the toll road was the "regular wagon road to the San Juans and will be the first transportation conjunction between steam and mule power." By 1884, the area on the hillside above the track at Osier was known as Jenkins Gardens, where Mr. William Jenkins was postmaster, tollgate keeper, as well as a saloon and restaurant owner. Mr. Jenkins had a homestead and is known to have lived in Osier until at least 1907. Crude corrals adjoined the log buildings, but no mention was found of a hotel for weary travelers.

Mrs. C.W. Romney, editor of the first newspaper in Durango, described her trip to Durango in December 1880:

> **Alta is the working terminus of the railroad, the tracks, however, being completed two or three miles farther on. A night in Alta, and in the morning we run down on a special to the end of the track, and betake ourselves to the carriage brought in the train with us, together with four splendid horses, eager for the journey of which they wot [sic] sot little.**
> **The railroad winds around the mountains for several miles to accomplish the same descent which the wagon road takes at one dread leap, as it were. A little farther on and we reach the beautiful Chama Valley.**
> **We take dinner at the village of Chama, an embryo town of some prospective importance, especially in the near future as it will be the working terminus of the railroad very shortly.**

No mention was made in this account of the route being a toll road.

The road between Antonito and Chama was used heavily during the construction of the San Juan Extension by the D&RG. Newspapers in March 1881 complained bitterly about the bad condition of the road. Again, no mention was made of its being a toll road.

The history of this old toll road is elusive, and many intriguing questions remain unanswered. Old maps show the route as a "toll road" as late as 1884 or 1885, several years after the completion of the railroad. The date when tolls were no longer collected, or when the road was turned over to the counties for maintenance, is unknown. Toll rates are not known, but probably were similar to rates in other areas. Most charged about 15¢ for a man on horseback and $1.75 for a twelve-horse team and wagon. Sheep cost ½¢ and cattle 2-½¢ to pass through the toll gate. After State Highway 17 was completed in 1923, this rugged old line of transportation to the San Juans soon fell into disuse.

EARLY D&RG RAILROAD HISTORY

The Denver and Rio Grande Railway Company (D&RG) was incorporated in the Territory of Colorado and the Territory of New Mexico October 27, 1870 to build a railroad from Denver south to El Paso, Texas. The company also planned to extend rails to Mexico City, Mexico. The route to El Paso was to go south to Pueblo, west through the Arkansas River Canyon (Royal Gorge), across Poncha Pass (then called Poncho Pass), and into the San Luis Valley to the Rio Grande. Tracks were to follow the Rio Grande southward to El Paso. Six branches were planned to the mining areas of Colorado and one branch was projected to reach Salt Lake City, Utah. President of this first narrow gauge railroad in Colorado was General William Jackson Palmer, who had served in the Civil War with distinction and had come west after the war to work on the Kansas Pacific Railroad that reached Denver August 15, 1870.

The D&RG decided to build its railroad "narrow gauge" (rails 3 ft apart) rather than "standard gauge" (rails 4 ft 8-½ in wide) which was used on most other railroads. The choice was made because narrow gauge construction was cheaper, equipment cost less, and sharper curves were possible. Thus it was better adapted to mountainous terrain. The railroad was only eleven years old when Palmer and his associates realized they were bucking great odds with a narrow gauge operation. Consequently, by late 1890, the main line to Salt Lake City was converted to standard gauge. Standard gauge rail was laid to Antonito in 1901. Some portions of the narrow gauge in Colorado and New Mexico managed to survive until the 1950s and 1960s. Of the surviving routes, only the D&RGW's Silverton Branch showed a profit by the early 1960s, when tourists discovered the pleasure of a leisurely journey along the Animas River to Silverton.

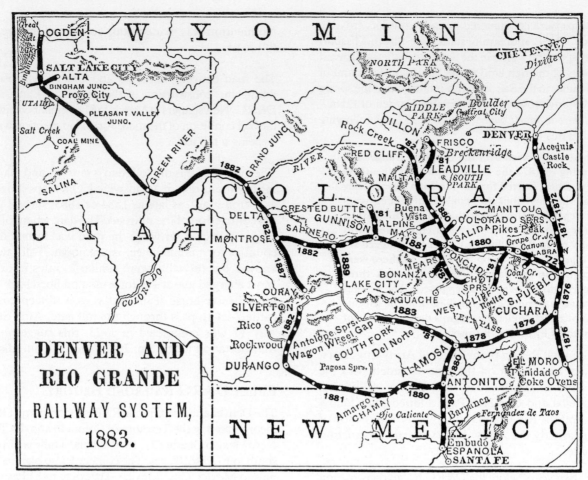

Route map from the Annual Report of the Board of Trustees to the Stockholders of the Denver & Rio Grande Railway, for 1882. (Colorado Historical Society)

Grading for the 75 miles between Denver and Colorado Springs commenced July 1, 1871 and the track to Colorado Springs was completed on April 15, 1872. The new narrow gauge railroad opened for business to Colorado Springs on June 15, 1872. Construction continued and Pueblo was reached in August 1872. Money problems delayed construction for several years, however, and track did not reach La Veta, Colorado, until 1876. By that time, mining activity in central and southwestern Colorado was booming, a fact which caused the D&RG to forget El Paso, and turn west toward the irresistible lure of mining riches. In 1877, rails were completed to El Moro coal mines, near Trinidad, and across Veta Pass to Garland City (now Ft. Garland) in the San Luis Valley. In July 1878, narrow gauge track lay beside the cottonwood trees along the Rio Grande River at the new company town of Alamosa. Thus eight years after its inception, the D&RG Railway could justify its name.

Financial problems continued to haunt the railroad. An expensive court fight with the Atchison, Topeka and Santa Fe Railroad (AT&SF) stopped all construction until a lawsuit was settled by a U.S. Supreme Court decision of April 21, 1879. This fight was over which railroad had first rights to build across Raton Pass and through the Royal Gorge of the Arkansas River to Leadville. A final settlement between the railroads was signed in Boston, Massachusetts, March 27, 1880. The terms stipulated that the D&RG could not build south of Espanola, New Mexico for ten years, and that the AT&SF was forbidden to construct any more track westward toward Leadville via the Royal Gorge.

BUILDING THE SAN JUAN EXTENSION

When the Rio Grande owners realized they had finally won the route to Leadville and other mining towns in Colorado, new money for construction appeared. D&RG stock advanced dramatically on the New York stock exchange and work officially began on the San Juan and New Mexico Extensions November 28, 1879. Thus began a period of incredible building and expansion for the ten-year-old company. During 1880, a total of 347 miles of track was completed and in 1881 another 383 miles were completed in Colorado, New Mexico, and Utah.

Contracts were let in December 1879 for track to be laid south of Alamosa on a grade that had been started two years before. In spite of bad weather and a scarcity of laborers, the grading between Alamosa and Antonito was completed by March 31, 1880 and the wobbly 40 lb per yard steel rails reached the new company "town" of Antonito on April 10, 1880. Early newspaper articles referred to this town as San Antonio, but in the 1880 annual report for the railroad it was called Antonito. Why the Cumbres Pass route won final approval of D&RG officials is outlined on p. 11.

It is believed this photo by William H. Jackson was taken on the first excursion of the new railroad, October 5, 1880. Obviously the trestle, at the west entrance to Toltec Tunnel,has just been completed. See page 20 for a description of this excursion..

(Doris Osterwald collection)

Proposals for work on the two extensions were published in the Colorado newspapers and in November, 100 teams of horses and mules and 200 men were ready to work for Carlile, Orman and Crook on grading. Along the San Juan Extension, other contracts were let to McGarrick and Tate for 24 miles of right-of-way. Clark, Lipe and Company was awarded a contract for another 21 miles, including a tunnel through the ridge opposite the Pinos canon (Toltec Tunnel). McCarthy and Holman got a contract for grading and masonry work on another four-mile section of the roadbed. Bridge and carpentry contracts were let to Donegan and Martel, while Carroll and Jones and other contractors agreed to deliver ties for the first 40 miles of the San Juan Extension.

The November 23, 1879 Colorado Springs *Weekly Gazette* ended the article about the Rio Grande's latest construction with the statement: "Track-laying will start January 1 and then the iron horse will continue to threaten the heels of the graders until he can quench his thirst in the Animas River." The rush to the San Juans was on.

Construction crews were housed in tents near Antonito and as grading and track-laying progressed, these primitive quarters were moved westward. In December 1879, the company placed orders for 52 new engines, 12 passenger cars, 40 freight cars, and rail for 400 miles of track for all the extensions being built in Colorado. Advertisements in newspapers all over the state offered jobs for tie cutters. In December, a five-car train passed through Colorado Springs crowded with men headed for the tie camps of the various extensions.

During the spring of 1880, grading and track-laying proceeded as fast as possible. The track reached Lava tank, eleven miles southwest of Antonito, April 30, and one month later rails were completed to the Big Horn wye. Toltec Siding was reached on June 30, 1880 and the line was open for business to that point on the same date. Grading crews passed Osier and arrived at Alta (Cumbres Pass) on July 31 and continued down the steep four percent grade, reaching Chama on Sept. 30. Track-laying could not keep up with that pace, however, and rails did not reach Osier until October 10 and Alta on December 15, 1880. Despite another bitter cold and snowy winter, crews continued to spike rails to the ties and the infant town of Chama greeted the first train on the last day of 1880. During January 1881, the line between Antonito and Chama was transferred from the Rio Grande Extension Company (the builders) to the D&RG Railway. L.C. Hamilton was appointed Superintendent for the new San Juan Division.

Chama became the railhead for construction that was proceeding west of the new company town. During January 1881, it was reported that with the exception of the railroad buildings and warehouses, the town was a collection of tents, slab and log cabins on the terrace above the railroad. The town had two blacksmith shops, two forwarding and commission houses, several hotels, restaurants and six saloons. Stages between Chama and Durango were operated by John Wall, who reported he did not have enough coaches to meet the demand. Barlow and Sanderson, the well-known stage company was reported to be en route to Chama with coaches, and Jim McGee had several six-mule teams available for hire at Chama to transport passengers on to Durango.

EXCURSIONS ON THE NEW RAILROAD

The first formal excursion over this portion of the San Juan Extension was October 4-5, 1880 for a group of editors and their wives who came from Denver, Colorado Springs, Pueblo, and other towns throughout the the state. This is also the date for the first C&TS excursion, exactly 90 years later.

Mr. F.C. Nims, General Passenger Agent for the D&RG, was in charge of the arrangements. The train consisted of a Pullman sleeper, chair car, and baggage car. (No mention is made of the engine used on the trip.) Among the guests were William H. Jackson, famous western photographer and his wife. Soon after this trip, Jackson started to work for the Rio Grande and other railroads as their publicity photographer.

A quote from a long article in the Pueblo *Weekly Colorado Chieftain* describes quite graphically this first passenger excursion and the country west of Antonito:

> I wish that all whose pulses thrill at the sight of nature's beauties might have been on the train with us that glorious afternoon. At first we glide smoothly across the plain toward a mesa that seems but a step for a giant; yet our train creeps up its side in a long zig zag. The cuttings show the underlying rock to be a lava; and we look more reverently upon the cold white peaks in the distance, at the thought that once smoke and ashes belched from their summits, and the fiery streams stained the snow upon their sides.

Another quote by the correspondent of that first excursion described the Whiplash Curve:

> Away we glide past romantic glades, whose velvety carpets of golden brown lie in folds of exquisite grace—clean and smooth as the ocean in a great swell. Pines are scattered picturesquely over glade and hill, casting sharp shadows upon the smooth turf. Now we have the rounded head of such a glade, in a curve that only a narrow gauge could describe; and now we are zigzaging up the side of a hill that bounds it on the right. The summit reached, we look down on the glade and could toss a stone upon two railway tracks, one above the other, and by which we have ascended, we are standing upon the third.

In, 1880, another correspondent described Toltec Tunnel in very dramatic terms:

> Having allured the railway into their awful fastnesses, the mountains seemed determined to baffle its further progress. But it was a strong-hearted railway, and although a little giddy at a thousand feet above the stream, it cut its way through the crags and among the monuments and bore onward for miles up the valley…At one point the cañon narrows into an awful gorge, apparently but a few yards wide and nearly a thousand feet in depth, between almost perpendicular walls of granite. Here a high point of granite has to be tunneled, and in this tunnel the rock men are at work drilling and blasting to complete the passage, which is now open to pedestrians. The frequent explosions of the blasts echo and re-echo among the mountains until they die away in the distance.

The October 4, 1880 excursion for newspaper editors traveled to Toltec Gorge where they spent the night:

> Then pine logs are brought and a fire kindled, for we camp here tonight. Think of it; camping in a Pullman car in the midst of the San Juan Mountains. Our thoughtful host has anticipated everything. A royal supper from the cuisine of the Glenarm is served by waiters from the same hotel. Was ever chicken more delicious? Had ever roast duck a finer flavor?
> Next morning we are out betimes, some to see the sun rise and shine visibly through the gorge, others to climb and explore at will.
> Breakfast is served and then we enter upon a day of unalloyed delight…The points of interest must be named. After much discussion the following were decided upon: The canon is to be known as "Toltec Gorge," the tunnel "Toltec Tunnel." A rocky promentory (sic) that juts out into the gorge is "Ella Cliff," in honor of Mrs. Nims.

The names chosen by this group are interesting. Why Toltec? The name probably referred to one of the tribes of Nahuatl Indians of Mexico. The D&RG's original plans were for the line to be built to Mexico City. In fact, General Palmer, President of the D&RG, had started construction of the Mexican National Railway in Mexico City during September 1880, just one month before this excursion. Ella Cliff was later mentioned by Ernest Ingersoll in his book, *Crest of the Continent*.

> The San Juan Extension was completed to Durango and opened for business on July 27, 1881. The track was hardly in place before a group of Durango citizens completed plans for a grand excursion to bring visitors to the new town along the Animas River. A special train left Denver August 3 and, as reported in the *Denver Tribune*, the trip was more than eventful. By the time the train reached Antonito it was running about 1-½ hours late. Five miles west of Sublette the second coach left the rails. "A delay of fifteen minutes was occasioned before the car could be again got on the track." Finally Toltec Gorge was reached and passengers "debarked" from the train to enjoy the scenery. At 12:30 p.m. on August 4, the train arrived at Osier. Upon reaching the wooded trestle across Cascade Creek, the second coach, in which the Colorado Springs delegation was located, again left the track. Only the guard rail saved the coach from falling more than 100 feet into the small canyon.

The train, which should have reached Cumbres by 11:00 AM, finally pulled into the station at 2:30 PM. After leaving Chama the special crossed the Continental Divide and arrived at Amargo, about 23 miles west of Chama to find that heavy rains had washed out the main track for a distance of two miles. By midnight, the passengers had run out of food, and were told that a bridge had also been washed away. A construction train was sent to the scene from Juanita, 20 miles west of Amargo, and men went to work to repair the washout. The article ended: "We will probably get to Durango by noon tomorrow." Such was life on the narrow gauge until the track settled and ballast was placed between the ties.

SUMMARY OF RIO GRANDE OPERATIONS

For 87 years, between 1881 and 1968, the D&RG (and later the D&RGW) operated the San Juan Division. During that time countless passengers enjoyed the narrow gauge, especially the daily *San Juan* that ran between Alamosa and Durango. The consist for this train was usually an RPO car, baggage car, coaches and one of the deluxe parlor cars. This train served the small communities along the route in many ways. In addition to carrying mail, the conductors could always be counted on to deliver newspapers, ice cream for the children, and supplies for families living along the way. In general, the train was their main source of communication and transportation. On February 1, 1951, when the *San Juan* ceased operation, a delightful, yet nostalgic chapter in narrow gauge railroading ended.

The popular concept of pioneer western railroads hauling solid trainloads of ore is not wholly correct, especially for the route across Cumbres Pass. Although the line was originally built to reach metal mining districts in the San Juan Mountains, most of the traffic consisted of mining machinery, supplies and other mining-related commodities, household goods, food, coal, and lumber. Most of the ore, however, was milled and smelted near the mines, at Silverton and Durango, so only refined metal or mill concentrates were shipped over Cumbres Pass.

Large numbers of livestock were shipped as ranching developed in the areas served by the D&RG. Large stands of timber south and west of Chama provided enormous quantities of lumber which went eastward across Cumbres Pass. During the 1940s, many carloads of pinto beans came from farming areas west of Durango. Fruit came from Farmington. Although not as glamorous as gold and silver, prosaic agricultural products probably accounted for much more traffic than mining.

The San Juan Basin's natural gas boom during the 1950s furnished the last traffic bonanza. In addition to solid trains of pipe, large amounts of drilling mud, oilfield machinery, and supplies were delivered via the Cumbres narrow gauge track. Crude oil was shipped eastward from Chama to a refinery at Alamosa. Additional details and photos of railroad operations start on p. 81.

The old story of more automobiles, better highways, fewer rail passengers, and a fairly slow trip combined to cause the cancellation of the daily *San Juan* in 1951. In addition, after World War II, the railroad's upper management decided to abandon all branch lines and passenger trains. They saw the railroad's future as a "bridge route" with no local carloadings. Freight service also began to dwindle during the late 1950s as the D&RGW shifted more and more freight loadings from rail to the Rio Grande Motorways, a trucking subsidiary company owned by the D&RGW. As a result, maintenance on right-of-way and rolling stock was reduced, causing further reductions in service to shippers and more justification to abandon the route.

Time eventually ran out for the last of the D&RGW narrow gauge lines. As suddenly as it began, the 1950s traffic boom disappeared, when the San Juan oil and gas fields reached maturity and as more pipe lines were completed. By October 1959, car loadings were down, and by December traffic had fallen to only one train per week. Traffic varied during the 1960s, and averaged about three trains per week. The Alamosa Division office closed in January 1960, and all the files were burned. Yet, in the fall of 1961, three-engine stock car freights were seen crossing Cumbres Pass. By November 1961, the extra board crews at Chama were laid off. Nine engines were retired in early 1962, and the last D&RGW rotary snowplow ran March 5-6, 1962. The Alamosa refinery (p. 88) closed in 1963, and the tank cars were scrapped or sold. The narrow gauge closed down completely for the first time during the winter of 1965. When it reopened in the spring, traffic was very light; some short freights pulled by a single engine were seen by sad railfans. The last dual gauge freights to Antonito ran in 1965, and by April 1966, the Alamosa transfer tracks had been removed. Only 20 trips were made in 1966, setting a "minimum activity" record. Service continued intermittently until 1968, when the last train ran west to Durango on December 5.

In spite of the increasing popularity of *"The Silverton"* train, after 1951 only occasional special passenger trains were run, especially in the autumn to see aspens in all their glory. During the fall of 1966 three separate excursions were operated from Alamosa to Cumbres. These were the last such trips. The final, and long-expected culmination occurred on September 18, 1967 when the Rio Grande filed an application with the Interstate Commerce Commission (ICC) to abandon the narrow gauge between Alamosa and Farmington.

In 1984, Denver billionaire Philip Anschutz purchased the D&RGW for half a billion dollars, stating that there would be no change in the operation of the company. On December 18, 1987, the Santa Fe Southern Pacific Corp. announced the sale of the SP to the Rio Grande. It was also announced the two companies would operate as separate entities and retain their own identities. But by 1989, the round SP herald began to replace the flying Rio Grande Herald. In May 1992, it was announced that the venerable D&RGW would no longer exist as an operating company, and would be completely absorbed into the Southern Pacific (SP) system. In another merger in 1995, the SP was absorbed by the Union Pacific Railroad.

SAVING THE NARROW GAUGE

By 1968, many individuals and organizations started to consider seriously the possibility of preserving at least a portion of the original San Juan Extension for use as a tourist line. After much discussion, the states of Colorado and New Mexico joined forces and through legislative action, each state created its Railroad Authority.

The New Mexico and Colorado Railroad Authorities purchased the 64 miles of track between Chama and Antonito for $547,120.00 in July 1970. The track from Chama to Durango and Farmington, N.M. was scrapped after the D&RGW refused to consider any extension of time for interested parties to make offers to purchase the entire line. Final terms between the Rio Grande and the states were completed by July, and on September 1, 1970 the first of three large shipments of engines, rolling stock, and non-revenue equipment was delivered at Antonito to the Cumbres & Toltec Scenic Railroad. Between July and September volunteer labor, estimated to be worth at least $50,000, spent untold hours and days repairing track so the shipments could be safely moved to Chama for winter storage, as Antonito had no available storage tracks or yards. Because the Rio Grande would not allow the new railroad to use its Antonito wye and storage tracks, engine 483 (the only operable engine available at that time) had to be turned at Lava or Big Horn, and run in reverse all the way to Antonito. The 483 received water from the Antonito fire department and coal donated by interested citizens.

On September 1, 1970, soon after the D&RGW made the first delivery of equipment to the new C&TS Railroad, volunteers painted out the Rio Grande lettering and relettered the tender of 483. On the far right is Ernest Robart, a volunteer from the New Mexico Railroad Club, and standing to his left is Robert W. Richardson, of the Colorado Railroad Museum. (Doris B. Osterwald)

The C&TS is owned by the citizens of Colorado and New Mexico. The Colorado-New Mexico Railroad Authorities are the governing body for the states and oversee the operation of the railroad. Two members from each state are appointed to serve on this board.

Through the years a number of companies have had contracts to operate the line for the Commission, paying a percentage of their gross income to the Commission, be responsible for day-to-day operations and maintenance of the equipment owned by the two states. During the fall of 1999 the Commission terminated the lease of the Cumbres & Toltec Scenic Railroad Corporation for breach of contract.

On March 1, 2000, after several companies made offers to operate the railroad that the Commission would not accept, the *Friends of the C&TS* volunteer organization (see pp. 98-101) submitted a bid to operate the railroad on a nonprofit basis. To accomplish this, the Rio Grande Railway Preservation Corpo-

ration (RGRPC) was formed as a separate company to operate the railroad. The *Friends* Board of Directors elected members to the new board of the RGRPC and hired Edward M. McLaughlin as General Manager for the 2000 season. He declined to renew his contract for 2001 and returned to his home in Salt Lake City.

Because of serious fires in New Mexico in the spring of 2000, the New Mexico Forest Service requested the railroad delay the opening for at least 30 days. But the C&TS suggested that the Jordan spreader OU be used to cut back all vegetation 18 feet from both sides of the track and all trains leaving Chama carry the 6,000 gallon water car from Rotary OY behind the engine rigged to spray water outward about 30 feet on both sides of the track. These proposals were accepted and the C&TS opened on schedule. Using the Jordan spreader also was an added bonus, and saved much time when new ballast was being spread later in the summer. No serious fires were started by the engines during the hot dry season. Cost of these fire suppression efforts, however, cost the C&TS an additional $124,000 (photos, pp. 94-97).

During December 2000, RGRPC, operator of the C&TS Railroad announced that Dan Ranger, former General Manager of the C&TS from 1983-1990 agreed to return as General Manager, even though he is also serves as Executive Director for the Tourist Railway Association, Inc. (TRAIN). Earl Knoob, former Superintendent of Operations also returned for the 2001 season as Superintendent.

Because the C&TS operates an an interstate common carrier, the railroad is subject to inspection and regulation by the Interstate Commerce Commission, U.S. Department of Transportation and the Federal Railroad Administration. Preservation standards have been adopted so that any work done on the property or to the equipment maintains historical accuracy.

The C&TS is listed in the National Register of Historic Places. Jointly, the New Mexico Register of Cultural Properties and the Colorado Historical Society work to preserve the historic integrity of all property, perform inspections, and supervise work done to maintain and restore equipment now owned by the two states. The C&TS has been honored by the National Trust for Historic Preservation and by the American Society of Civil Engineers. In 1999 the railroad was also selected as one of the 20 Best Rail Trips by the Society of International Railway Travelers.

Probably nowhere else in the United States is there a comparable living and working museum of steam railroading. It has been established that the best way to preserve historic railroad equipment is to use it. Countless individuals have worked long and hard to preserve this railroad for future generations to enjoy. We owe them a huge Thank You!

USING THE MILE-BY-MILE GUIDES®

This mile-by-mile guide is written so that points of interest, scenic highlights, historic locations, geology, and nature notes are keyed to mileposts set along the track. Most mileposts are white, 12 in. square, wooden posts set in the ground during construction of the San Juan Extension. Many of the original posts have been replaced, repainted, and renumbered by the volunteers of the *The Friends of the C&TS*. A few sites have metal posts. Mileposts are graphically shown on all the guide maps. Cross-ties are ¹⁄₁₀ mile apart to aid the reader in following the map and the text.

The numbers indicate the distance, by rail, from Denver where the D&RG started in 1870. Thus, the beautiful old D&RG stone depot at Antonito is 280.3 miles from Denver because milepost 280 is 0.3 mile north of the depot. The new C&TS depot is at milepost 280.7.

Two mile-by-mile guides are included. Passengers boarding the train at Antonito will use the Westbound Guide, while those passengers leaving Chama will follow the Eastbound Guide. If you plan on traveling just to Osier and return to your departure point, the appropriate portions of both guides will be used.

Before we leave this morning, the conductor will explain safety regulations that will be strictly enforced. Please listen; do not let an accident spoil your trip. When moving around in your coach or walking to the open gondola car, brace yourself against any sudden jostling. Do not throw anything out of the cars. One smoldering cigarette can cause irreversible damage to this beautiful region.

SYMBOLS USED ON GUIDE MAPS

309	C&TS mainline with milepost marker Crossties are ¹⁄₁₀ mile apart	— — —	State line
	Other C&TS track	— ᵕ —	County line
	Other railroads	— — —	National forest boundary
	Abandoned railroad grade	·	Water tank
(17)	Highway	·	Building
	Roads and streets	⚲	Church
	Dirt road	⋀	Campground
	Route of toll road	⬛	School
	Streams and rivers	✕	Site of train wreck
	Lake		Trestle
	Edge of flat-topped mountain or mesa	⋋	Tunnel
		LOBATO el 8,303' (2,532 m)	C&TS station
		Tanglefoot Curve	Point of interest
		el 10,562' (3,219 m) ✕	Mountain location and elevation

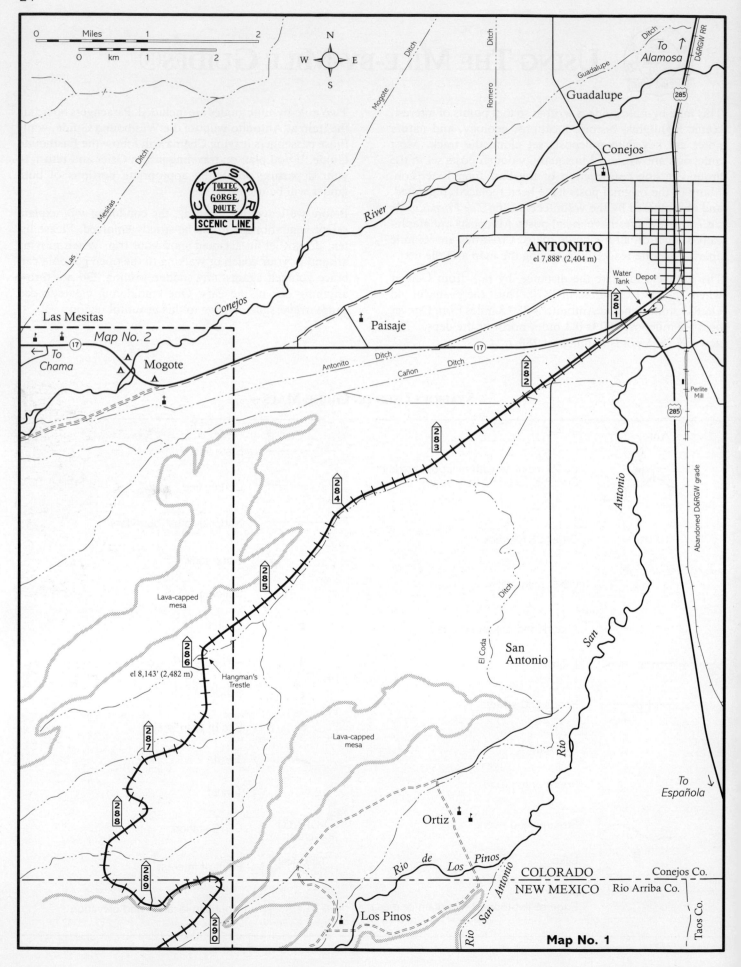

Miles
0   1   2

km
0   1   2

N
W   E
S

C&TSRR
TOLTEC
GORGE
ROUTE
SCENIC LINE

To
Alamosa

D&RGW RR

Ditch

Guadalupe

Guadalupe

Mogote

Romero

Ditch

Conejos

River

ANTONITO
el 7,888' (2,404 m)

Water
Tank

Depot

285

281

Las Mesitas

Map No. 2

Conejos

Paisaje

Antonito   Ditch

Cañon   Ditch

17

17

282

To
Chama

Las Mesitas   Ditch

Mogote

283

Perlite
Mill

285

Abandoned D&RGW grade

284

285

Lava-capped
mesa

El Coda   Ditch

San
Antonio

Rio   San   Antonio

286
el 8,143' (2,482 m)

Hangman's
Trestle

Lava-capped
mesa

To
Española

287

288

Ortiz

289

Rio   de   Los   Pinos

COLORADO   Conejos Co.

NEW MEXICO   Rio Arriba Co.

290

Rio   San   Antonio

Los Pinos

Taos Co.

Map No. 1

WESTBOUND GUIDE

Mile
280.70 ANTONITO, COLORADO.
elev 7,888 ft (2,404 m)

This station is the eastern terminus of the Cumbres & Toltec Scenic Railroad (C&TS). None of the buildings and railroad facilities surrounding the present C&TS depot were here until after the states purchased the line from the Denver & Rio Grande Western Railroad (D&RGW) in 1970. They were largely built with volunteer labor and a number of financial grants. With a great deal of hard work and community effort, local residents built the small depot, a wye, storage tracks, and facilities for servicing engines by the summer of 1971 when the C&TS officially opened for business.

Antonito came into existence March 31, 1880 when D&RG construction crews reached their newly platted company "town." From Antonito, two lines were built. The mainline San Juan Extension turned west toward the mining camps in the San Juan Mountains, while the New Mexico Extension was built southward to Santa Fe, New Mexico (ref. C). The beautiful old stone depot (p. 13, 76) on the east side of Main Street in Antonito was built by the Denver & Rio Grande Railway (D&RG) in 1882, replacing a wooden depot which became the freight house.

Railroad profits were made by land speculation and development as much as by carrying passengers and freight. Laying out a new town, selling lots, and bringing newcomers to the new settlement were more important than becoming a part of the old established town of Conejos. This policy was repeated many times by the D&RG.

While in Antonito, perhaps you will have time to tour the facilities using the brochure prepared by the volunteer organization, *Friends of the C&TS*. Don't miss the dual gauge display.

Four long—and loud—blasts of the whistle remind passengers to get on board immediately.

As the train slowly pulls away from the depot, plumes of black coal smoke billow upward into the morning sky. Wide, sweeping vistas of distant mountain peaks offer a sneak preview of scenes to come as the day progresses. There will be plenty of chances to see and photograph the sights, especially from the open gondola car. Between Antonito and Cumbres, your engine will burn about two to three tons of coal.

Mileposts are set on the **right** side of the track.

Mile
280.86 CROSS U.S. HIGHWAY 285.

Between mile 280.90 and milepost 283 is one of three locations on the C&TS route where the track is actually straight. As your journey progresses, the novelty of this will become apparent. The meandering, convoluted route chosen by the D&RG was explained by one wit who said the surveying crews simply turned their mule loose and followed it to the summit of Cumbres Pass!

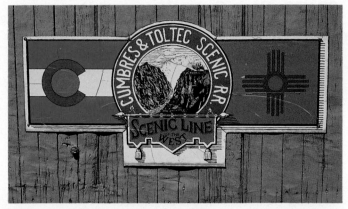

(Jim Ozment)

Antonito, Colorado depot of the C&TS Railroad. The building was completed in 1977.   *(Jim Ozment)*

The infamous Hangman's Trestle at mile 285.87. This photo was taken in June 1990 after the bridge had been rebuilt following the fire during the filming of "Where the Hell's That Gold." Engine 488 is pulling a special freight train chartered by Jim Trowbridge.

(Gerald M. Blea)

Just beyond the highway crossing, an old, weathered D&RGW Railroad sign stands along the right side of the track that reads "End of Standard Gauge." This is the point where the wider standard gauge from Denver ended. Beyond this point is "narrow gauge country." The standard gauge third rail was laid from Alamosa to Antonito in 1901 (ref. F).

Mile
281.20 CROSS CAÑON IRRIGATION DITCH.

The oldest irrigation projects in Colorado are near Antonito, where many ditches bring water from the mountains to the valley to irrigate crops and pastureland. The first ditch was dug by hand in 1852 near San Luis, Colorado.

Milepost
283.00 TRACK ON FLAT VALLEY FLOOR.

Vegetation is typical of the semiarid west. Much sagebrush, rabbitbrush, and native grasses grow with little water. A wide variety of wildflowers bloom when sufficient moisture is present. Purple bee plants, yellow clovers, and cream-colored stickweeds bloom during the summer. In the fall, purple asters and other composites are a delight to see.

A number of standard pile trestles cross intermittent stream drainages throughout this portion of the valley. These bridges were built between 1885 and 1890 to replace the first hastily constructed wooden bridges of 1880. Many others have been replaced with culverts and fills.

Mile
285.87 CROSS BRIDGE.

This bridge crosses an intermittent stream channel. The original 80 ft, five-panel frame trestle, built in 1886 (ref. A), was inadvertently burned in 1988 during the filming of "Where the Hell's That Gold." Passenger traffic was halted for a week while a temporary culvert and fill were built. The next spring, the present structure was completed which duplicates the burned bridge as much as possible (photo, p. 25).

This bridge is also called "Hangman's Trestle" or "Ferguson's Trestle." It seems a Mr. Ferguson of Antonito had the dubious honor of being hung from the bridge for an unknown capital crime. Those responsible for this act supposedly commandeered a locomotive sitting in the Antonito yards and ran it out to the trestle where there was enough height for him to hang without touching the ground.

On both sides of the track are large gray-green shrubs with dark-colored bark that shreds in long strips. This is big sagebrush or wormwood, *Artemisia tridentata*. Some interesting facts about this shrub are on p. 109.

On October 4-5, 1880, the first formal excursion on the San Juan Division was held. Excerpts of the newspaper accounts of this momentous occasion are on p. 20 and graphically describe the country you are now passing through.

Mile
288.55 LEAVE COLORADO.

This is the first of eleven crossings of the Colorado-New Mexico state boundary. The D&RG placed stone monuments at each of these crossings, and most are still in place today.

Watch for deer, antelope, jackrabbits, cottontail rabbits, gophers, and perhaps a coyote or mountain lion along the track and on the hillsides.

Milepost
289 VIEW OF LOS MOGOTES PEAK.

The twin summits of Los Mogotes, elev 9,818 ft (2,993 m), are visible to the northwest. Los Mogotes is a small volcano from which basalt poured onto the surface between four and five million years ago. The Spanish translation is vague; some sources say the word means "hummocks," while others say it means "the horns of young animals." The peak was originally called Prospect Mountain.

Mile
289.48 CROSS COLORADO–NEW MEXICO STATE BOUNDARY.

Another crossing is also at mile 289.71. The boundary between the two states was first surveyed in 1868 along the 37th parallel. Later, errors were found and in 1902-3 a second survey was authorized by Congress. This survey would have reduced the size of Colorado considerably, which brought forth loud protests from property owners along the boundary line. Arguments between the two states continued until 1925 when the U.S. Supreme Court ruled that the 1868 boundary was legal. The boundary has since been re-surveyed and portions have been moved about 1,200 ft southward near Cresco, Colorado. The boundary fence between the two states is easy to see to the west.

Mile
290.77 SITE OF LAVA PHONE BOOTH AND SIDING.

A telephone booth was on the north side of the track until about 1973 when it was destroyed by vandals. The D&RGW used telephones, placed in booths along the route, so trainmen could contact the dispatcher in Alamosa to report problems and get instructions. *The Friends of the C&TS* is attempting to preserve the remaining booths.

This is also the site of the 1,084 ft LAVA SIDING, which was removed in 1955 (ref. B). It had a 25-car capacity. Track-laying reached this point April 30, 1880.

In 1923, second-hand 70 pound rail was laid between Antonito and Lava, in preparation for using the heavier K-27 locomotives.

Milepost
291 LOWER CURVE OF LAVA LOOP.
elev 8,479 ft (2,584 m)

Between mileposts 291 and 292, the curving track makes a tight loop and passes LAVA TANK. This 15° curve is connected by an 826 ft section of track which was built some years after the San Juan Extension was completed, and was frequently used to turn snowplow trains. There are no curves sharper than 20° on the C&TS route (ref. B).

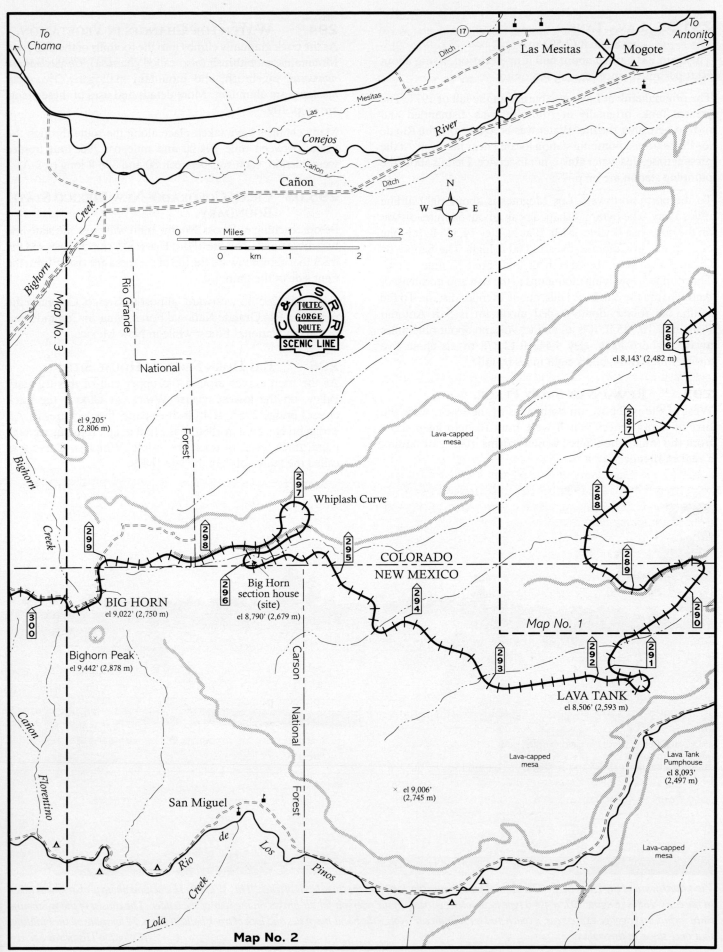

To Chama

To Antonito

(17)

Las Mesitas

Mogote

Conejos   River

Las   Mesitas

Cañon

Ditch

Cañon

Ditch

N
W   E
S

0   Miles   1   2

0   km   1   2

C&TSRR
TOLTEC
GORGE
ROUTE
SCENIC LINE

Bighorn   Creek

Map No. 3

Rio Grande

National

Forest

el 9,205'
(2,806 m)

el 8,143' (2,482 m)

286

287

288

289

290

Lava-capped
mesa

297   Whiplash Curve

298

299

295

296

Big Horn
section house
(site)
el 8,790' (2,679 m)

COLORADO
NEW MEXICO

Map No. 1

294

293

292

291

300

BIG HORN
el 9,022' (2,750 m)

Bighorn
Creek

Bighorn Peak
el 9,442' (2,878 m)

Carson   National   Forest

LAVA TANK
el 8,506' (2,593 m)

Lava Tank
Pumphouse
el 8,093'
(2,497 m)

Cañon   Florentino

San Miguel

× 9,006'
(2,745 m)

Lava-capped
mesa

Lava-capped
mesa

Rio   de   Los   Pinos

Creek

Lola

Map No. 2

Mile
291.55 LAVA TANK.
elev 8,506 ft (2,593 m)

The train has gained about 600 ft in elevation, rising about 50 ft per mile, since leaving Antonito.

The original tank at Lava was burned in the fall of 1971. The present tank, originally at Antonito, was dismantled and moved here after the fire. Water was brought from the Rio de los Pinos from a pumping station located near the river. At the present time, this water tank is not in service. Details about the pumping station are on p. 77.

To the north-northwest, Los Mogotes is about eight airline miles away. The pyramid-shaped peak, about 54 miles distant on the northeast skyline, is Mt. Blanca, elev 14,345 ft. It is one of 53 peaks in Colorado over 14,000 ft high. The Sangre de Cristo Range is on the eastern skyline about 32 miles away. The rounded, low-lying mountains to the east and northeast of Antonito are the San Luis Hills, about 18 miles distant. To the south, the round, dome-shaped mountain is San Antonio Peak, elev 10,935 ft. It is an extinct volcano about nine miles away. Bighorn Peak, elev 9,442 ft (2,878 m), is about five airline miles away, but is eight miles by rail.

Milepost
293 REMAINS OF SNOW FENCE.

West of the milepost, on both sides of the track, were the first of many fences which were built to help keep snow from the track when fierce winter storms made railroading a real challenge.

Milepost
294 WATCH FOR CHANGES IN VEGETATION.

As the track gradually climbs into the foothills of the San Juan Mountains, rabbitbrush (also called chamisa), *Chrysothamnus nauseosus*, sagebrush, and mountain mahogany, *Cercocarpus montanus*, are abundant. More details and uses of these plants are on p. 109.

Many changes have taken place along the route through the years. Between mile 294.20 and milepost 296, four trestles were filled in; each was between 80 and 336 ft long (ref. A).

Mile
295.08 CROSS COLORADO–NEW MEXICO STATE BOUNDARY.

Before reaching milepost 296, the train will cross the state line two more times. The site of BIG HORN SECTION HOUSE and the track that climbs toward the top of the mesa are visible from the right side of the train.

From mile 295.40 westward, almost to Cresco, Colorado the route is in Rio Grande National Forest while in Colorado and in Carson National Forest while in New Mexico.

Milepost
296 BIG HORN SECTION HOUSE SITE.

As the train curves around the upper end of this tributary valley, on the lowest reverse WHIPLASH CURVE, the track crosses bridge 296A, a 48 ft three-panel fire-deck trestle. An earlier bridge, built in 1886, was 112 ft long. From this vantage point, three levels of track are visible. Whiplash Curve was called the "three-ply" in the late 1880s.

View northward of Big Horn Section House and bunk house (far Left) and the three levels of track. This William H. Jackson photo probably was taken in the early-1880s. Engine 107, a 4-4-0 type locomotive, carried an air reservoir for air brakes on the rear of the tender. The consist of the westbound train includes a baggage-express car, a coach and a Pullman car. Notice the hand-hewn ties and lack of track ballast. See p. 77 for more on the buildings that once stood in this valley.

(Colorado Historical Society)

Milepost
297 NORTHERN END OF WHIPLASH CURVE.

Don't miss the the lovely view of the Conejos valley below and of Los Mogotes Peak to the north. Remains of several snow fences are along the right side of the track. This mesa is capped with dark loose pieces of lava of the Cisneros Formation that probably flowed from the Los Mogotes volcano (see Geology, p. 111).

Milepost
299 MONTANE ZONE WILDFLOWERS.
elev 8,997 ft (2,742 m)

Between Lava Tank and Big Horn, wildflowers are more common than at lower elevations. White or cream-colored blossoms include stickweeds and yuccas; paintbrushes, scarlet gilias and beard-tongues; buckwheats are reddish-colored. Flowers with yellow blossoms include mustards, mulleins, ragged sunflowers, sulfur flowers, and golden asters. Common blue or purple blossoms are bee plants, several species of lupines, fleabanes, and thistles.

Ponderosa pines, *Pinus ponderosa,* the dominant trees of the mesas, foothills, and south-facing slopes of the montane life zone, grow abundantly along here. The long needles, bright reddish-brown bark, and large drooping cones make this tree easy to identify. Other trees that dot the hillsides include junipers, pinyon pines, a few aspens, firs, and spruces.

Mile
299.09 ENTER NEW MEXICO.

Mile
299.41 BIG HORN WYE AND SIDING.
elev 9,022 ft (2,750 m)

Track was completed to Big Horn wye May 31, 1880 and the line immediately opened for business to this point (photo, p. 104).

Just east of the east switch for the siding was a 24-panel snow fence. The tail of this long, curving wye was extended in 1953 during the oil and gas boom in the San Juan Basin. In addition to the snow-fighting equipment which turned here, helper engines frequently used the wye. The siding is 1,184 ft long and will hold 28 cars. This was a frequent meeting point for trains. The station sign was located 400 ft east of the west switch.

Bighorn Peak, elev 9,442 ft (2,878 m), south of the track, is capped with a layer of basalt.

Mile
299.70 BIG HORN PHONE BOOTH.

Another old booth is on the right side of the track, 200 ft west of the west switch. The train has climbed a steady 1.42 percent grade most of the way from Antonito. One K-36 engine can pull 36 loaded freight cars. Longer trains need a helper engine cut into the middle for westbound trips. Many snowfences were necessary along this section of track.

Mile
300.50 SITE OF BIG HORN BELL.

A metal relay box was located here. It was used to signal the dispatcher in Alamosa that a train had passed this point, as no block signals or radios were ever used on the narrow gauge during D&RGW ownership. The box was removed by unauthorized persons.

Milepost
301 ASPEN GROVES.

Aspens, also called quaking aspens or "quakies," *Populus tremuloides,* are the dominant tree as the train continues west. Aspens reproduce from shallow roots which spread laterally. They send shoots upward to form a grove in which all the trees are related—called "clones." The genetics of clone groves determine when the first leaves appear in the spring, and when and to what color the leaves turn in the fall. Amounts of moisture, temperature, and soil composition also affect these traits. Genetics also determine the shapes of the branches and the color of the bark, which varies from light gray-green to brownish-green to whitish. Bark of older aspen trees may be whitish due to oxidation. Aspens also produce some seeds, which explains why one clump will turn a saffron yellow color in the fall, and an adjacent grove will be a brilliant red color.

Beavers are very fond of aspen wood for food and for building lodges. The soft white wood is used in industry for pulp, excelsior, boxes, and matches.

Westward there will be many chances to see and photograph the aspens in all their glory, especially during the crisp, clear autumn days. Backlighted photos with the sunlight filtering through the dancing leaves can be very dramatic.

Even on a cloudy autumn afternoon, the aspens are glorious.
(Doris B. Osterwald)

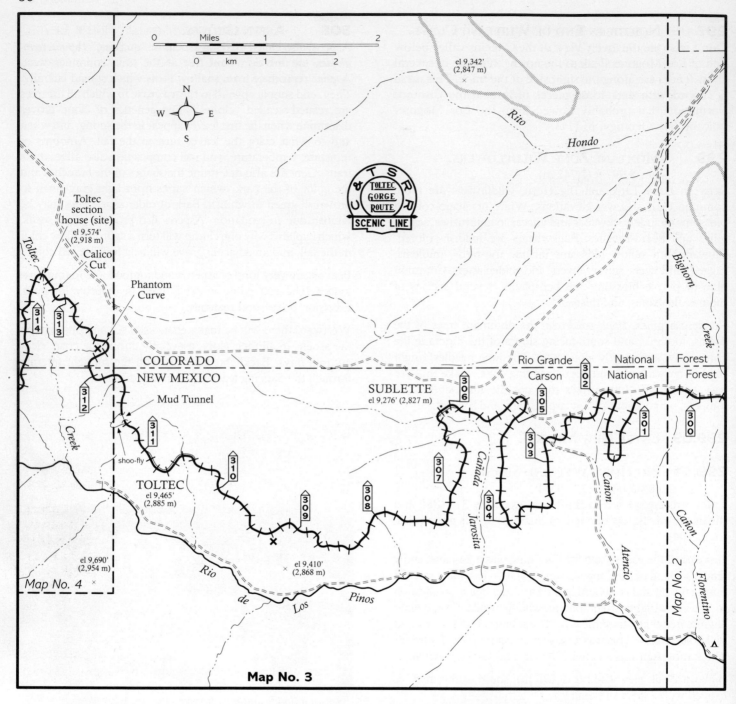

Map No. 3

Mile
303.50 Loose Gravel in Railroad Cut.

The loose, rounded pebbles and cobbles in this cut are part of the 26 million year old Los Pinos Formation. In 1925, rock from this cut was used for badly-needed railroad ballast.

To the south are many nice views into the Rio de los Pinos Valley. San Antonio Peak is still visible on the southeastern skyline.

Mile
303.90 Southernmost Sharp Curve.

This curve winds around the hill between Cañon Atencio and Cañada Jarosita. Westward, the aspen leaves are brilliantly colored during the all-too-short autumn days.

Near milepost 304, the track is about 500 ft above Cañada Jarosita.

Mile
305.20 Cross Headwaters of Cañada Jarosita.

Mile
306.06 SUBLETTE, NEW MEXICO.
elev 9,276 ft (2,827 m)

This station was first called Boydsville; why the name was changed is not known. The San Juan Extension was completed and opened for business to this point by early June 1880 (ref. E).

Originally there was a wooden water tank along the left side of the track; today a metal standpipe serves the same purpose. Engine water is piped from a small cistern above the track which is filled from a small stream. The water was noted in 1891 as being "good and plenty" (ref. A). See page 77 for more on the structures here.

The large frame building was the section foreman's home. The hand-hewn log bunk house to the east is identical to the one at Chama. Both were built soon after the line was completed. During 1990 and 1991, *The Friends of the C&TS Railroad* completed major repairs and painting of these structures. The Sublette siding is 949 ft long, and has a capacity of 25 cars (photos, p. 61, 77, 83, 95, 100).

After the train leaves Sublette the track makes two 20° double-S curves as it winds through the aspen forest.

Sublette, New Mexico in the early 1900s. This westbound passenger train had stopped for water, and perhaps to let off passengers for a summer picnic. The wooden water tank was removed in 1937 and replaced with the present water plug. By this date, the hand-hewn ties had been replaced with sawed ones. (W.D. Joyce Collection)

Milepost
307 TRACK WINDS THROUGH ASPEN GROVES.

Nestled among the aspens are some Douglas firs and white firs, *Abies concolor*. This tall, stately tree with an ash-gray, deeply furrowed bark, is from 70 to 160 ft tall. The cones may be from 5 to 7 in. long.

A wide variety of wildflowers bloom during the summer months along this shady moist hillside. Purple bull thistles, scarlet gilias, white yarrows, blue lupines, and penstemons, yellow gumweeds, wallflowers, and orange mallows are easy to find. Ferns, wild roses, gooseberries, chokecherries, and raspberries are also very common.

Milepost
308 CONEJOS FORMATION AT TRACK LEVEL.

A small fault just beyond the milepost brings the Conejos Formation upward to track level. This formation is the oldest volcanic unit in the eastern San Juan Mountains and is from 31 to 34 million years old. At mile 308.50, a deep cut with vertical sides offers an opportunity to see the rusty-red to pink breccias of the Conejos Formation.

At mile 308.40, the track is about 900 ft above Rio de los Pinos, and the canyon is about ¾ mile wide.

Mile
309.35 SITE OF HEAD-ON COLLISION.

On September 23, 1922 the westbound *San Juan* passenger train #115, pulled by engine 169, was hit by an eastbound light locomotive, number 411. Engineer R.L. Smith misread his orders and collided head-on with the passenger train. Smith believed he had more time to reach Sublette siding. He received minor injuries, but D.M. Wright, engineer, and L.J. Knee, fireman, on the passenger train were killed. Three railroad employees and 20 passengers were injured. The remains of one locomotive pilot and a coupler are down the hill about 50 ft from the nearest telephone pole. The Rio Grande built a ramp to drag engine 169 up the slope to track level. Some coal and bricks from the fire box are still litter the ground. Engine 169 is now on display in Cole Park at Alamosa, Colorado.

Mile
310.30 EAST SWITCH OF TOLTEC SIDING.
elev 9,465 ft (2,885 m)

As construction of the San Juan Extension continued at a feverish pace, track was completed to this point June 30, 1880.

Toltec Siding was originally 1,166 ft long, but was lengthened to 3,400 ft during the 1950s to handle the long pipe trains that operated between Alamosa, Colorado, and Farmington, New Mexico. With a capacity of 75 cars, most of the longer trains met here. Another phone booth is located on the left at mile 310.46. The Toltec station sign stood about 450 ft east of the west switch.

Milepost
311 WEST SWITCH OF TOLTEC SIDING.

Beautiful views of the tree-covered slopes make this section of track a delight—and so different from the scenery near Antonito (photo, p. 32).

Mile
311.30 MUD TUNNEL (TUNNEL NO. 1).

This 342 ft tunnel (ref. B) was dug through soft, weathered volcanic ash and mud of the Conejos Formation. The Rio Grande had many problems here because the soft rock and mud slides when wet. It was also necessary to line the tunnel with timber—an additional hazard for steam locomotives.

On April 14, 1889, an engine pulling a westbound freight struck a mud slide that forced the engine into the timbers at the east portal. Engineer George Riddle and fireman Fred Wendle were injured. The Alamosa *San Luis Valley Courier* reported on April 17, 1889: "The engine No. 68 was pretty badly demolished but very little damage was done to the cars with the exception of breaking a few draw head bolts."

West switch of Toltec siding, milepost 311. This photograph was taken by geologist L.S. Robbins, who did consulting work on the Gramps oil field (p. 88) and also enjoyed riding the narrow gauge. The work train is powered by a K-27 (possibly the 464) and is pulling the pile driver and five outfit cars for the bridge gang. A great deal of bridge work was done during 1936, the date of this photo. The work train has gone into the siding to let the westbound passenger train pass. Notice the four-wheel caboose with its square signal box on the cupola roof.   *(Earl G. Knoob collection)*

Shoo-fly roadbed around Mud Tunnel. According to Robert W. Richardson of the Colorado Railroad Museum, sometime in the early 1900s, the wooden timbering in the tunnel caught fire. In order to keep traffic moving, a sharp loop of track (called a "shoo-fly") was laid around the tunnel. During the several weeks it took to repair the tunnel, eastbound and westbound trains traveled to the shoo-fly where the passengers disembarked, walked around the brown of the hill and boarded another train for the remainder of their journey. Freight cars were pulled around the hill by teams of horses or oxen. This view looks west along the roadbed at the eastern end of the shoo-fly.   *(Gordon Chappell)*

During the spring of 1982, the C&TS installed concrete sills so the timbers do not sit on mud, and rebuilt both portals.

Chances for good photographs are at both portals. As the train leaves the west portal, take a quick look to the left to see the "shoo-fly" built in the early 1900s while the tunnel was being rebuilt after a fire (photo, p. 32).

Several scenes of the popular movies, "Bite the Bullet," "Where the Hell's That Gold," and "Indiana Jones and the Last Crusade" were filmed here (photo, p. 61).

Mile
312.10 ENTER COLORADO.
From here to milepost 316 is some of the most spectacular scenery on the entire trip. (Have another roll of film handy for quick camera loading.) The rugged country to the south is largely uninhabited and has changed little since the railroad was built.

Milepost
312
to
313
VOLCANIC SPIRES.

The track winds back and forth around tall pinnacles, spires, and pedestal rocks formed from breccias of the Conejos Formation. These weird shapes are the result of alteration by hot water, by weathering, and by erosion of the volcanic rock. Alteration also causes the wide variety of colors seen in the rocks along this section of track (photos, p. 61, 115).

Mile
312.30 PHANTOM CURVE.
This location was named by early-day D&RG trainmen, who often made the trip at night. They saw in the dim shadows, strange shapes darting back and forth in front of the engine headlight beam during long, tiring trips. The squealing noises of the wheel flanges rubbing against the rails as the trains rounded the sharp curve added an eerie effect.

On February 11, 1948 the *San Juan*, with well-known engineer Bill Holt at the throttle, was en route to Alamosa from Durango when a snow avalanche came down the steep cliff above the track and plowed into the train at about 6:30 PM. The lights went off as the coaches started to slide slowly down the side of the canyon; some of the passengers were not even moved off their seats. The locomotive and two baggage cars were not involved and stayed on the track. Most seriously injured was the conductor, George Ottoway, who was pinned in a coach by a timber. The passengers suffered most from the bitter cold. After climbing back up the hill, they were able to get warm in the baggage cars. A "hospital train" arrived at the wreck site about 11:00 PM and returned to Alamosa by 4:00 AM the next morning.

Mile
313.20 CALICO CUT.
A very descriptive name for the soft, rusty-red, orange, purple, maroon, and tan-colored loose clays and weathered rock that are the result of the alteration of hard and soft portions of the chaotic breccias of the Conejos Formation (photo, p. 61).

Avalanches and mudslides caused many problems along here for the Rio Grande, particularly during the winter and early spring months when the rocks were wet.

Salvage operations for the <u>San Juan</u> passenger train wreck of February 11, 1948 at mile 312.30. This eastward view is along the track toward the engine of the wreck train, which is backing down the track pulling a long cable through a block and tackle attached to a large rock to the left of the photograph. In this manner, the coach was pulled up the steep slope to track level.

Derrick OP, located west of the wreck site, was also used to pull this <u>San Juan</u> coach up to track level.

(K.C. Flansburg collection)

Mile
313.44 CROSS TOLTEC CREEK.
elev 9,574 ft (2,918 m)

Until 1942 there was a five-panel standard pile trestle across this small stream.

Just west of Toltec Creek, in the open area on the left side of the track, was the site of TOLTEC SECTION HOUSE, bunk house and coal house (photos, p. 78). Details on the buildings once located here are on p. 77.

On both sides of Toltec Creek, the aspens are glorious in the fall. The red and yellow leaves, and the multi-colored rocks, combine to offer superb photographic opportunities.

Milepost
314 GREAT VIEWS ACROSS TOLTEC CREEK CANYON.

From the left side of the train are many chances to again enjoy the scenery at CALICO CUT and PHANTOM CURVE. The flat-topped mesa on the skyline is capped with resistant layers of Masonic Park Tuff. The track is about 600 ft above the stream at this point and is about ½ mile wide.

Mile
314.32 ENTER NEW MEXICO.

Mile
314.75 TOLTEC PHONE BOOTH.

On April 23, 1881, a special passenger train with one coach and a caboose left Antonito at 11:00 AM bound for Chama. Near the phone booth, engine number 170 and the coach derailed and rolled down the hillside The coach was demolished. Unfortunately, eight people were killed and six others were injured. Heavy rains caused the rails to spread on the new roadbed. There were many derailments until the roadbed had settled and enough ballast was added to stabilize the track.

Milepost
315 GEOLOGIC CONTACT AND TUNNEL TELLTALE.

From here to mile 315.60 is the only place on the entire trip where ancient Precambrian igneous and metamorphic rocks are visible along the track and in Toltec Gorge. These crystalline gneisses and schists are about 1,700 million years old and have been intruded by 1,450 million year old granites and pegmatites.

Outcrops of the jagged Precambrian rocks on both sides of the Rio del los Pinos canyon are quite different from outcrops of the volcanic Conejos Formation. At this point the canyon is very narrow because the stream had a difficult time cutting a channel through the harder, more resistant crystalline rocks.

Soon after reaching the crystalline rocks, the track passes beneath a telltale, a tall, inverted U-shaped metal contraption with wires hanging down from a horizontal bar. When brakemen are on top of a car and get hit in the head by the wires hanging down, they know it is time to get off the roof for the approaching tunnel portal! Photos, p. 57.

Mile
315.20 ROCK OR TOLTEC TUNNEL (TUNNEL NO. 2).
elev 9,631 ft (2,936 m)

At this point, the track is about 600 ft above the stream. It is about 800 ft to the opposite side of the gorge. This 366 ft tunnel was blasted out of the Precambrian rocks using black powder. Because these rocks are so hard, the tunnel did not need to be lined.

Of the approximately 1,600 miles of narrow gauge built by the Rio Grande, only two other narrow gauge tunnels were ever built. In 1882, one was bored at Grassy Trail, Utah, and in 1884 a tunnel was built at Bridgeport in the Gunnison River canyon south of Grand Junction. Later, four tunnels on Tennessee Pass and three in Glenwood Canyon were built to standard gauge dimensions. With so much mountain construction, it is amazing that so few tunnels were needed.

Another interesting quotation (p. 20) from the 1880 excursion describes Toltec Tunnel and how the group spent the night in their Pullman car.

The afternoon sun streams down on a brake wheel on one of the passenger coaches at the west portal of Toltec Tunnel.

(Doris B. Osterwald)

View east from the ridge above Toltec Tunnel. Judging from the hand-hewn ties, this photograph also must have been taken in the early 1880s. A telegraph pole, to the right of the stack of ties, has a cross-arm to carry two wires instead of the original single wire attached to the top of the pole. This area was burned in the 1879 fire, judging from the number of dead trees still standing around the east portal. Outcrops of Precambrian crystalline rocks are in the foreground.

Jackson turned his camera west while standing above Toltec Tunnel and recorded this unusual view of Toltec Gorge, the narrow Rio de los Pinos, and outcrops of cracked and fractured Precambrian granites, gneisses, and schists in the foreground. The forest above the track was destroyed by the 1879 fire. Today, aspens have replaced the burned evergreens.
        (Both photos, W.H. Jackson, Colorado Historical Society)

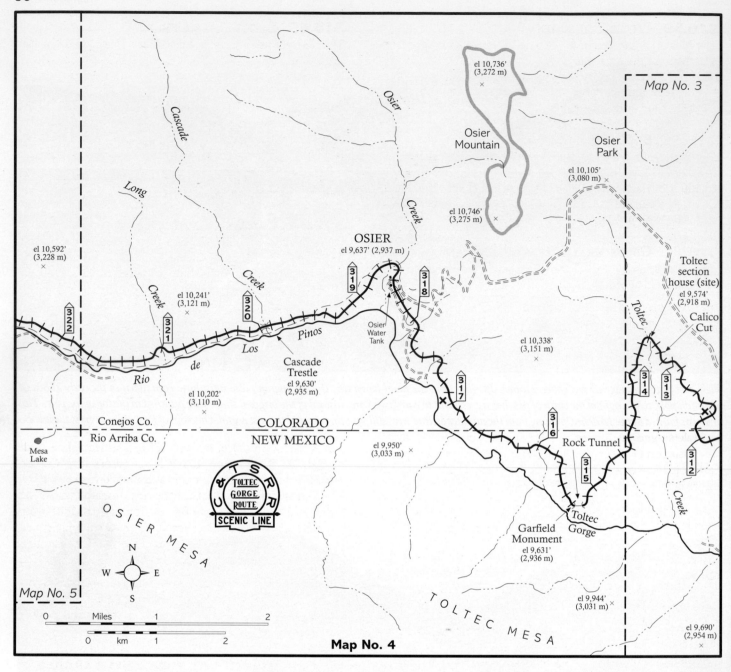

el 10,736' (3,272 m) ×

Osier Mountain

Map No. 3

Osier Park

el 10,105' (3,080 m) ×

Toltec section house (site) el 9,574' (2,918 m)

Calico Cut

el 10,592' (3,228 m) ×

Long

Creek

Creek

el 10,241' (3,121 m) ×

OSIER el 9,637' (2,937 m)

el 10,746' (3,275 m) ×

319

318

320

322

321

Los Pinos de Rio

Cascade Trestle el 9,630' (2,935 m)

Osier Water Tank

el 10,338' (3,151 m) ×

Toltec

314

313

315

316

317

312

Conejos Co.
Rio Arriba Co.

COLORADO
NEW MEXICO

el 10,202' (3,110 m) ×

el 9,950' (3,033 m) ×

Rock Tunnel

Mesa Lake

C&TSRR TOLTEC GORGE ROUTE SCENIC LINE

Creek

OSIER MESA

N
W E
S

Toltec Gorge

Garfield Monument el 9,631' (2,936 m)

el 9,944' (3,031 m) ×

Map No. 5

el 9,690' (2,954 m) ×

Miles
0   1   2

0   km   1   2

TOLTEC MESA

Map No. 4

Mile
315.32 GARFIELD MONUMENT AND TOLTEC GORGE.

The monument (photo, p. 58), along the left side of the track, was erected in honor of President James A. Garfield. He was shot by Charles J. Guiteau, a disappointed office-seeker, in the Washington, D.C. railroad station on July 2. Garfield died on September 19, 1881. The excursion train stopped at the gorge, and after viewing the canyon, members of the Association of General Passenger and Ticket Agents held an impromptu memorial service, which was on September 26, the same day concluding funeral services were held in Cleveland, Ohio. The association later financed the erection of the monument which reads:

IN MEMORIAM
JAMES ABRAM GARFIELD
PRESIDENT OF THE UNITED STATES
DIED SEPTEMBER 19, 1881.
MOURNED BY ALL THE PEOPLE

ERECTED BY MEMBERS OF THE NATIONAL ASSOCIATION OF GENERAL PASSENGER AND TICKET AGENTS, WHO HELD MEMORIAL BURIAL SERVICE ON THIS SPOT SEPTEMBER 26, 1881.

Beyond the monument is another telltale.

A short distance beyond the boundary sign, at mile 315.60, is the contact between the Precambrian rocks and the younger Conejos Formation (see geologic map, p. 116).

Milepost
316.59 ENTER COLORADO.
The hills on both sides of the Rio de los Pinos have very few trees because the area was ravaged by fire in 1879. That year must have been very dry, as fires raged out-of-control in the Lime Creek area between Durango and Silverton, around Leadville, and at many other locations in Colorado.

Mile
317.11 SITE OF SNOWSHED.
This was the first of 24 wooden snowsheds built to protect the track from blowing and drifting snow. At one time at least 13,000 ft of track was covered with sheds between here and Coxo. A complete list of the snowsheds built between 1884 and 1908 is on p. 124.

Milepost
318 CROSS SMALL DRAINAGE CHANNEL.
One-tenth of a mile east of the milepost is a large railroad cut in the Conejos Formation.

Snow fences once covered the entire north side of the track from here to the west switch at Osier. The few wooden timbers left standing are stark reminders of places where blowing and drifting snows filled cuts and caused many blockades.

Mile
318.40 OSIER, COLORADO.
elev 9,637 ft (2,937 m)
Grading crews reached Osier July 31, 1880. Track-laying was completed and the line opened for business between Denver and Osier on October 10, 1880. During those early years, the fare from Denver was $20.30, and a "good meal" cost 75 cents. More details on the history of Osier are on p. 77.

Following a morning of enjoying the sights, sounds, and smells of the narrow gauge, the arrival at Osier offers a change of pace. This lonely outpost is host to a hungry, bustling, crowd of excursionists for several hours every day during the summer season. Lunch is served cafeteria style—quite different from how members of the very first excursion in October 1880 (p. 20) were fed!

The new $600,000 dining facility was dedicated June 30, 1989 with a number of officials and invited guests attending the ceremonies. Following the ribbon-cutting, about 500 hungry passengers and guests entered the dining hall for lunch. The kitchen is on the lower level, along with a gift shop and additional dining tables. Restrooms are on the main level.

After the eastbound train arrives, a second wave of hungry, camera-carrying excursionists join the westbound crowd for lunch. Following lunch, there is plenty of time to inspect the engines, see the remaining buildings at this old station, and to change trains if you are continuing on to Chama. When the train crews complete the necessary switching, check the engines and cars, four long and <u>loud</u> blasts of the whistle summon everyone back to their respective trains for the remainder of the day's excursion on the C&TS. Photos of this area are on p. 38, 57, 79, 96, 115.

Mile
318.45 CROSS OSIER CREEK.
This stream was formerly called Bear Creek. In 1882, two bridges were built to replace the first rickety ones thrown together in the rush to complete the line. One bridge was a 28 ft, three-panel bridge. The second was a 112 ft, seven-panel structure. These bridges lasted until 1936 when much-needed work was done on the line and a culvert was installed (ref. B). Many snow fences were along the right side of the track, but few remnants remain today.

Traces of the old toll road are still visible on the left side of the train from here to about milepost 323.

Mile
319.95 CASCADE TRESTLE.
In the rush to complete the San Juan Extension, a wooden trestle was built across Cascade Creek during 1880. According to bridge record books unearthed by former D&RGW employee Jackson C. Thode, the original bridge was 432 ft long, 116 ft high, and had 28 bents (ref. G).

The *Denver Tribune* wrote of an excursion made over the new line in August 1881 and reported that one coach derailed on the bridge. "Within sight of Osier is a long bridge, built of wood and supported on wooden trestles." If there had not been a guard rail on the bridge, "the whole train would have been thrown off the bridge and plunged into the gully below, a depth of several hundred feet."

The present structure, built in 1889, is a deck-plate girder bridge 137 ft high and 408 ft long, across tiny Cascade Creek. It has seven 54 ft spans and one 30 ft span on steel bents. Iron for both the Cascade and Lobato trestles was fabricated by the Keystone Bridge Company in 1881, using a unique German design. There is no cross-bracing between the bents (photos, p. 38, 56). More details on the complicated history of this bridge are on p. 73.

No doubleheading has ever been allowed over this bridge. During the years the D&RGW ran long freight trains, helper engines were inserted into the middle of trains, and ahead of the caboose.

Milepost
320 MILEPOST AT WEST END OF TRESTLE.
During the early summer, large clumps of wild blue iris are abundant (p. 109). Later yellow-blossomed shrubby cinquefoils are common. During the fall, bright, indigo-blue gentians peek through the native grasses. Few trees have grown back since the 1879 fire.

The track is almost level for several miles—a good place in earlier days for westbound engineers to "make up time."

Milepost
321 CROSS LONG CREEK.
The track was completed to this point October 16, 1880.

D&RGW right-of-way and track maps indicate portable snow fences once stood along this area. Just west of the bridge, a snowshed stood until 1911 when it was blown down by a gale-force wind. According to long-time D&RGW crewmen, from here to Cumbres was the most difficult section to keep open. The straight track at Los Pinos was probably the worst place

Eastbound passenger train 2, pulled by engine 488, rounds the last large curve west of Osier, June 30, 1989.

Westbound passenger train arriving at Osier, June 30, 1989 just in time for the dedication ceremonies before the opening of the new dining facility.
(Both photos, Doris B. Osterwald)

Author's note: in January 2004 I received an unexpected letter from Vernon J. Glover, well-known for his carefully documented research on New Mexico's railroads, lumbering, and mining history. He confirmed that the Cascade and Lobato trestles were designed by consulting engineer C. Shaler Smith.
I have long believed AT&SF locating engineer A.A. Robinson invited Smith to Colorado in 1878 or 1879 to design the Hanging Bridge in the Royal Gorge for the AT&SF, and that Smith probably met Robert Morley and James DeRemer, locating engineers for the D&RG who accompanied him to the sites of the Cascade and Lobato bridges. Smith and Robinson then traveled south across Raton Pass to Apache Canyon of the Rio Galisteo east of Lamy NM where Smith designed three more AT&SF bridges. These four bridges were described in the May 1892 Amer. Soc. of Civil Eng. Transactions, but the author neglected to state who designed them.
Glover also documented that during a later trip west in 1880 or 1881 C. Shaler Smith designed at least 23 spans for the AT&SF, a number for the A&P RR (an AT&SF subsidiary that built west from Albuquerque), and the Johnson Canyon viaducts west of Williams AZ.

where winds would whip across the top of the ridge and pile the white stuff into huge drifts, 20 to 30 ft high.

During the early summer, yellow holly grapes, wallflowers, puccoons, senecios, and tiny cinquefoils are common. Later, blue flax and pink to reddish scarlet gilias, and brilliant fuchsia-colored locoweeds may be spotted from the train. Purple asters are common during the fall.

Milepost
322 NICE VIEWS OF LOS PINOS VALLEY.
The stream is now less than 100 ft below the track. The tree-covered slopes across the valley obviously escaped the 1879 fire.

Mile
322.12 SITE OF OLD LOS PINOS SIDING.
The original Los Pinos siding was here and could hold 18 cars. You'll need a sharp eye to find any trace of it, as it was moved west to its present location in the 1920s. An account of a Rio Grande train getting stuck at this point is on p. 93.

Mile
322.95 LOS PINOS PHONE BOOTH.
This dilapidated, unused booth probably was moved from mile 322.12 sometime after 1923. Another phone booth can be seen due west across the valley at a higher elevation.

The rounded, hummocky, irregular slopes on both sides of the stream are small landslides that formed when loose debris, left by small glaciers, gradually moved downward and outward.

Neff Mountain, elev 10,888 ft (3,319 m) is the flat-topped mountain to the northwest. Layers of volcanic Masonic Park Tuff cap the peak.

Mile
324.50 STRAIGHT TRACK.
For almost a mile the track is actually straight. In 1920, second-hand 57 pound rail was laid from here to Cumbres (ref. F).

On October 2, 1971, a special excursion, pulled by old-reliable engine 483, stopped at Cascade Trestle for a photo run-by.

(Frank W. Osterwald)

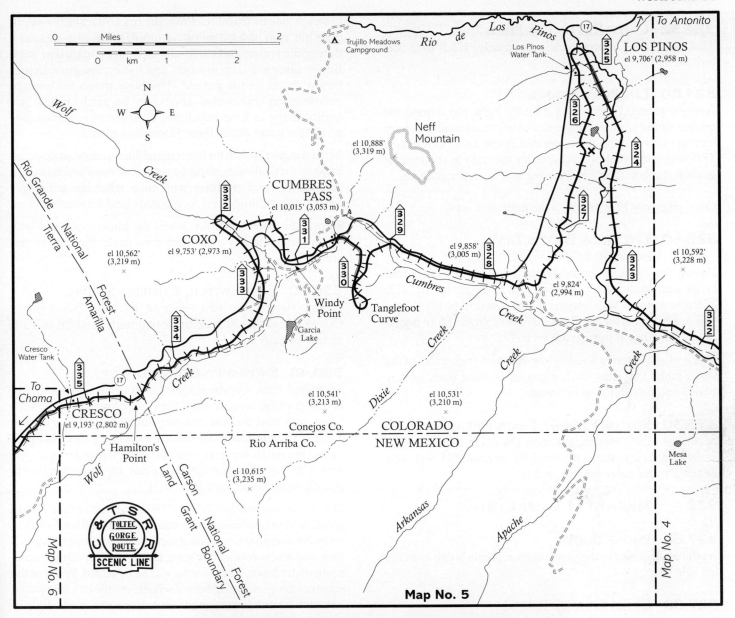

Map No. 5

A photographer's special on October 21, 1990, got an unexpected heavy snowstorm, as this view of Los Pinos Tank shows. (Gerald M. Blea)

Mile
324.52 CROSS RIO DE LOS PINOS.

This fire-decked, eleven-panel, pile trestle, 175 ft long was built in 1886.

Mile
324.80 LOS PINOS SIDING.

A 46-car siding, 1,850 ft long is on the right, just beyond the bridge. At the west end of the siding, the track makes a sharp hairpin curve around the upper end of the Los Pinos valley. This long curve makes it possible for the train to continue its gradual climb to Cumbres Pass without a steeper gradient.

Colo. Highway 17 is visible to the north and west.

Mile
325.50 LOS PINOS WATER TANK.
elev 9,710 ft (2,960 m)

During the 1920s, a section house, bunk house, and a coal house were located here. The first coal house burned in 1912, and was replaced with another which lasted until 1929. Coal was needed for refueling the rotary snowplows. More details on the buildings at this site are on p. 77.

Many swallow nests are just below the overhanging roof of the water tank. You may catch glimpses of these birds as they swoop and dive, hunting for insects.

Mile
326.30 SITE OF FREIGHT TRAIN DERAILMENT.

In the last major derailment during D&RGW ownership, an eastbound freight train, powered by engines 498 and 497, derailed at this curve (photos, p. 53).

Milepost
327 MILEPOST AT SHARP CURVE.

Mile
327.60 PHONE BOOTH.

As the track curves to the right, another phone booth is on the left side.

Mile
327.80 CROSS GRAVEL ROAD.

This road leads southward onto private land which was originally part of the Tierra Amarilla Mexican Land Grant of 1832 (p. 14).

Milepost
328 TRACK BELOW COLORADO HWY. 17.
elev 9,858 ft (3,005 m)

To reach the summit of Cumbres, the train must still climb another 159 ft in 2.6 miles.

Mile
329 CROSS CUMBRES CREEK.

From here are great views of TANGLEFOOT CURVE, the hairpin-shaped loop the track makes to reach Cumbres Pass.

Mile
329.76 TANGLEFOOT CURVE.

At the lower end of the sharp loop was the site of three snowsheds and two wooden trestles during the early years (photos, p. 55, 90). Until recent times, this 20° curve was also called the "Cumbres Loop" or "The Balloon" by railroad crews.

On each side of Cumbres Pass, the track reaches the subalpine life zone. Much snow accumulates in this area, and during the spring and early summer, it is a luxuriant wildflower garden. Iris, primroses, and buttercups grow in profusion on the moist ground. The large plants with bright yellow-green leaves that appear to be partly rolled, are cornhusk lily or false hellebore, *Veratrum tenuipetalum*. See p. 109 for more about these interesting plants.

In the summer, watch for blue columbines, yellow arctic paintbrushes, arctic thistles, shrubby cinquefoils and potentillas. In August, this area is ablaze with color when the tall purple asters, lupines, sunflowers, goldenrods, and fireweeds bloom.

During the winter months, when the track is covered with snow, snowmobilers make their own tracks throughout this area.

Mile
330.10 EAST SWITCH, CUMBRES SIDING.

At this switch, the two levels of track at TANGLEFOOT CURVE are about 70 ft apart horizontally, and 20 to 25 ft apart vertically.

Mile
330.48 SNOWSHED-COVERED WYE.

Snowshed 330A was about 526 ft long and covered portions of both legs of the wye. It is the last covered wye in the United States and also the last standing snowshed on the narrow gauge. Due to lack of maintenance, most of the shed collapsed during the rough winters of the late 1970s. Near the tail of the wye is the same beautiful little lake that Lt. Anderson (p. 16) and his men camped beside in 1874.

During the summer of 1990 and 1991, members of the *Friends of the C&TS* volunteered time, money, lumber and hard work to begin rebuilding this historic structure. Also completed at this time was a new roof and bracing for the car inspectors house, north of the depot. The building was also painted. Without the efforts of this group of dedicated volunteers, the building would not have survived many more winters (photos, p. 99, 100).

Mile
330.60 CUMBRES, COLORADO.
elev 10,015 ft (3,053 m)

Cumbres means "crests" or "summits" in Spanish. During construction days, this station was referred to as "Alta." Grading crews reached this point July 31, 1880 and the San Juan Extension was opened for travel from Antonito to Cumbres (or Alta) December 15, 1880. When completed, it was one of the highest railroads in the United States. Cumbres Pass is not on the Continental Divide, which is about 10 miles west of Chama.

One wonders how the construction crews for the Rio Grande felt when they finally reached Alta, looked down into Wolf Creek valley, and realized their difficult job was far from over. Many more sharp curves, steep grades, rock cuts, and bridges remained to be built, which were additional challenges to their skill and ingenuity. The back-breaking labor of placing hand-hewn ties on the prepared grade, and spiking the rails to the ties was done during December and January, hardly an ideal time to complete a railroad.

In the early years, a number of people lived at Cumbres Pass year round. A post office was here until 1937. Most structures were built between 1880 and 1882. There are about 3,000 ft of sidings. Additional details on the structures and facilities at Cumbres are on p. 79.

Just west of the water plug is a "hump" in the track. This is where the four percent grade starts. This means that for every 100 ft the train moves forward, it descends 4 ft vertically. East of the "hump," the grade is nearly level, gradually increasing to an easy 1.42 percent ruling grade. After the train crew has filled the engine tender with water, performed a brake test, and set the retainers for the steep descent from Cumbres, your narrow gauge railroading adventure continues. Additional photos are on p. 80, 82-85, 94, 99, 100.

Mile
330.75 CROSS WOODEN TRESTLE.
This 84 ft, six-panel standard pile trestle was the railroad overpass above Colo. Hwy. 17 until the late 1960s, when the highway was relocated.

Milepost
331 WINDY POINT.
For the next mile, have your camera ready for the spectacular scenery of the valley of Wolf Creek. The sharp curves, steep hillsides, and colorful rocks make this area another of the dramatic highlights of the trip. The track is about 250 ft above the valley floor (photos, p. 52, 94, 97).

The valley below Windy Point was partly filled with slow-moving ice during the most recent ice age. After the ice melted, blocks of loose rock and soil in lateral moraines moved or slid downward (landslides) to form the rounded hills visible along the sides of the valley.

On the skyline, above the right side of the train, are more volcanic rocks that have been altered and weathered to produce the bright red, yellow, and orange-colors. During July, Colorado's state flower, the blue columbine blooms along the track, adding yet another color to the landscape.

An interesting account of D&RGW crews fighting huge snowdrifts along this section of track is on p. 93.

Milepost
332 MILEPOST JUST EAST OF WOLF CREEK.
Another 20° curve is at the upper end of Wolf Creek Valley.

Notice how the trunks of the aspen trees are bowed close to the ground. This is a sign of unstable ground that is moving. The trees continue to grow upward while the ground slowly moves downward.

Between mile 331.28 and 332.78 were eight snowsheds that covered more than 1,000 ft of track. All were burned by the D&RG.

Mile
332.20 COXO, COLORADO
elev 9,753 ft (2,973 m)
Until 1965 there was an 800 ft siding here (photo, p. 82) which had a capacity of 18 cars. The one building located here was retired in 1938.

Mile
332.75 CROSS COLORADO HWY 17.
This is a popular stop for railfans following the train by automobile. Innumerable photographs have been taken from here, as eastbound trains labor up the steep four percent grade to Windy Point.

This is a good location to compare the environmental impact on the land of a railroad grade more than 110 years old with that of the automobile highway built in the 1960s.

Mile
332.85 COXO PHONE BOOTH.
This booth was rebuilt by volunteers in 1973.

For the next several miles the train winds among thick aspen groves which are favorite habitats for scarlet gilias, blue monkshoods and penstemons, and yellow golden banners. Trees include white pine, Douglas firs, river willows, birches and some blue spruces. Occasionally deer are spotted in the timber.

Mile
334.50 HAMILTON'S POINT.
This location may be named for L.C. Hamilton, a D&RG Division Superintendent in 1881. An early W.H. Jackson photograph referred to this locality as "White Rock Point." The track is now about 300 ft above Wolf Creek and the canyon is about 1,000 ft wide.

The track enters land of the former Tierra Amarilla Mexican Land Grant, which was one of many grants given Mexican citizens to encourage settlement on the northern frontier of the Mexican state of Nuevo Mejico (p. 14).

As the track descends into Wolf Creek Valley, outcrops of sedimentary rocks of Tertiary and Jurassic age are visible on each side of the track.

Mile
335.10 CRESCO, COLORADO.
elev 9,193 ft (2,802 m)
The present water tank was built in 1893. Several families lived here year round, and their only continuous contact with the "outside world" was with the daily trains. A 64 ft, four-panel pile trestle crosses a small stream just west of the water tank. More on the buildings that once stood here is on p. 79.

Aspen trees along here were infected by millions of tent caterpillars, *Malacosma americana*, during the early 1970s. Many acres of trees were killed or badly damaged by these insects. The larvae live in a web-like nest suspended on the branches of aspens. When the insects hatched, the rails became so coated with creeping worms that the locomotives were unable to maintain any traction. Two persons then sat on the front of the engine and removed the insects by holding brooms on each rail. In that manner eastbound trains were able to ascend the four percent grade.

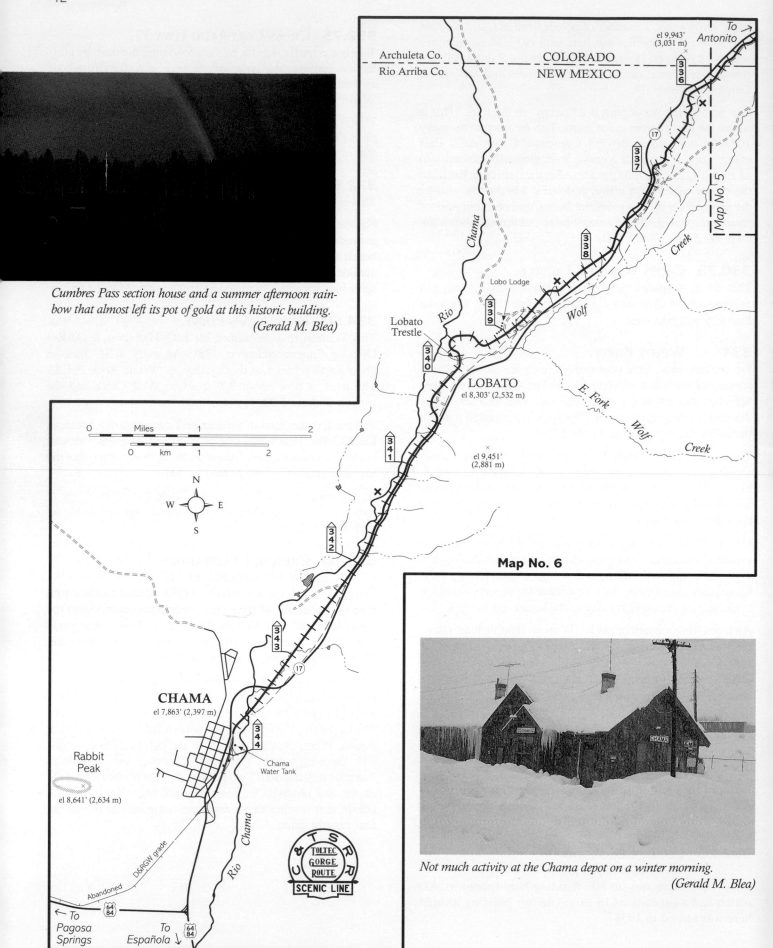

Cumbres Pass section house and a summer afternoon rainbow that almost left its pot of gold at this historic building.
(Gerald M. Blea)

Archuleta Co.
Rio Arriba Co.

COLORADO
NEW MEXICO

To
Antonito

el 9,943'
(3,031 m)

336

337

Map No. 5

338

Lobo Lodge

Rio Chama

339

Wolf

Creek

Lobato
Trestle

340

E. Fork

Wolf

LOBATO
el 8,303' (2,532 m)

Creek

341

el 9,451'
(2,881 m)

Miles
0   1   2
0   1   2
km

N
W   E
S

342

Map No. 6

343

17

CHAMA
el 7,863' (2,397 m)

344

Rabbit
Peak

Chama
Water Tank

el 8,641' (2,634 m)

D&RGW grade

Rio Chama

Abandoned

64
84

← To
Pagosa
Springs

To
Española ↓

64
84

C&TSRR
TOLTEC
GORGE
ROUTE
SCENIC LINE

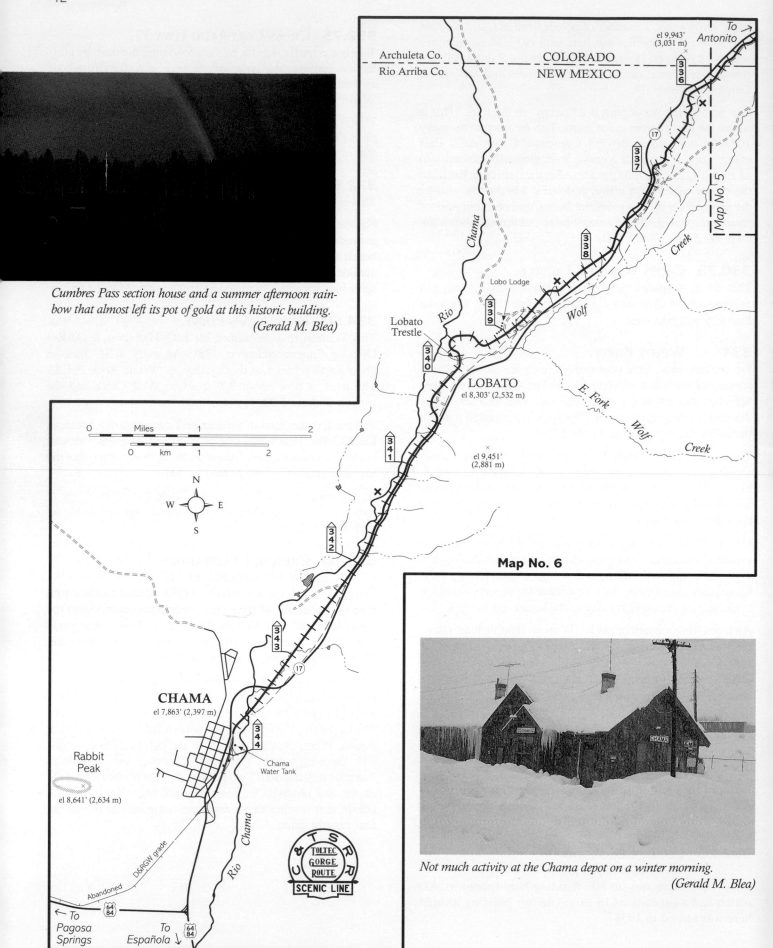

Not much activity at the Chama depot on a winter morning.
(Gerald M. Blea)

Mile
335.60 CROSS COLORADO–NEW MEXICO STATE BOUNDARY.

This is the last crossing of the state line before reaching Chama.

Throughout this portion of Wolf Creek Valley are lovely views of the open rounded hills. The lush grasses, bracken ferns, wildflowers, some blue spruces, white firs, and clumps of scrub oaks or Gambel oaks, are a decided change from the dense aspen groves at higher elevations or from the sagebrush country near Antonito.

Gambel oak, *Quercus gambelii,* grows in dense thickets of tall shrubs or small trees. In the fall, the leaves change from a shiny green color to shades of yellow, orange, and red. The acorns from this tree were an important food for Indians and early settlers because the seeds are sweet and tasty. Dried acorns can be ground into flour or meal.

The very conspicuous 3 to 5 ft tall spiked plant with lance-shaped, bright-green leaves up to 1 ft long are monument plants, also called green gentians or elkweeds, *Frasera speciosa.* A biennial, it blooms in the early summer. Another tall, spiked biennial is mullein, *Verbascum thapsus.* Fireweed, *Epilobium angustifolium,* is one of the most beautiful and distinctive plants found in the mountains. The four-petaled, pink or reddish-purple blossoms form a symmetrical unbranched stem from 1 to 5 ft tall. More on these interesting species is on p. 109.

Mile
336.20 SITE OF ENGINE DERAILMENT.

According to newspaper accounts and D&RG company records, light engine 489 derailed at this point on May 3, 1926. Details and photographs are on p. 50.

Mile
337.45 CROSS NEW MEXICO HWY 17.

The largest family of wildflowers, the composite or sunflower family, grow in abundance throughout this area. Some common members that are easy to see from the train include several species of sunflowers, thistles, yarrows, gumweeds, asters, daisys, salsifys, rabbitbrushes, senecios, dandelions, and sneezeweeds. Composites are usually shades of yellow, white, blue, purple, or reddish purple; red blossoms are very rare.

Mile
338.35 HURLEY'S CURVE.

This reverse curve was named by Rio Grande railroaders for an early-day engineer, Ed J. Hurley, who was killed in a derailment at this location. The photo on p. 48 is of another wreck at this site on May 20, 1904.

Mile
338.65 CROSS GRAVEL ROAD.

This U.S. Forest Service road leads to the upper Rio Chama Valley. As the train continues toward Chama, the sound of air escaping from the retainer valves at the end of each car offers more unusual sounds.

Mile
338.91 DALTON.

A ten-car lumber-loading spur was at this site until 1913. The name may be for John C. Dalton of Manassa, Colorado, a contractor who worked for the D&RG Chief Engineer's Office in the late 1890s.

Milepost
339 LOBO LODGE.

Cabins on the right side are rented to hikers, hunters, and fishermen. They are built on glacial debris.

Mile
339.75 LOBATO TRESTLE.

The original bridge across the East Fork of Wolf Creek was a hastily built wooden trestle. The present iron trestle is a deck-plate girder bridge,100 ft high and 310 ft long, that was installed in 1883 (ref. G). There are five 54 ft spans and one 40 ft span supported by five riveted bents. Iron for both the Lobato and Cascade trestles was fabricated by the Keystone Bridge Company in 1881 using a unique German design. There is no cross-bracing between the bents. A walk-way and hand rails were added in 1945. It is amazing that this beautiful, tall bridge crosses such an insignificant stream (photos p. 49, 74).

The name Lobato (which means "young wolf" in Spanish) may be for the J.J. Lobato Land Grant in Rio Arriba County, New Mexico.

Mile
339.99 LOBATO SIDING.
elev 8,303 ft (2,532 m)

First known as Wolf Creek siding, the name was changed by General Manager Dodge of the D&RG Railway in December 1880. This 28-car siding is 1,190 ft long. The cattle pens on the right side of the track were last used in the fall of 1966.

A small, flimsy depot and strange looking fake water tank were built in the fall of 1970 for the first movie filmed on the C&TS, "Shootout," starring Gregory Peck. The "town" was called Weed City. Through the years, several other movies have used this location for movie sets. During the winter of 1991-92 a portion of the depot collapsed.

Mile
340.50 ENTER "THE NARROWS."

The valley at this point is more narrow and V-shaped because a small glacier, which flowed down Wolf Creek from Cumbres Pass, met another small mass of ice that flowed from the upper Rio Chama Valley. These two small glaciers met to form a terminal moraine at Lobato. Below the moraine, the valley was not sculptured and carved by ice into the characteristic U-shape seen in Wolf Creek Valley to the east. The track, however, is built on glacial debris washed from the moraines.

The term "Narrows" was coined by early-day railroaders for this portion of the route located in the narrow Wolf Creek Valley that was not glaciated.

Taking water at Chama, August 29, 1967.   *(Carl R. Osterwald)*

Mile
341.65 FAULT IN DAKOTA FORMATION.
On the right side of the train, across the canyon, a small fault is visible (photo, p. 119).

Between mile 341.90 and 343.50 is the second longest stretch of straight track—all of a mile and a half long. The train is still on the four percent grade.

Milepost
342 LEAVE "THE NARROWS."

Mile
342.50 END FOUR PERCENT GRADE.
The track is built on glacial outwash debris from the melting Chama and Wolf Creek glaciers. Rabbit Peak, elev 8,641 ft, is the prominent flat-topped peak on the southwestern skyline.

Mile
343 SITE OF BROAD SPUR.
A lumber-loading spur track, named for F.W. Broad, a Chama lumberman, was located at this milepost at one time.

Mile
343.20 CROSS NEW MEXICO HWY 17.

Mile
343.60 CROSS RIO CHAMA.
The 230 ft steel truss bridge was installed in the 1920s. The trees on both sides of the river are cottonwoods and willows.

Mile
343.70 RIO CHAMA RV CAMPGROUND.

Mile
343.12 CHAMA, NEW MEXICO.
elev 7,863 ft (2,397 m)
The western terminus and main headquarters for the Cumbres & Toltec Scenic Railroad. As the train slowly pulls to a stop in front of the depot, and after the last echo of the whistle and bell have faded away, remember the sights, sounds, and smells of your day on the narrow gauge. Imagine how it must have been to travel this route a century ago, and be thankful that this bit of western America has been preserved for future generations to enjoy. Do return for another ride on this very special railroad.

Grading crews camped here in September 1880, and the first train arrived December 31, 1880. The San Juan Division opened for business between Denver and Chama January 18, 1881. Chama is a railroad town. It was the division point on the San Juan Extension. The roundhouse and other facilities were built to service the engines and cars before heading east up "the hill" or west to Durango.

While in Chama, perhaps you will have time to take a tour of the Chama yards using the brochure prepared by the *Friends of the C&TS*. These yards are a living and working museum of narrow gauge railroading. Please follow the safety instructions listed in the brochure, if you plan on visiting the equipment in the yards. More information and photos on the structures and equipment in the Chama yards are on p. 15, 42, 46, 70, 75, 76.

EASTBOUND GUIDE

Mile
344.12 CHAMA, NEW MEXICO.
elev 7,863 ft (2,397 m)

Western terminus and main headquarters for the Cumbres & Toltec Scenic Railroad (C&TS).

Construction of the San Juan Extension started at Antonito on March 31, 1880. Grading crews were dispatched to various points along the proposed route and by September 1880, crews camped along the Rio Chama. The first train arrived in Chama December 31, and the San Juan Division opened for business between Denver and Chama January 18, 1881.

Chama is a railroad town. It was a division point on the San Juan Extension of the Denver and Rio Grande Railway (D&RG). The roundhouse and other facilities were built to service the engines and cars before heading east up "the hill" or west to Durango. The coaling tower or coal tipple, on the right, is believed to be the last remaining wooden tipple in the United States.

Perhaps on your return to Chama, you will have time to tour the Chama yard using the brochure prepared by the *Friends of the C&TS.* These yards are a living and working museum of narrow gauge railroading. Additional data on the facilities is on p. 75. Please follow the safety instructions listed in the brochure, if you plan on visiting the equipment in the yards.

As the train slowly pulls away from the depot, plumes of black coal smoke billow upward into the morning sky. The eastbound trip is always exciting, especially if your train is pulled by two engines up the steep, winding four percent grade to Cumbres Pass. There will be many chances to photograph the engines and train as it labors up the grade, especially from the open gondola car.

Between Chama and Cumbres, your engine will use 2-½ to 3-½ tons of coal and about 3,500 gallons of water. For the remaining 51 miles between Cumbres and Antonito, the engine will use an additional two to three tons of coal.

Mileposts are on the **left** side of the train.

Mile
343.70 RIO CHAMA RV CAMPGROUND.

Mile
343.60 CROSS RIO CHAMA.
The 230 ft steel truss bridge was installed in the 1920s. The trees on both sides of the river are cottonwoods and willows.

Mile
343.20 CROSS NEW MEXICO HWY 17.

Milepost
343 GAMBEL OR SCRUB OAKS.
These trees, *Quercus gambelii,* grow in dense thickets of tall shrubs or small trees along the track. In the fall, the leaves change from a shiny green color to shades of yellow, orange, and red. The acorns from this tree were an important food for Indians and early settlers because the seeds are sweet and tasty. Dried acorns can be ground into flour or meal.

A lumber-loading spur track, named BROAD SPUR for Chama lumberman F.W. Broad, was located at this milepost at one time.

Mile
342.50 START FOUR PERCENT GRADE.
A decided hump indicates the point where the track begins the four percent ruling grade. This means that for every 100 ft the train moves forward, it climbs 4 ft vertically.

The track is built on glacial outwash debris from the Chama and Wolf Creek glaciers. Rabbit Peak, elev 8,641 ft (2,634 m), is the prominent flat-topped peak on the southwestern skyline. Ahead is the steep, tree-covered valley of Wolf Creek through which the train will climb to Cumbres Pass.

Milepost
342 ENTER "THE NARROWS."
The valley at this point is more narrow and V-shaped because a small glacier, which flowed down Wolf Creek from Cumbres Pass, met another small mass of ice that flowed from the upper Rio Chama Valley. These two small glaciers met to form a terminal moraine at Lobato. Below the moraine, the valley was not sculptured and carved by ice into the characteristic U-shape in Wolf Creek Valley farther to the east. The track is, however, built on glacial debris washed from the moraines.

The term "Narrows" was coined by early-day railroaders for this portion of the route located in the narrow V-shaped Wolf Creek Valley that was not glaciated.

Mile
341.65 FAULT IN DAKOTA FORMATION.
On the left side of the train, across the canyon, a small fault is visible (photo, p. 119).

Between mile 343.50 and mile 341.90 is the second longest stretch of straight track—all of a mile and a half long! As your journey progresses the novelty of this will become apparent. The meandering, convoluted route chosen by the D&RG was explained by one wit who said the surveying crews simply turned their mule loose and followed it across the mountains!

Aspen trees line both sides of the track through "The Narrows." These trees, *Populus tremuloides,* reproduce from shallow roots which spread laterally. They send shoots upward to form a grove in which all the trees are related—called "clones." The genetics of clone groves determine when the first leaves appear in the spring and when and to what color the leaves turn in the fall. Amounts of moisture, temperature, and soil composition also affect these traits. Genetics also determine the shapes of the branches and the color of the bark, which varies from light gray-green to brownish-green to whitish. Bark of older

The Chama depot of the C&TS on the bright morning of June 12, 1988.　*(Jim Ozment)*

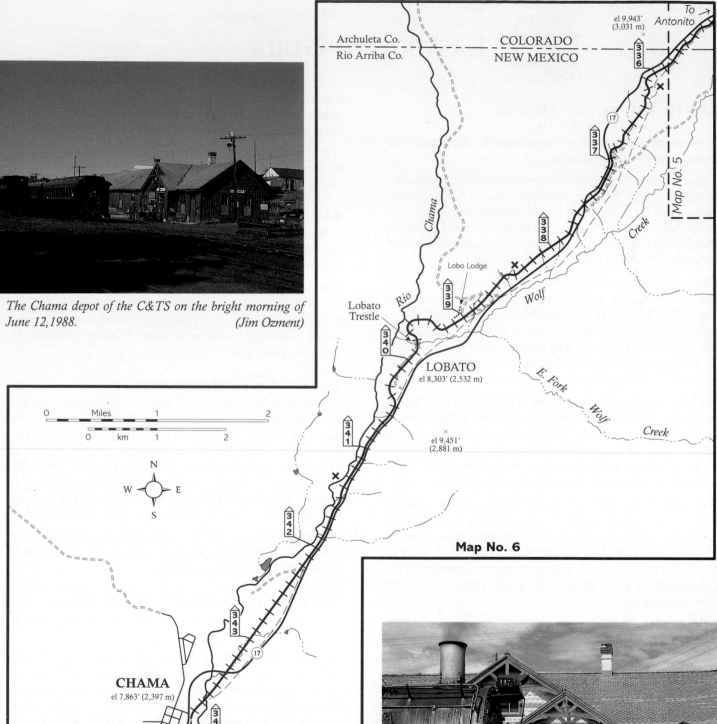

Archuleta Co.
Rio Arriba Co.

COLORADO
NEW MEXICO

To Antonito

el 9,943'
(3,031 m)

336

337

17

Map No. 5

338

Rio Chama

Creek

Lobo Lodge

339

Wolf

Lobato Trestle

340

Rio

LOBATO
el 8,303' (2,532 m)

E. Fork Wolf

341

el 9,451'
(2,881 m)

Creek

Map No. 6

0　Miles　1　2
0　km　1　2

N
W　E
S

342

343

17

CHAMA
el 7,863' (2,397 m)

344

Rabbit
Peak

Chama Water Tank

el 8,641' (2,634 m)

Rio Chama

D&RGW grade

Abandoned

64 84

← To Pagosa Springs

To Española ↓

64 84

C&TSRR
TOLTEC GORGE ROUTE
SCENIC LINE

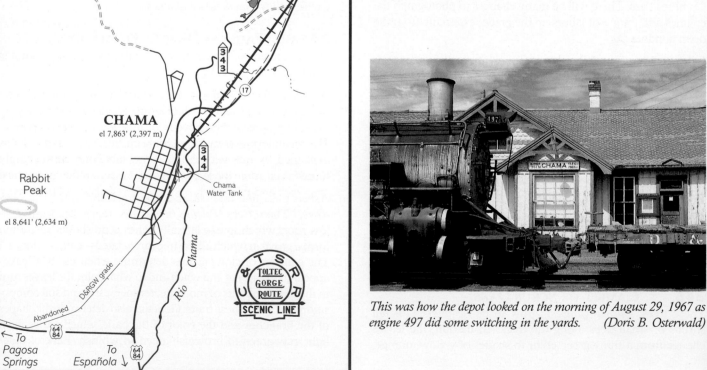

This was how the depot looked on the morning of August 29, 1967 as engine 497 did some switching in the yards.　*(Doris B. Osterwald)*

aspen trees may be whitish due to oxidation. Aspens also produce some seeds, which explains why one clump will turn a golden yellow color in the fall, and an adjacent grove will be a brilliant red color.

Beavers are very fond of aspen wood for food and for building their lodges. The soft white wood is used in industry for pulp, excelsior, boxes, and matches.

As the train continues eastward there will be many chances to see and photograph the aspens in all their glory, especially during the crisp, clear autumn days. Backlighted photos with the sunlight filtering through the dancing leaves can be very dramatic.

Mile 340.50 LEAVE "THE NARROWS."
Ahead, watch for the rounded slopes of morainal debris through which the Rio Chama has cut a channel.

Mile 399.99 LOBATO SIDING.
elev. 8,303 ft. (2,532 m)

First known as Wolf Creek siding, the name was changed by General Manager Dodge of the D&RG Railway in December 1880.

This 28-car siding is 1,190 ft long. The cattle pens on the left side of the track were last used in the fall of 1966.

A small, flimsy depot and strange looking fake water tank were built in the fall of 1970 for the first movie filmed on the C&TS, "Shootout," starring Gregory Peck. The "town" was called Weed City. Through the years, several other movies have used this location for movie sets. During the winter of 1991-92 a portion of the depot collapsed.

Mile 339.75 LOBATO TRESTLE.
The original bridge across the East Fork of Wolf Creek was a hastily built wooden trestle. The present iron trestle is a deck-plate girder bridge, 100 ft high and 310 ft long, that was fabricated by the Keystone Bridge Company in 1881, and installed in 1883 (ref. G). There are five 54 ft spans and one 40 ft span supported by five riveted bents. There is no cross-bracing between the bents. A walk-way and hand rails were added in 1945. It is amazing that this beautiful, tall bridge crosses such an insignificant stream (photos, p. 49, 74).

Because of weight restrictions, when double-headed trains reach this trestle, the head engine is cut off. Then the rest of the train proceeds across the trestle where the two engines are again coupled up.

The name Lobato (which means "young wolf" in Spanish) may be for the J.J. Lobato Land Grant in Rio Arriba County, New Mexico.

Milepost 339 LOBO LODGE.
Cabins on the left are rented to hikers, hunters, and fishermen. They are built on glacial debris.

Mile 338.91 DALTON.
A ten-car lumber loading spur was at this site until 1913. The name may be for John C. Dalton of Manassa, Colorado, a contractor who worked for the D&RG Chief Engineer's Office in the late 1890s.

Train No. 2 will stop here to board eastbound passengers, if notified by radio.

Mile 338.65 CROSS GRAVEL ROAD.
A U.S. Forest Service road leads to the upper Rio Chama Valley. There is a fascinating rhythm in the sound of the engine (or engines) laboring up the four percent grade.

Mile 338.35 HURLEY'S CURVE.
This reverse curve was named by Rio Grande railroaders for an early-day engineer, Ed J. Hurley, who was killed in a derailment at this location. The photo on p. 48 is of another wreck at this site on May 20, 1904.

Mile 337.45 CROSS NEW MEXICO HWY 17.
The largest family of wildflowers, the composite or sunflower family, grow in abundance throughout this area. Some common members that are easy to see from the train include several species of sunflowers, thistles, yarrows, gumweeds, asters, daisys, salsifys, rabbitbrushes, senecios, dandelions, and sneezeweeds. Composites are usually shades of yellow, white, blue, lavender, or reddish-purple; red blossoms are very rare.

Mile 336.20 SITE OF ENGINE DERAILMENT.
According to newspaper accounts and D&RG company records, light engine 489 derailed at this point on May 3, 1926. Details and photographs are on p. 50.

Mile 335.60 ENTER COLORADO.
This is the first of eleven crossing of the the Colorado-New Mexico state boundary. The D&RG placed stone monuments at each of these crossings, and most are still in place today.

The boundary between the two states was first surveyed in 1868 along the 37th parallel. Later, errors were found and in 1902-3 a second survey was authorized by Congress. This survey would have reduced the size of Colorado considerably, which brought forth loud protests from property owners along the boundary line. Arguments between the two states continued until 1925 when the U.S. Supreme Court ruled that the 1868 boundary was legal. The boundary has since been re-surveyed and portions have been moved about 1,200 ft southward near Cresco, Colorado.

From here to mile 295.08 the route is in Rio Grande National Forest while in Colorado and Carson National Forest while in New Mexico.

Throughout this portion of Wolf Creek Valley, are lovely views of the open rounded hills. The lush grasses, ferns, wildflowers, some blue spruces, white firs, and clumps of scrub or Gambel oaks are always a delight to see.

This photo taken by D&RG carman Monte Ballough show the result of engine 170 jumping the track at mile 338.35 in 1904. This engine was involved in many accidents during its service on the Rio Grande. It was finally dismantled in 1926. The baggage and mail car left the track and turned over on the north side, while two coaches tipped over on the opposite side of the track. No one was killed, although passengers were shaken up and had to crawl out of the coach through the windows. A relief train with a doctor came from Chama.

One month before the above photo was taken, a westbound freight piled up in "The Narrows" at mile 341.35. According to newspaper accounts of this wreck, engineer George Lewis lost control of the train and the engine plunged down a steep embankment. The engineer suffered rib, ankle, and hip injuries, but conductor W.K. Newcomb and the brakeman, Killian, were not injured. They had uncoupled the caboose from the train so it was not wrecked.   *(Both photos by Monte Ballough)*

Author's note: in January 2004 I received an unexpected letter from Vernon J. Glover, well-known for his carefully documented research on New Mexico's railroads, lumbering, and mining history. He confirmed that the Cascade and Lobato trestles were designed by consulting engineer C. Shaler Smith.

I have long believed AT&SF locating engineer A.A. Robinson invited Smith to Colorado in 1878 or 1879 to design the Hanging Bridge in the Royal Gorge for the AT&SF, and that Smith probably met Robert Morley and James DeRemer, locating engineers for the D&RG who accompanied him to the sites of the Cascade and Lobato bridges. Smith and Robinson then traveled south across Raton Pass to Apache Canyon of the Rio Galisteo east of Lamy NM where Smith designed three more AT&SF bridges. These four bridges were described in the May 1892 Amer. Soc. of Civil Eng. Transactions, but the author neglected to state who designed them.

Glover also documented that during a later trip west in 1880 or 1881 C. Shaler Smith designed at least 23 spans for the AT&SF, a number for the A&P RR (an AT&SF subsidiary that built west from Albuquerque), and the Johnson Canyon viaducts west of Williams AZ.

Engine 489 running light across Lobato Trestle in October 1991. Details of the bridge construction show quite clearly.

Typical summer scene near milepost 337, as Train No. 2 climbs eastward toward Cumbres Pass. The curved, grass-covered area to the right of the train is the roadbed for Highway 17 before it was realigned.
(Both photos, Gerald M. Blea)

Just eight months old and still wearing its factory paint, engine 489 derailed and turned over near mile 336.2 while returning to Chama from a Cumbres turn, May 3, 1926. According to D&RGW personal injury records, the engine hit a broken rail, and rolled over twice before coming to rest. The engineer, Roy Cretcher, did not survive. His fireman, Joe Dalla, although seriously injured, returned to service and worked on the line until his retirement.

The <u>Durango Evening Herald</u> for May 4, 1926 was very critical of the condition of the track, stating: "it is to be hoped that the D&RGW will either return to the use of smaller engines, even tho it does mean a heavier payroll, or else use some of the money that the San Juan Basin has poured into its coffers to put the roadbed in a condition that will guarantee the safety of the lives of its passengers and employees."

(Three photos, Earl G. Knoob collection)

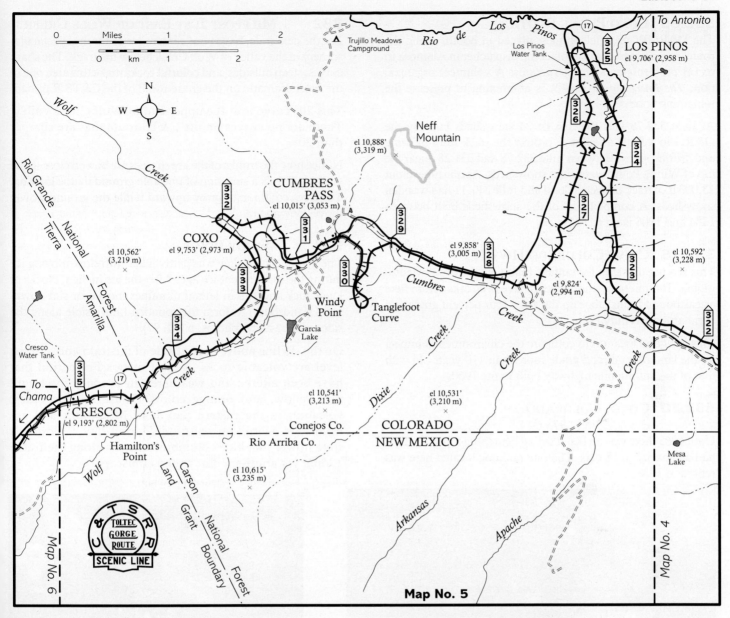

Map No. 5

Mile
335.10 CRESCO, COLORADO.
elev 9,193 ft (2,802 m)

The present water tank was built in 1893. Several families lived here year round, and their only continuous contact with the "outside world" was with the daily trains. A 64 ft, four-panel pile trestle crosses a small stream just west of the water tank. More on the buildings that once stood here is on p. 79.

Aspen trees along here were infected by millions of tent caterpillars, *Malacosma americana*, during the early 1970s. Many acres of trees were killed or badly damaged by these insects. The larvae live in a web-like nest suspended on the branches of aspens. When the insects hatched, the rails became so coated with creeping worms that the locomotives were unable to maintain any traction. Two persons then sat on the front of the engine and removed the insects by holding brooms on each rail. In that manner eastbound trains were able to ascend the four percent grade.

Mile
334.50 HAMILTON'S POINT.

This location may be named for L.C. Hamilton, a D&RG Division Superintendent in 1881. An early W.H. Jackson photograph referred to this locality as "White Rock Point." The track is now about 300 ft above Wolf Creek and the canyon is about 1,000 ft wide.

The track enters land of the former Tierra Amarilla Mexican Land Grant, which was one of many grants given Mexican citizens to encourage settlement on the northern frontier of the Mexican state of Nuevo Mejico (p. 14).

As the track continues its steady climb, outcrops of sedimentary rocks of Tertiary and Jurassic age are visible on each side of the track.

For the next several miles the train winds among thick aspen groves which are favorite habitats for scarlet gilias, blue monkshoods and penstemons, and yellow golden banners. Trees include blue spruces, white pines, Douglas firs, river willows, and birches. Occasionally deer are spotted in the timber.

Mile
332.85 COXO PHONE BOOTH.

The D&RGW used telephones, placed in booths along the route, so trainmen could contact the dispatcher in Alamosa to report problems and get instructions. A volunteer organization, *The Friends of the C&TS,* is attempting to preserve the remaining booths.

At mile 332.78 was the first of 24 snowsheds built by the D&RG in a futile attempt to protect the track from blowing and drifting snow. Between mile 332.78 and 331.28 , near the top of Windy Point, were eight snowsheds. At one time about 13,000 ft of track between Coxo and mile 317.11 had wooden snowsheds. A complete list of the snowsheds built between 1884 and 1908 is on p. 124.

Mile
332.75 CROSS COLORADO HWY 17.

This is a popular stop for railfans following the train by automobile. Innumerable photographs have been taken from here as eastbound trains labor up the steep four percent grade and wind around Windy Point.

This is a good location to compare the environmental impact on the land of a railroad grade more than 110 years old with that of the automobile highway built in the 1960s.

Mile
332.20 COXO, COLORADO.
elev 9,753 ft (2,973 m)

Until 1965 there was an 800 ft siding here (photo, p. 82) which had a capacity of 18 cars. The one building located here was retired in 1938.

Milepost
332 MILEPOST JUST EAST OF WOLF CREEK.

For the next mile, have your camera ready for the spectacular scenery of the valley of Wolf Creek below the track. The sharp curves, steep hillsides, and colorful rocks make this area one of the most dramatic on the entire route of the C&TS Railroad.

This 20° curve is at the upper end of Wolf Creek Valley. There are no curves on the C&TS route that are sharper than 20°.

Notice how the trunks of the aspen trees are bowed close to the ground. This is a sure sign of unstable ground that is moving. The trees continue to grow upward while the ground slowly moves downward.

Milepost
331 WINDY POINT.

The Wolf Creek Valley was partly filled with slow-moving ice during the most recent ice age. After the ice melted, blocks of loose rock and soil in lateral moraines moved or slid downward (landslides) to form the rounded hills visible along the sides of the valley (photos, p. 94, 97).

On the skyline above the left side of the train and at track level are volcanic rocks of the Conejos Formation that have been altered and weathered to produce the bright red, yellow, and orange colors. These are the oldest volcanics in the eastern San Juan Mountains and are from 31 to 34 million years old. During July, Colorado's state flower, the blue columbine blooms along the track, adding yet another color to the landscape.

Light engine 484 rounds the big curve just east of Windy Point on a crisp and cool fall afternoon in October 1990.   (Gerald M. Blea)

Eastbound passenger train stalled at Cresco siding when engine 489 broke a piston rod. Engine 497 has arrived to rescue the stranded train. June 12, 2001.   (Earl Knoob)
(Earl Knoob)

An interesting account of D&RGW crews fighting huge snow-drifts along this section of track is on p. 93.

Mile
330.75 CROSS WOODEN TRESTLE.
This 84 ft, six-panel standard pile trestle was the railroad overpass above Colo. Hwy. 17 until the late 1960s, when the highway was relocated.

Mile
330.60 CUMBRES, COLORADO.
elev. 10,015 ft (3,053 m)
Cumbres means "crests" or "summits" in Spanish. During construction days, this station was referred to as "Alta." Grading crews reached this point July 31, 1880 and the San Juan Extension was opened for travel from Antonito to Cumbres (or Alta) on December 15, 1880. When completed, it was one of the highest railroads in the United States. Cumbres Pass is not on the Continental Divide, which is about 10 miles west of Chama.

One wonders how the construction crews for the Rio Grande felt when they finally reached Alta, looked down into Wolf Creek valley, and realized their difficult job was far from over. Many more sharp curves, steep grades, rock cuts, and bridges remained to be built, which were additional challenges to their skill and ingenuity. The back-breaking labor of placing hand-hewn ties on the prepared grade, and spiking the rails to the ties was done during December and January, hardly an ideal time to complete a railroad.

In the early years, a number of people lived at Cumbres Pass year round. A post office was here until 1937. There are about 3,000 ft of sidings. Just west of the water plug is a "hump" in the track. This is where the four percent grade ends. East of the hump, the grade is nearly level, gradually increasing to an easy 1.42 percent ruling grade for the remainder of the trip to Antonito. After the engine takes water, your narrow gauge railroading adventure continues. Additional photos and details on the structures and facilities at Cumbres are on p. 79, 80, 82-85, 94, 99, 100.

During the winter months, when the track is covered with snow, snowmobilers make their own tracks throughout this area.

Mile
330.48 SNOWSHED-COVERED WYE.
A snowshed, about 526 ft long, covered portions of both legs of the wye. It is the last covered wye in the United States and also the last standing snowshed on the narrow gauge. Due to lack of maintenance, most of the shed collapsed during the rough winters of the late 1970s. Near the tail of the wye is the same beautiful little lake that Lt. Anderson (p. 16) and his men camped beside in 1874.

During the summer of 1990 and 1991, members of the *Friends of the C&TS* volunteered time, money, lumber and hard work to begin rebuilding this historic structure. Also completed at this time was a new roof, bracing and paint for the car inspector's house, north of the depot. Without the efforts of this group of dedicated volunteers, the building would not have survived many more winters (photos, p. 99, 100).

Mile
330.10 EAST SWITCH, CUMBRES SIDING.
At this switch, the two levels of track at TANGLEFOOT CURVE are about 70 ft apart horizontally, and 20 to 25 ft apart vertically.

In the last major derailment during D&RGW ownership of the line, an eastbound doubleheader, powered by engines 498 and 497, derailed at mile 326.30, February 10, 1960. Engine 498 just kept going when it went into the curve, turning over on its right side. The helper, 497, uncoupled and slid past the 498 and down the hill. Luckily neither the engineer, Ben Hindelang, or the head-end brakeman was seriously injured. The engines were left at Cumbres until late July 1960, when they were taken to Alamosa and rebuilt. The year 1960 was rough winter. In late February, a train had to return to Alamosa from Sublette because of snow, and in March the rotary made its first trip west of Chama since 1916!

(Jim Shawcroft)

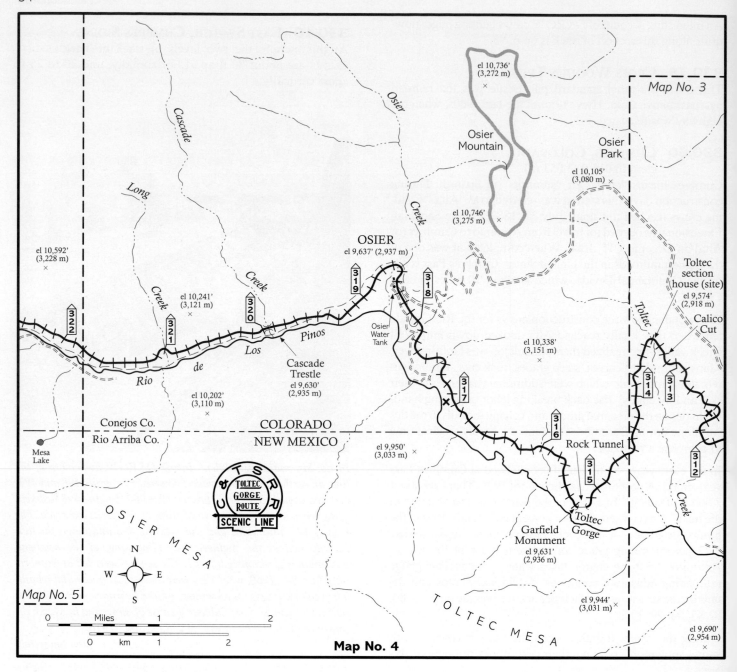

Map No. 3

Map No. 5

Map No. 4

Mile
329.76 TANGLEFOOT CURVE.

At the lower end of the sharp loop was the site of three snowsheds and two wooden trestles during the early years (photo, p. 55, 90). This 20° curve has also been called the "Cumbres Loop" or "The Balloon" by railroad crews.

On each side of Cumbres Pass, the track reaches the subalpine life zone. Much snow accumulates in this area, and during the spring and early summer, it is a luxuriant wildflower garden. Iris, primroses, and buttercups grow in profusion on the moist ground. The large plants with bright yellow-green leaves that appear to be partly rolled, are cornhusk lily or false hellebore, *Veratrum tenuipetalum.* See p. 109 for more about these interesting plants.

In the summer, watch for blue columbines, yellow arctic

paintbrushes, arctic thistles, shrubby cinquefoils and potentillas. In August, this area is ablaze with color when the tall purple asters, lupines, sunflowers, goldenrods, and fireweeds bloom.

Mile
329   CROSS CUMBRES CREEK.

From here are great views of TANGLEFOOT CURVE, the hairpin-shaped loop the track makes to reach Cumbres Pass.

Milepost
328   TRACK BELOW COLORADO. HWY. 17.
elev 9,858 ft (3,005 m)

A 112 ft, seven-panel pile trestle, built in 1887, was located at mile 329.90. Along the entire route, a number of standard pile trestles cross stream drainages. These bridges were built between 1885 and 1890 to replace the original, hastily-constructed wooden bridges of 1880.

NO. 2009. TANGLEFOOT CURVE, CUMBRES PASS. D.R.G.RR.

Snowsheds at Tanglefoot Curve sometime between 1908 and 1921. The left snowshed, built in 1908, was 314 ft long and had sloping sides and a narrow flat roof. It was replaced with a snow fence in 1924. The shed on the right, built in 1884, was burned in 1921. It was 472 ft long with vertical sides and a broad flat roof. Hand-hewn ties were still in use, but the track was well ballasted. The dead trees still standing were killed in the 1879 fire.

(George E. Mellon photo, Colorado Historical Society)

Mile
327.80 CROSS GRAVEL ROAD.

This road leads southward onto private land which was originally part of the Tierra Amarilla Mexican Land Grant of 1832 (p. 14).

Mile
327.60 PHONE BOOTH.

As the track curves to the left, a phone booth is on the right side of the train.

Milepost
327   MILEPOST AT SHARP CURVE.

Mile
326.30 SITE OF FREIGHT TRAIN DERAILMENT.

In the last major derailment during D&RGW ownership, an eastbound freight train, powered by engines 498 and 497, derailed at this curve (photos, p. 53).

Mile
325.50 LOS PINOS WATER TANK.
elev 9,710 ft (2,960 m)

During the 1930s, a section house, bunk house, and a coal house were located here. The first coal house burned in 1912 and was replaced with another which lasted until 1929. Coal was needed for refueling the rotary snowplows. More details on the buildings at this site are on p. 77 (photo, p. 39).

Many swallow nests are just below the overhanging roof of the water tank. You may catch glimpses of these birds as they swoop and dive, hunting for insects.

Mile
324.80 LOS PINOS SIDING.

A 46-car siding 1,850 ft long, is on the left side of the track. For almost a mile the track is actually straight. According to long-time D&RGW crewmen, from here to Cumbres was the most difficult section to keep open. In winter, the straight track at Los Pinos was probably the worst place where winds would whip across the top of the ridge and pile the white stuff into huge drifts, 20 to 30 ft high.

Mile
324.52 CROSS RIO DE LOS PINOS.

This bridge is a fire-decked, eleven-panel, pile trestle, 175 ft long. Colo. Highway 17 is visible to the north and west. In 1920, second-hand 57 pound rail was laid from here to Cumbres (ref.F).

Mile
323.30 SITE OF SNOW FENCES.

Many snow fences were along the right side of the track, but few remnants remain today.

Traces of the old toll road are still visible on the left side of the train from here to about milepost 323.

Mile
322.95 LOS PINOS PHONE BOOTH.
This dilapidated, unused booth probably was moved from mile 322.12 sometime after 1923. Another phone booth can be seen due west across the valley at a lower elevation.

The rounded, hummocky, irregular slopes on both sides of the stream are small landslides that formed when loose debris, left by small glaciers, gradually moved downward and outward.

Neff Mountain, elev 10,888 ft (4,180 m) is the flat-topped mountain to the northwest. Layers of volcanic Masonic Park Tuff cap the peak.

Mile
322.12 SITE OF OLD LOS PINOS SIDING.
The original Los Pinos siding was here and could hold 18 cars. You'll need a sharp eye to find any trace of it, as it was moved west to its present location in the 1920s. An account of a Rio Grande train getting stuck at this point is on p. 93.

Milepost
322 NICE VIEWS OF LOS PINOS VALLEY.
The stream is less than 100 ft below the track. The tree-covered slopes across the valley escaped destruction in a 1879 forest fire that destroyed timber along both sides of the valley, eastward to about milepost 313. Other forest fires raged out-of-control in the Lime Creek area between Durango and Silverton, around Leadville, and at other locations in Colorado.

Milepost
321 CROSS LONG CREEK.
The track was completed to this point on October 16, 1880.

D&RGW right-of-way and track maps indicate portable snow fences once stood along this area.

The track is almost level in this area—a good place in earlier days for westbound engineers to "make up time."

During the early summer, yellow holly grapes, wallflowers, puccoons, senecios, and tiny cinquefoils are common. Later, blue flax and pink to reddish scarlet gilias, brilliant fuchsia-colored locoweeds may be spotted from the train. Purple asters are common during the fall.

Milepost
320 MILEPOST AT WEST END OF TRESTLE.
During the early summer, large clumps of wild blue iris are abundant (p. 109). Later yellow-blossomed shrubby cinque-foils are common. During the fall, bright indigo blue gentians peek through native grasses. Notice how few trees have grown back since the 1879 fire.

Mile
319.95 CASCADE TRESTLE.
In the rush to complete the San Juan Extension, a wooden trestle was built across Cascade Creek during 1880. According to bridge record books unearthed by former D&RGW employee Jackson C. Thode, the original bridge was 432 ft long, 116 ft high, and had 28 bents (ref. G).

The *Denver Tribune* wrote of an excursion made over the new line in August 1881 and reported that one coach derailed on the bridge. "Within sight of Osier is a long bridge, built of wood and supported on wooden trestles." If there had not been a guard rail on the bridge, "the whole train would have been thrown off the bridge and plunged into the gully below, a depth of several hundred feet."

The present iron trestle, built in 1889, is a deck-plate girder bridge 137 ft high and 408 ft long, across tiny Cascade Creek. It has seven 54 ft spans and one 30 ft span on steel bents. Iron for both the Cascade and Lobato trestles was fabricated by the Keystone Bridge Company in 1881, using a unique German design. There is no cross-bracing between the bents (photo, p. 38). More details on the complicated history of this bridge are on p. 73.

No doubleheading has ever been allowed over this bridge. During the years the D&RGW ran long freight trains, helper engines were inserted into the middle of trains, and ahead of the caboose.

Engine 483 at Cascade Creek Trestle eastbound with the first Moonlight Excursion on the C&TS, August 25, 1972. The large car behind the engine is the steel Hinman coach. Note the tapered bents of the trestle. (Ed Osterwald)

Mile
318.45 CROSS OSIER CREEK.
This stream was formerly called Bear Creek. In 1882, two bridges were built to replace the first rickety ones thrown together in the rush to complete the line. One bridge was a 28 ft, three-panel bridge. The second was a 112 ft, seven-panel structure. These bridges lasted until 1936 when much needed work was done on the line and a culvert was installed (ref. B).

Mile
318.40 OSIER, COLORADO.
elev 9,637 ft (2,937 m)
Grading crews reached Osier on July 31, 1880. Track-laying was completed and the line opened for business between Denver and Osier on October 10, 1880. During those early years, the fare from Denver was $20.30, and a "good meal" cost 75 cents. More details on the history of Osier are on p. 77.

After a morning of enjoying the sights, sounds, and smells of the narrow gauge, the arrival at Osier offers a change of pace. This lonely outpost is host to a hungry, bustling, camera-carrying crowd of excursionists for several hours every day during the summer season. Lunch is served cafeteria style—quite different from how members of the very first excursion in October, 1880 (p. 20) were fed!

The new $600,000 dining facility was dedicated June 30, 1989 with a number of officials and invited guests attending the ceremonies. Following the ribbon-cutting, about 500 hungry passengers and guests entered the dining hall for lunch. The kitchen is on the lower level, along with a gift shop and additional dining tables. Restrooms are on the main level.

Your train usually arrives after the westbound train. Don't worry, there is plenty of food for all. Following lunch, there is plenty of time to photograph the trains, engines, and remaining buildings at this old station, and to change trains if you plan on continuing to Antonito. When the train crews complete the necessary switching, check the engines and cars, four long and <u>loud</u> blasts of the whistle summon everyone back to their respective trains for the remainder of the day's excursion on the C&TS. Additional photos of this area are on p. 38, 79, 96, 115.

At mile 318.10 a large railroad cut is in the Conejos Formation.

Milepost
318   CROSS SMALL DRAINAGE CHANNEL.
This stream channel is 1/10 mile east of the milepost.

A number of snow fences once stood along the left side of the track. The few wooden timbers left standing are stark reminders of places where blowing and drifting snows filled cuts and caused many blockades.

Mile
317.11   SITE OF SNOWSHED.
This is the last of 24 wooden snowsheds built to protect the track from blowing snow.

From here to about milepost 312 be ready enjoy the dramatic vistas along the steep canyon at Toltec Gorge and the weird, eroded rock spires and pedestal rocks of Calico Cut and Phantom Curve. (Have another role of film handy for quick camera loading.)

Milepost
316.59   ENTER NEW MEXICO.

Mile
315.60   GEOLOGIC CONTACT.
From here to milepost 315 is the only place on the entire trip where ancient Precambrian crystalline metamorphic and igneous rocks are visible along the track and in the gorge. These crystalline gneisses, schists, and granites are about 1,700 million years old and have been invaded by 1,450 million year old granites and pegmatites. On the right, the jagged Precambrian rocks on both sides of the Rio del los Pinos canyon are visible. At this point the canyon is very narrow because the stream had a difficult time cutting a channel through the harder, more resistant crystalline rocks.

A typical mid-summer scene at Osier in 1990, showing the new eating house and train numbers 1 and 2.   (Gerald M. Blea)

Eastbound train approaching Toltec Gorge at the telltale, just west of the Garfield Monument. September 1991.   (Doris B. Osterwald)

Engine 487 passing under the telltale at the east portal of Toltec Tunnel. September 1973.   (Doris B. Osterwald)

Mile
315.32 GARFIELD MONUMENT AND TOLTEC GORGE.

Just before reaching the monument stands a telltale. This tall, inverted U-shaped metal contraption above the track has wires hanging down from a horizontal bar. When brakemen are on top of a car and get hit in the head by the wires hanging down, they know it is time to get off the roof for the approaching tunnel portal! Photos, p. 35, 57.

The monument, along the right side of the track, was erected in honor of President James A. Garfield. He was shot by Charles J. Guiteau, a disappointed office-seeker, in the Washington, D.C. railroad station on July 2. Garfield died on September 19, 1881. The excursion train stopped at the gorge, and after viewing the canyon, members of the Association of General Passenger and Ticket Agents held an impromptu memorial service on September 26, the same day concluding funeral services were held in Cleveland, Ohio. The association later financed the erection of the monument which reads:

IN MEMORIAM
JAMES ABRAM GARFIELD
PRESIDENT OF THE UNITED STATES
DIED SEPTEMBER 19, 1881.
MOURNED BY ALL THE PEOPLE

———

ERECTED BY MEMBERS OF THE NATIONAL
ASSOCIATION OF GENERAL PASSENGER AND
TICKET AGENTS, WHO HELD MEMORIAL
BURIAL SERVICE ON THIS SPOT
SEPTEMBER 26, 1881.

Mile
315.20 ROCK OR TOLTEC TUNNEL (TUNNEL NO. 2).
elev 9,631 ft (2,936 m)

At this point, the track is about 600 ft above the stream. It is about 800 ft to the opposite side of the gorge. This 366 ft tunnel was blasted out of the Precambrian rocks using black powder. Because these rocks are so hard, the tunnel did not need to be lined.

Of the approximately 1,600 miles of narrow gauge built by the Rio Grande, only two other narrow gauge tunnels were ever built. In 1882, one was bored at Grassy Trail, Utah, and in 1884 a tunnel was built at Bridgeport in the Gunnison River canyon south of Grand Junction. Later, four tunnels on Tennessee Pass and three in Glenwood Canyon were built to standard gauge dimensions. With so much mountain construction, it is amazing that so few tunnels were needed.

The first formal excursion on the San Juan Extension was held on October 4-5, 1880. On p. 20 are some interesting quotations from that trip. The group spent the night in their Pullman car "camped" at the tunnel portal.

Beyond the east portal of the tunnel is another telltale.

Milepost
315 GEOLOGIC CONTACT.

Near this milepost on the left side of the track, is the contact (boundary) between the ancient Precambrian crystalline gneisses, schists, and granites and the younger volcanic Conejos Formation (see geologic map, p. 116).

D&RG employee Monte Ballough was at the the west portal of Toltec Tunnel in the early 1900s to record the passage of this work train. It is a cold winter day, as the section men on the flat car are bundled up to keep warm. The engine is a 200-class, 2-8-0 with a diamond stack and an oil head lamp.

(Collection Margaret B. Palmer)

Mile
314.75 TOLTEC PHONE BOOTH.

On April 23, 1881, a special passenger train with one coach and a caboose left Antonito at 11:00 AM bound for Chama. Near the phone booth, engine number 170 and the coach derailed and rolled down the hillside. The coach was demolished. Unfortunately, eight people were killed and six others were injured. Heavy rains caused the rails to spread on the new roadbed. There were many derailments until the roadbed had settled and enough ballast was added to stabilize the track.

Mile
314.32 ENTER COLORADO.

Milepost
314 GREAT VIEWS ACROSS TOLTEC CREEK CANYON.

From the left side of the train are many chances to again enjoy the scenery at CALICO CUT and PHANTOM CURVE. The flat-topped mesa on the skyline is capped with resistant layers of Masonic Park Tuff. The track is about 600 ft above the stream at this point and is about ½ mile wide.

Mile
313.44 CROSS TOLTEC CREEK.
elev 9,574 ft (2,918 m)

Until 1942 there was a five-panel standard pile trestle across this small stream.

Just west of Toltec Creek, in the open area on the left side of the track, was the site of TOLTEC SECTION HOUSE, bunk house and coal house (photo, p. 78). Details on the buildings once located here are on p. 77.

On both sides of Toltec Creek, the aspens are glorious in the fall. The red, and yellow leaves, and the multi-colored rocks, combine to offer superb photographic opportunities.

Mile
313.20 CALICO CUT.

A very descriptive name for the soft, rusty-red, orange, purple, maroon, and tan-colored loose clays and weathered rock that are the result of the alteration of hard and soft portions of the chaotic breccias of the Conejos Formation (photo, p. 61).

Avalanches and mudslides caused many problems along here for the Rio Grande, particularly during the winter and early spring months when the rocks were wet.

Milepost
313
to
312 VOLCANIC SPIRES.

The track winds back and forth around tall pinnacles, spires, and pedestal rocks formed from breccias of the Conejos Formation. These weird shapes are the result of alteration by hot water, by weathering, and by erosion of the volcanic rock. Alteration also causes the wide variety of colors seen in the rocks along this section of track (photos, p. 61, 115).

Mile
312.30 PHANTOM CURVE.

This location was named by early-day D&RG trainmen, who often made the trip at night. They saw in the dim shadows, strange shapes darting back and forth in front of the engine headlight beam during long, tiring trips. The squealing noises of the wheel flanges rubbing against the rails as the trains rounded the sharp curve added an eerie effect.

On February 11, 1948 the *San Juan,* with well-known engineer Bill Holt at the throttle, was en route to Alamosa from Durango when a snow avalanche came down the steep cliff above the track and plowed into the train at about 6:30 PM. The lights went off as the coaches started to slide slowly down the side of the canyon; some of the passengers were not even moved off their seats. The locomotive and two baggage cars were not involved and stayed on the track. Most seriously injured was the conductor, George Ottoway, who was pinned in a coach by a timber. The passengers suffered most from the bitter cold. After climbing back up the hill, they were able to get warm in the baggage cars. A "hospital train" arrived at the wreck site about 11:00 PM and returned to Alamosa by 4:00 AM the next morning (photo, p. 33).

Mile
312.10 ENTER NEW MEXICO.

Mile
311.30 MUD TUNNEL (TUNNEL NO. 1).

This 342 ft tunnel (ref. B) was dug through soft, weathered volcanic ash and mud of the Conejos Formation. The Rio Grande had many problems here because the soft rock and mud slides when wet. It was also necessary to line the tunnel with timber—an additional hazard for steam locomotives. During the spring of 1982, the C&TS installed concrete sills so the timbers do not sit on mud and rebuilt both portals.

On April 14, 1889, an engine pulling a westbound freight struck a mud slide that forced the engine into the timbers at the east portal. Engineer George Riddle and fireman Fred Wendle were injured. The Alamosa *San Luis Valley Courier* reported on April 17, 1889: "The engine No. 68 was pretty badly demolished but very little damage was done to the cars with the exception of breaking a few draw head bolts."

Chances for good photographs are at both portals. Just before the train enters the tunnel, take a quick look to the right of the "shoo-fly" built in the early 1900s while the tunnel was being rebuilt after a fire (photo, p. 32).

Several scenes of the popular movies, "Bite the Bullet," "Where the Hell's That Gold," and "Indiana Jones and the Last Crusade" were filmed here (photo, p. 61).

Milepost
311 WEST SWITCH OF TOLTEC SIDING.

Beautiful views of the tree-covered slopes make this section of track a delight (photo, p. 32).

Another phone booth is located on the right at mile 310.46.

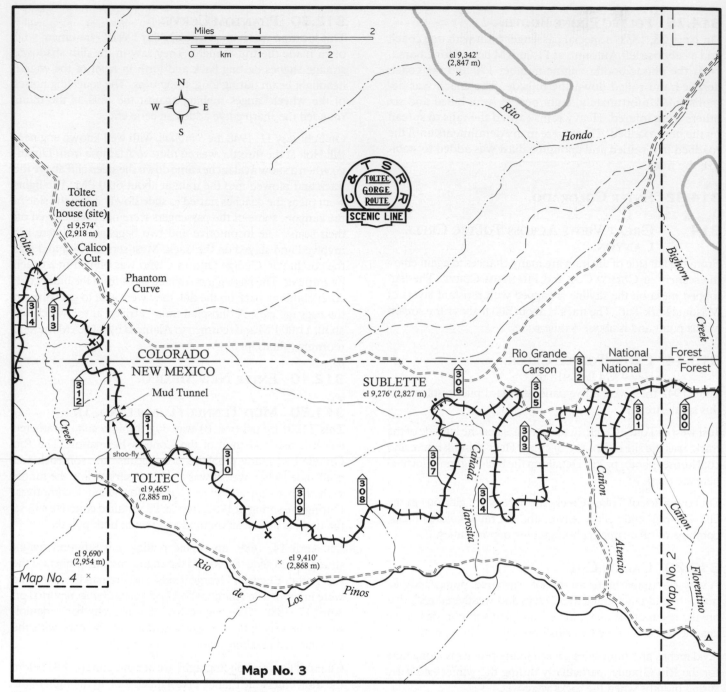

Map No. 3

Mile
310.30 East Switch of Toltec Siding.
elev 9,465 ft (2,885 m)

As construction of the San Juan Extension continued at a feverish pace, track was completed to this point June 30, 1880.

Toltec Siding was originally 1,166 ft long, but was lengthened to 3,400 ft during the 1950s to handle the long pipe trains that operated between Alamosa, Colorado and Farmington, New Mexico. With a capacity of 75 cars, most of the longer trains met here. The Toltec station sign stood about 450 ft east of the west switch.

Mile
309.35 Site of Head-On Collision.

On September 23, 1922 the westbound *San Juan* passenger train #115, pulled by engine 169, was hit by an eastbound light locomotive, number 411. Engineer R.L. Smith misread his orders and collided head-on with the passenger train. Smith believed he had more time to reach Sublette siding. He received minor injuries, but D.M. Wright, engineer, and L.J. Knee, fireman, on the passenger train were killed. Three railroad employees and 20 passengers were injured. The remains of one locomotive pilot and a coupler are down the hill about 50 ft from the nearest telephone pole. The Rio Grande built a ramp to drag engine 169 up the slope to track level. Some coal and bricks from the fire box are still litter the ground. Engine 169 is now on display in Cole Park at Alamosa, Colorado.

Calico Cut from the western side of Toltec Creek Canyon. September 1973. *(Doris B. Osterwald)*

View to the northwest of the reddish-colored volcanic spires and pedestal rocks between mile 312 and 313. June 6, 1971. *(Doris B. Osterwald)*

Engine 488, at the west portal of Mud Tunnel, is carrying the white flags that indicate an extra, the Jim Trowbridge special freight train of 1990. *(Gerald M. Blea)*

In the fall of 1990, a work extra, pulled by engine 489, was "in the hole" at Sublette. This train was dropping off ties for installation along the line. This photo was taken before the section house roof was replaced and the buildings repainted by the <u>Friends of the C&TS</u>. *Gerald M. Blea)*

Milepost

308   CONEJOS FORMATION AT TRACK LEVEL.
A small fault, just beyond the milepost, brings the Conejos Formation upward to track level.

Milepost

307   TRACK WINDS THROUGH ASPEN GROVES.
Nestled among the aspens are some Douglas firs and white firs, *Abies concolor*. This tall, stately tree with an ash-gray, deeply furrowed bark, is from 70 to 160 ft tall. The cones may be from 5 to 7 in long.

A wide variety of wildflowers bloom during the summer months along this shady moist hillside. Purple bull thistles, scarlet gilias, white yarrows, blue lupines, and penstemons, yellow gumweeds, wallflowers, and orange mallows are easy to find. Wild roses, gooseberries, chokecherries, and raspberries are also very common

Just before reaching Sublette, the track makes two 20° double-S curves as it winds through the aspen forest.

Mile

306.06   SUBLETTE, NEW MEXICO.
             elev 9,276 ft (2,827 m)
This station was first called Boydsville; why the name was changed is not known. The San Juan Extension was completed and opened for business to this point by early June 1880 (ref. E).

Originally there was a wooden water tank along the right side of the track; today a metal standpipe serves the same purpose. Engine water is piped from a small cistern above the track which is filled from a small stream. The water was noted in 1891 as being "good and plenty" (ref. A). See p. 77 for more on the structures here.

The large frame building was the section foreman's home. The hand-hewn log bunk house is identical to the one at Chama. Both were built soon after the line was completed. During 1990 and 1991, *The Friends of the C&TS Railroad* completed major repairs and painting of these structures. The Sublette siding is 949 ft long, and has a capacity of 25 cars (photos, p. 61, 77, 83, 95, 100).

Mile

**305.20   CROSS HEADWATERS OF CAÑADA
                   JAROSITA.**

Mile

303.90   SOUTHERNMOST SHARP CURVE.
This curve winds around the hill between Cañon Atencio and Cañada Jarosita.

Mile

303.50   LOOSE GRAVEL IN RAILROAD CUT.
The loose, rounded pebbles and cobbles in this cut are part of the 26 million year old Los Pinos Formation. In 1925, rock from this cut was used for badly-needed railroad ballast.

To the south are many nice views into the Rio de los Pinos Valley. San Antonio Peak is still visible on the southeastern skyline.

Milepost

301   ASPEN GROVES.

Mile

300.50   SITE OF BIG HORN BELL.
A metal relay box was located here. It was used to signal the dispatcher in Alamosa that a train had passed, as no block signals or radios were ever used on the narrow gauge during D&RGW ownership. The box was removed by unauthorized persons.

Mile

299.70   BIG HORN PHONE BOOTH.
Another old booth is on the left side of the track, 200 ft west of the west switch. The train has descended a steady 1.42 percent grade most of the way from Cumbres. One K-36 engine can pull 36 loaded freight cars. Longer trains need a helper engine cut into the middle for westbound trips. Many snowfences were necessary along this section of track.

Mile

299.41   BIG HORN WYE AND SIDING.
             elev 9,022 ft (2,750 m)
Track was completed to Big Horn wye May 31, 1880 and the line immediately opened for business to this point (photo, p. 104).

Just east of the east siding switch was a 24-panel snow fence. The tail of this long, curving wye was extended in 1953 during the oil and gas boom in the San Juan Basin. In addition to the snow-fighting equipment which turned here, helper engines frequently used the wye. The siding is 1,184 ft long and will hold 28 cars. This was a frequent meeting point for trains. The station sign was located 400 ft east of the west switch.

Bighorn Peak, elev 9,942 ft (3,030 m), south of the track, is capped with a layer of basalt.

Mile

299.09   ENTER COLORADO.

Milepost

299   MONTANE ZONE WILDFLOWERS.
             elev 8,997 ft (2,742 m)
White or cream-colored blossoms include stickweeds and yuccas; paintbrushes, scarlet gilias and beard-tongues; buckwheats are reddish-colored. Flowers with yellow blossoms include mustards, mulleins, ragged sunflowers, sulfur flowers, and golden asters. Common blue or purple blossoms are bee plants, several species of lupines, fleabanes, and thistles.

Ponderosa pines, *Pinus ponderosa*, the dominant trees of the mesas, foothills, and south-facing slopes of the montane life zone, grow abundantly along here. The long needles, bright reddish-brown bark, and large drooping cones make this tree easy to identify. Other trees that dot the hillsides include junipers, pinon pines, a few firs and spruces.

Milepost

297   NORTHERN END OF WHIPLASH CURVE.
Don't miss the the lovely view of the Conejos valley below and of Los Mogotes Peak to the north. Remains of several snow fences are along the right side of the track. This mesa is capped with dark loose pieces of lava of the Cisneros Formation that probably flowed from the Los Mogotes volcano (see Geology, p. 111).

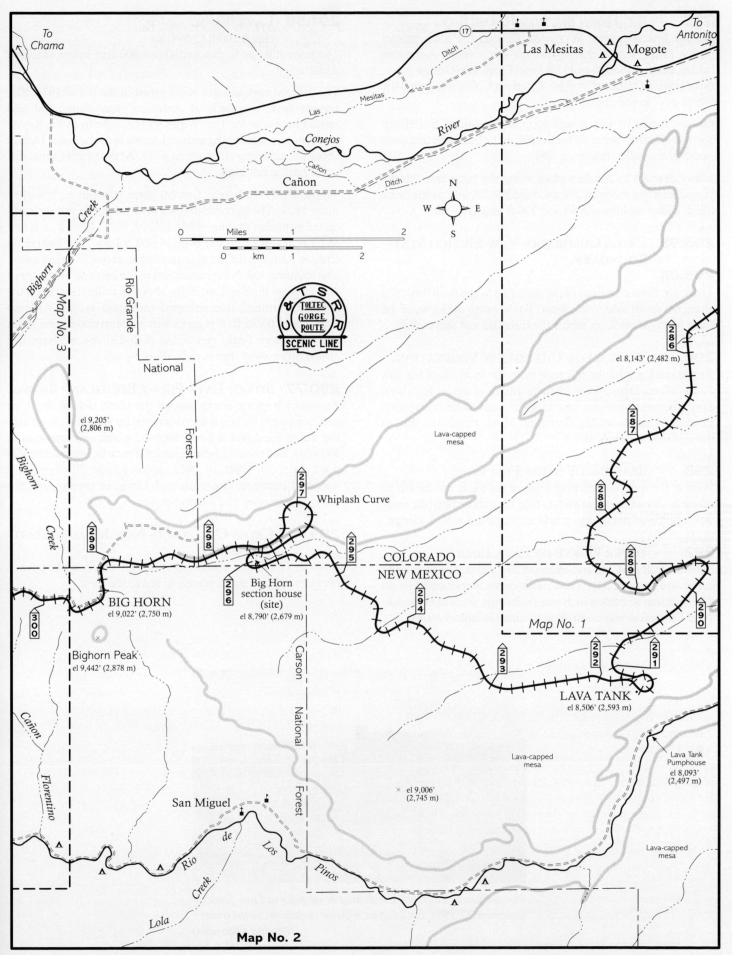

To Chama

Las Mesitas

Mogote

To Antonito

17

Ditch

Las   Mesitas

Conejos   River

Cañon   Ditch

Cañon

N
W · E
S

0   Miles   1   2

0   km   2

C & T S R R
TOLTEC
GORGE
ROUTE
SCENIC LINE

Lava-capped
mesa

286
el 8,143' (2,482 m)

287

288

289

Map No. 3

Rio Grande

National

Forest

el 9,205'
(2,806 m)

Bighorn

Creek

297
Whiplash Curve

298

299

295

COLORADO
NEW MEXICO

290

Map No. 1

296
Big Horn
section house
(site)
el 8,790' (2,679 m)

BIG HORN
el 9,022' (2,750 m)

300

294

293

292

291

LAVA TANK
el 8,506' (2,593 m)

Bighorn Peak
el 9,442' (2,878 m)

Carson

National

Forest

Cañon

Florentino

San Miguel

Rio   de

Creek

Los

Pinos

Lola

× el 9,006'
(2,745 m)

Lava-capped
mesa

Lava Tank
Pumphouse
el 8,093'
(2,497 m)

Lava-capped
mesa

Map No. 2

Milepost
296   BIG HORN SECTION HOUSE SITE.

On the lowest reverse WHIPLASH CURVE, the track crosses bridge 296A, a 48 ft three-panel fire deck trestle. An earlier bridge, built in 1886, was 112 ft long. From this vantage point, three levels of track are visible. Whiplash Curve was called the "three-ply" in the late 1880s.

On the inside of this lowest loop is the site of BIG HORN SECTION HOUSE. See p. 77 for details on the buildings that once stood in the valley (photo, p. 28).

Many changes have taken place along the route through the years. Between milepost 296 and mile 294.20, four trestles were filled; each was between 80 and 336 ft long (ref. A).

Mile
295.98   CROSS COLORADO–NEW MEXICO STATE
to
295.08   BOUNDARY.

There are three crossings of the state line as the train descends along the south side of the mesa. To the north are views of the three levels of track on which the train has just descended.

Milepost
294   WATCH FOR CHANGES IN VEGETATION.

As the track gradually descends from the foothills of the San Juan Mountains, rabbitbrush (also called chamisa), *Chrysothamnus nauseosus*, sagebrush, and mountain mahogany, *Cercocarpus montanus*, are abundant. More details and uses of these plants are on p. 109.

Milepost
293   REMAINS OF SNOW FENCE.

West of the milepost, on both sides of the track, are the last of many fences which were built to help keep snow from the track when fierce winter storms made railroading a real challenge.

Milepost
292   UPPER CURVE OF LAVA LOOP.

Between milepost 292 and milepost 291, the track makes a 15° curve and passes LAVA TANK. This curve is connected by an 826 ft section of track which was built some years after the San Juan Extension was completed to turn snowplow trains.

Mile
291.55   LAVA TANK.
elev 8,500 ft (2,591 m)

The train still has to descend about 600 feet before reaching Antonito.

The original tank at Lava was burned in the fall of 1971. The present tank, originally at Antonito, was dismantled and moved here after the fire. Water was brought from the Rio de Los Pinos by a pumping station located near the river. Details about the pumping plant are on p. 77. At the present time, this water tank is not used.

To the north-northwest, Los Mogotes is about eight airline miles away. The pyramid-shaped peak, about 54 miles distant on the northeast skyline, is Mt. Blanca, elev 14,345 ft. It is one of 53 peaks in Colorado over 14,000 ft high. The Sangre de Christo Range is on the eastern skyline about 32 miles away. The rounded, low-lying mountains to the east and northeast of Antonito are the San Luis Hills, about 18 miles distant. To the south, the round, dome-shaped mountain is San Antonio Peak, elev 10,935 ft. It is an extinct volcano about nine miles away. Bighorn Peak, elev 9,442 ft (3,030 m), is about five airline miles away, but is eight miles by rail.

Mile
290.77   SITE OF LAVA PHONE BOOTH AND SIDING.

Another telephone booth was on the north side of the track until about 1973 when it was destroyed by vandals. This is also the site of the 1,084 ft LAVA SIDING, which was removed in 1955 (ref. B). It had a 25-car capacity. Track laying reached this point April 30, 1880. In 1923, second-hand 70 pound rail was laid between Antonito and Lava, in preparation for using the heavier K-27 locomotives.

Mile
289.71   CROSS COLORADO–NEW MEXICO STATE
          BOUNDARY.

Another crossing is also at mile 289.48. The boundary fence between the two states is easy to see to the west.

The eastbound, Train No.4, is drifting down grade at Lava Tank on September 20, 1988. Los Mogotes is on the horizon above the train.

(Ray W.Osterwald)

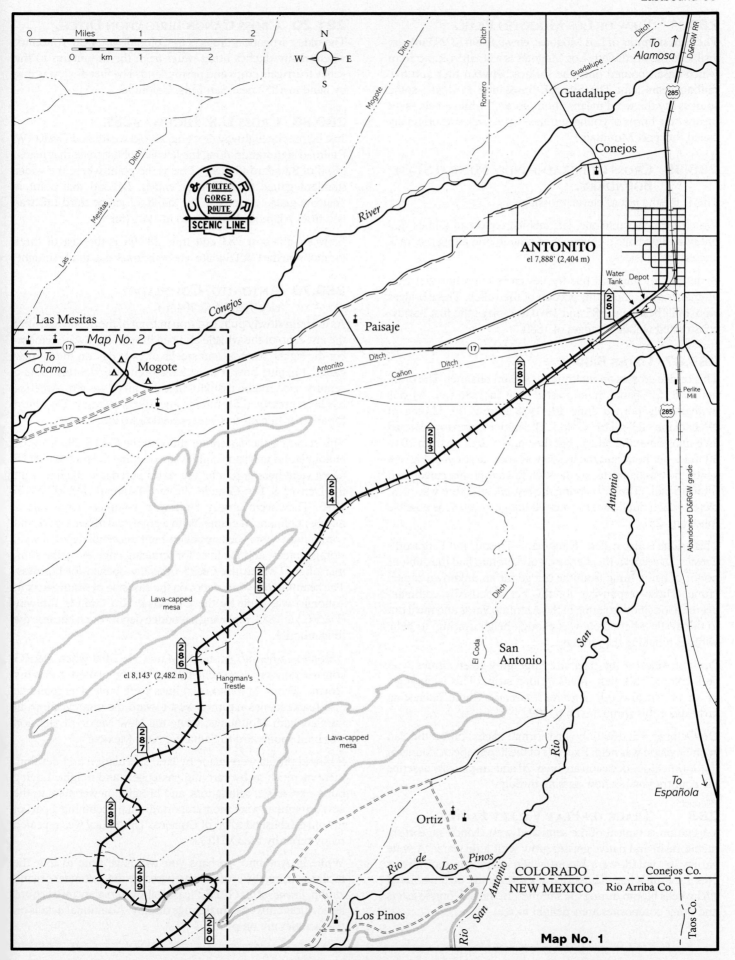

Map No. 1

Milepost
289 VIEW OF LOS MOGOTES PEAK.

The twin summits of Los Mogotes, elev 9,818 ft (2,993 m), are visible to the northwest. Los Mogotes is a small volcano from which basalt poured onto the surface between four and five million years ago. The Spanish translation is vague; some sources say the word means "hummocks," while others say it means "the horns of young animals." The peak was originally called Prospect Mountain.

Mile
288.55 CROSS COLORADO–NEW MEXICO STATE BOUNDARY.

This is the the last of eleven crossings.

Watch for deer, antelope, jackrabbits, cottontail rabbits, gophers, and perhaps a coyote or mountain lion along the track and on the hillsides.

A number of standard pile trestles cross intermittent stream drainages throughout this portion of the valley. These bridges were built between 1885 and 1890 to replace the first hastily-constructed wooden bridges of 1880.

Mile
285.87 CROSS BRIDGE.

This bridge crosses an intermittent stream channel. The original 80 ft, five-panel frame trestle, built in 1886 (ref. A) was inadvertently burned June 13, 1988 during the filming of "Where the Hell's That Gold." The movie company planned an explosion at the bridge, but the wind picked up from 10 to 40 miles per hour and the trestle was soon destroyed. Passenger traffic was halted for six days while a temporary culvert and fill were built. The next spring the present structure was completed which duplicates the burned bridge as much as possible (photo, p. 25).

This bridge is also called "Hangman's Trestle" or "Ferguson's Trestle." It seems a Mr. Ferguson of Antonito had the dubious honor of being hung from the bridge for an unknown capital crime. Those responsible for this act supposedly commandeered a locomotive sitting in the Antonito yards and ran it out to the trestle where there was enough height for him to hang without touching the ground.

On both sides of the track are large gray-green shrubs with dark-colored bark that shreds in long strips. This is big sagebrush or wormwood, *Artemisia tridentata*. Some interesting facts about this shrub are on p. 109.

On October 4-5, 1880, the first formal excursion on the San Juan Division was held. Excerpts of the newspaper accounts of this momentous occasion are on p. 20 and graphically describe the country you are now passing through.

Milepost
283 TRACK ON FLAT VALLEY FLOOR.

Vegetation is typical of the semi-arid west. Much sagebrush, rabbitbrush, and native grasses grow with little water. A wide variety of wildflowers bloom when sufficient moisture is present. Purple bee plants, yellow clovers, and cream-colored stickweeds bloom during the summer. In the fall, purple asters and other composites are a delight to see.

Mile
281.20 CROSS CAÑON IRRIGATION DITCH.

The oldest irrigation projects in Colorado are near Antonito, where many ditches bring water from the mountains to the valley to irrigate crops and pastureland. The first ditch was dug by hand in 1852 near San Luis, Colorado.

Mile
280.86 CROSS U.S. HIGHWAY 285.

Just before the highway crossing, an old weathered D&RGW Railroad sign stands along the left side of the track that reads: "End of Standard Gauge." This is the point where the wider standard gauge from Denver ended. Beyond this point is "narrow gauge country." The standard gauge third rail was laid from Alamosa to Antonito in 1901 (ref. F).

Between milepost 283 and mile 280.96 is the last of three locations on the C&TS route where the track is actually straight!

Mile
280.70 ANTONITO, COLORADO.
elev 7,888 ft (2,404 m)

As the train slowly pulls to a stop in front of the depot, and after the last echo of the whistle and bell have faded away, remember the sights, sounds, and smells of your day on the narrow gauge. Imagine how it must have been to travel this route a century ago, and be thankful that this bit of western America has been preserved for future generations to enjoy. Do return for another ride on this very special railroad.

This station is the eastern terminus of the C&TS. None of the buildings and railroad facilities surrounding the present C&TS depot were here until after the states purchased the line from the Denver & Rio Grande Western Railroad (D&RGW) in 1970. They were largely built with volunteer labor and a number of financial grants. With a great deal of hard work and community effort, local residents built the small depot, a wye, storage tracks, and facilities for servicing engines by the summer of 1971 when the C&TS officially opened for business. The beautiful old stone depot on the east side of Main Street in Antonito was built by the Denver & Rio Grande Railway (D&RG) in 1882, replacing a wooden depot which became the freight house.

Antonito came into existence March 31, 1880 when D&RG construction crews reached their newly platted company "town." From Antonito, two lines were built. The mainline San Juan Extension turned west toward the mining camps in the San Juan Mountains, while the New Mexico Extension was built southward to Santa Fe, New Mexico.

Railroad profits were made by land speculation and development as much as by carrying passengers and freight. Laying out a new town, selling lots, and bringing newcomers to the new settlement were more important than becoming a part of the old established town of Conejos. This policy was repeated many times by the D&RG.

While in Antonito, perhaps you will have time to tour the facilities, using the brochure prepared by the volunteer organization, *Friends of the C&TS*. Please follow the safety instructions listed. Don't miss the dual gauge display. Additional details on the facilities are on p. 75.

RAILROADING ACROSS CUMBRES PASS

At the throttle, 1990.   *(Gerald M. Blea)*

HOW THE ENGINE WORKS

One of the thrills of a trip on the C&TS is the chance to watch a narrow gauge steam locomotive working its way up the four percent grade, or drifting along the wide curves near Lava Tank as the train descends to Antonito. Steam locomotives have become quite rare. Although most people know that coal and water go into the tender, many may not know how these materials are converted into power to pull the train.

Coal is shoveled into the firebox in the engine cab. Heat from the fire passes through dozens of flues in the boiler, which is the part of the engine ahead of the firebox. The flues are surrounded by water, and the water is pumped against steam pressure into the boiler with a steam-powered injector. The heat is transferred to the water, and the water is converted into steam.

It takes many hours to steam up a cold locomotive. During this time, parts of the boiler expand as they are heated. Unless this is done slowly, to allow for gradual expansion, the boiler steel may be damaged. It is for this reason that engines are kept "steamed up" or "alive" after the day's run is completed.

Live steam from the top of the boiler is fed through the throttle valve inside the steam dome to two cylinders, one on each side of the engine, ahead of the drive wheels (drivers). These cylinders, which are similar to the cylinders in an automobile engine, contain movable pistons that are connected to the main rods which pivot on the drive wheels. Valves with adjustable travel control the admission of steam to the ends of the cylinders. The engineer's reverse lever changes the horizontal position of the valves with respect to the pistons, so that more

or less steam is admitted to the cylinders as required, and also that the engine can be reversed.

Steam expands in the front of one cylinder, driving the piston and main rod backward, and also expands in the rear of the cylinder on the other side of the engine, driving that piston and rod forward. This backward and forward motion of the rods causes the wheels to turn. Motion of the wheels reverses the motion of the rods and pistons, forcing spent steam out of the cylinders and up the stack along with smoke from the burning coal. This exhausted steam makes the unforgettable sound that is so characteristic of steam locomotives: four exhaust sounds for each turn of the drivers.

On the top of the boiler is a steam-driven electric dynamo, which generates electricity for the engine's lamps. On the left side of the engine is a contraption made up of small cylinders and pipes that usually leak steam and water and makes the characteristic "fla-thunk-fla-thunk" sound. This is the steam-driven air compressor that provides air pressure to operate the brakes and engine appliances.

Beneath the couplers on each car and on the engine are large rubber hoses that are connected to form a continuous air line from the engine to the rear of the train. Railroad brakes operate differently from automobile brakes, however. When you step on the brake pedal of your car, you *increase* the pressure in the brake system. About 70 to 90 pounds per square inch of air pressure is maintained in the air line while the train is moving. When the engineer operates the brake valve in locomotive cab, air pressure is *reduced*, which causes the brake rigging underneath the car to force the brake shoes against the wheels, thus slowing the train. If the air line is opened or broken anywhere along the train, the brakes will "go into emergency" and the train will stop until the line is again closed and repressurized. The train crew can also "pull the air" from the rear of the train in an emergency. For safety, while descending steep hills, "retainer valves" on the cars can be set to force the brakes to drag slightly. Large steel brake wheels on one end of each car are used to lock the brakes by hand when cars are stored, much like the parking brake in your car. They are also used in winter, when ice forms in the air line, making air reduction difficult.

Air brakes are nothing new to the Cumbres Pass narrow gauge. George Westinghouse's "straight" air brakes were installed on D&RG equipment in 1872; the Rio Grande then became the first U.S. railroad to have air brakes on its freight equipment. The "straight" air brakes, however, operated by increasing rather than reducing the air pressure.

C&TS ENGINES

The steam locomotives (engines) at the heads of the C&TS trains are of particular interest to visitors in narrow gauge country. Three types of steam locomotives are owned by the C&TS. All are outside-frame 2-8-2[1] Mikado engines (K-27, K-36, K-37 series) that came originally from the D&RGW; they are still numbered as they were on the Rio Grande. On outside-frame engines, the drive wheels are inside the engine frames, with counterweights, side rods, and main rods connected to the ends of the axles which stick out through the frames. Outside-frame engines are heavier and more powerful than comparable-sized inside-frame types. This type of construction makes for a lot of interesting action when all the exposed machinery is in motion. These narrow gauge 2-8-2 engines are as large as medium-sized standard gauge engines, and the whistles are just as loud (and melodious). The nickname "Little Train," sometimes applied to C&TS operations, simply does not fit.

K-27 CLASS

Engines of the K-27 class are almost extinct. In 1903, fifteen of these engines were built by Baldwin Locomotive Works for the D&RG, but only two have escaped the scrap pile. When new, they were regarded as "monsters," being the largest narrow gauge engines built to date. Number 463[2] was used until 1955 when actor Gene Autry purchased the locomotive for use in western movies and had it shipped to his ranch near Newhall, California. After a fire destroyed most of his sets, the engine sat idle until 1971, when it was given to the city of Antonito by Autry. In 1989, the city of Antonito leased the 463 to the Railroad Commission for $1.00. Major rebuilding of the boiler, running gear, and the tender was required before the 463 could be used. On April 27, 1994, after two winter's of work by C&TS employees in the Chama shops, the engine was returned to active service (photo, p. 70).

The only other K-27 not scrapped is number 464, which stood for years in the Durango yards as a neglected derelict after its flue time ran out in 1959. In November 1973, it was sold by the D&RGW to Knott's Berry Farm in Buena Park, California. It was reconditioned, but was too large for the available trackage, and sold to the Huckleberry Railroad in Michigan where it is now in service. Engine specifications are on p. 122.

K-36 CLASS

The real work-horses on the C&TS are the 480-series engines (D&RGW K-36 class). Ten of these locomotive were built by Baldwin for the Rio Grande in 1925. These were the last new

Engine 463 was often used out of Durango during the 1930s and 1940s. On October 2, 1949, 463 headed for Farmington, New Mexico with a 14-car train. This trestle, at mile 450.52, is south of Durango near Carbon Junction. This bridge was still standing in 1992.
(Otto Perry, Denver Public Library, Western History Dept.)

narrow gauge engines purchased by the Rio Grande, and were part of the general upgrading and rebuilding of their narrow gauge routes during the 1920s. They were specifically designed for Colorado narrow gauge, and were evolved from 50 years of mountain railroading experience. In the many years they have been in service, the 480s have proven to be some of the most efficient, tough, and well-liked locomotives ever built. Their original assignments were on the Marshall Pass line between Salida and Gunnison, Colorado, and in helper service between Chama and Cumbres Pass.

The C&TS Railroad Commission owns half of the K-36 engines still in existence: numbers 483, 484, 487, 488, and 489. The 483 has served the C&TS with distinction. It was the only operable engine when the states took possession of the railroad in 1970, and everyone who either worked on the railroad, or followed the progress in moving equipment to Chama, in those early days, developed a special, sentimental attachment for the 483. It was retired in 1977 because of worn out running gear and rear tube sheet. It is hoped this engine will be restored and returned to service, as ridership on the railroad continues to grow. The 483 pulled the last eastbound passenger train from Durango to Alamosa in November 1968, wearing its dubious paint job for the movie *"The Good Guys and the Bad Guys."* This special excursion was for the citizens group that was trying to interest the National Park Service in operating the line as a national monument (photo, p. 74).

Engine 484 has been in service since the first C&TS public excursion on June 26, 1971. During the winter of 1991-92 this engine received a major overhaul and rebuilding and is ready for many more years of active service. The 484 worked on the *San Juan* passenger train as well as on thousands of freights. It was the helper engine to Cumbres on the last eastbound *San Juan* January 31, 1951, having been the eastbound road engine from Durango to Chama. When the New Mexico Public Utilities Commission refused abandonment of the *San Juan* in their state, the 484 sometimes pulled a one-car passenger train from Chama westward to Dulce, New Mexico. The last chartered D&RGW excursion train from Alamosa to Cumbres and return, October 9, 1966, was pulled by 484.

---

[1]The Whyte system of classifying steam locomotives, as used in the United States, describes the wheel arrangement. Thus a 2-8-2 engine has two non-powered pilot wheels in front, eight powered drive wheels, and two non-powered trailing wheels, in addition to the tender wheels.
[2]The Friends of the C&TS published a comprehensive account of the history and rebuilding of engine 463 in Vol. 9, Nos, 1, 2 of the <u>C&TS Dispatch</u>.

Restoration of engine 487 started in 1973 and was completed in 1974, using matching funds from the two states. The 488 was restored with matching federal and state grant money, and was first used in June. 1979. More grant money was received in 1980 and by July 1981, the 489 ran for the first time since 1961. Number 488 was the road engine on the last *San Juan* from Chama to Alamosa and 489 was a helper engine on the last revenue train over Marshall Pass, from Gunnison to Salida. It also pulled the scrap train on Marshall Pass after abandonment. The 489 was one of the first of the 480s assigned to Chama for helper duty in early 1926—and paid dearly for that honor by derailing at mile 336.20 (photos, p. 50).

Engines 480, 481 and 482 are owned and operated by the D&SNG Railroad in Durango, Colorado. The 482 returned to Durango in October 1991 in a historic locomotive swap. The D&SNG traded their fully-operational K-37, 497 for the 482 owned by the C&TS. Photos of this trade are on p. 70.

The 486 which was on display at the Royal Gorge Park from 1966 until 1999 when the D&SNG Railroad traded their inoperable K-37 Class 499 for the 486. After a complete overhaul and restoration, the 486 returned to service on *The Silverton* August 26, 2000. Number 485 was not so lucky. It tumbled into the Salida turntable pit and was to badly damaged to repair. It was scrapped in 1955.

K-37 Class

Four D&RGW class K-37 engines are owned by the C&TS. Engines of this class, numbered in the 490 series, were the last narrow gauge engines put into service by the Rio Grande. The C&TS owns numbers. 492, 494, 495, and 497. During October 1991 engine 497, owned by the D&SNG, was traded for engine 482, owned by the C&TS. Engine 497, although in need of inspection and repair, was returned to service. The 494 and 495 are out of service.

The 491 is now owned by the Colorado Historical Society and is on display at the Colorado Railroad Museum in Golden, Colorado; 493 and 498 are owned by the D&SNG Railroad. The 490 was retired by the D&RGW in 1962 and scrapped during 1963-4. The 496 suffered a cracked boiler and was scrapped in Alamosa. The boiler and frame were hauled to Pueblo and scrapped in 1955. As an interesting side note, several of the 490s were equiped with three-position couplers so they could pull standard gauge cars on dual-gauge track. The 494 has one of these couplers.

The 490s have had checkered careers—they were originally built in 1902 by Baldwin as standard gauge 2-8-0s (D&RG Class C-41). In 1928 and 1930, 10 of the C-41 engines were rebuilt into narrow gauge 2-8-2s in the D&RGW's Burnham Shops at Denver. The 490-series engines had a reputation for being 'stiff' and subject to derailments. Look under the tender on a 490 at Antonito or Chama to see evidence of their history—the tender wheels were simply shoved closer together to fit narrow gauge track, using the original axles and truck sideframes. The K-37s can be distinguished from the 480s by the old-fashioned fluted sand and steam domes, and by the straight profile of the boiler tops. Engine specifications are on p. 122.

One other engine in the Chama yards is diesel-electric engine 19, a 44-ton General Electric locomotive that was purchased from the Oahu Railway in Hawaii in 1972 by Scenic Railways, Inc. Later the Railroad Commission purchased the engine from Scenic Railways. Affectionately known as "The Pineapple," during its early years in Chama, railroad crews now call it the "Bumble Bee." The number 19 is used in yard switching, on work trains, and is occasionally used for special chartered passenger trains. During shipment to Chama, it was discovered that the 19 actually weighs 47 tons—three tons of concrete ballast had been added to increase traction.

ENGINE 497 RETURNS TO THE C&TS

Between October 8 and 11, 1991, a historic event took place, quite unusual in the annals of narrow gauge railroading. After approval by the C&TS Railroad Commission, the D&SNG Railroad traded their fully operational K-37, engine 497, to the C&TS Railroad for the long-out-of-service K-36 engine 482.

On October 8, 1991, the tender for 497 was loaded onto a lowboy truck and transported to Chama. The following day, locomotive 482 was loaded and moved to Durango. The lowboy truck called into service for this historic exchange, was then loaded with locomotive 497 and moved to Chama. The next day, the truck returned to Durango with the tender for 482.

With this trade, in which both railroads are very satisfied, engine 497 returns to familiar territory after seven years of service on *The Silverton*. The D&SNG found that the larger and longer 497 had trouble going around the sharper curves of the Silverton Branch (the D&RGW never used K-36 and K-37 locomotives between Durango and Silverton). The engine can also pull one more coach up the four percent grade between Chama and Cumbres. The C&TS is delighted to have another fully operational locomotive added to its roster.

During the winter of 1991-92, 497's boiler was checked and ten broken staybolts were replaced. A hydrostatic test was run and needed minor repairs and adjustments were made. The hand rails on the tender tank were welded to the tank, but had to be removed and bolted on in order to meet Federal Railroad Association standards.

On opening day for the D&SNG, newly restored engine 482 pulled the first train of the season to Silverton and return. Likewise, on the C&TS, engine 497 started service on May 16 when it pulled a chartered special to Big Horn and return. It also was the helper engine on the first train of the 1992 season, May 23, 1992, and the following day pulled Train No. 2 to Antonito.

In the fall of 1991 for the first time in over 25 years, four K-36 class locomotives were under steam at Chama.   *(Three photos, Gerald M. Blea)*

Late in the afternoon of October 8, 1991, engine 497 arrived in Chama by truck as part of the "great locomotive swap."

The next day, October 9, engine 482 was loaded onto a low-boy trailer for a ride to Durango, where it was restored by the D&SNG Railroad

On April 28, 1994, the day after it was returned to service, engine 463 is under steam in Chama. The engine, last used by the D&RGW in 1955, has been completely rebuilt by C&TS employees.

(Jeff Johnson)

CARS

The first passenger cars for the C&TS were converted from D&RGW 3000-series boxcars and from 6000-series flatcars. Twenty-six of the 30 ft boxcars were purchased from the Rio Grande by the Colorado & New Mexico Railroad Authorities; a few additional ones were purchased by Scenic Railways and Kyle Railways. The boxcars were originally built during 1904 for the D&RG. During various modifications and rebuildings, modern couplers and air brake equipment were added. During a major rebuilding in 1924-26, the cars received metal roofs. Rebuilt, the cars can carry 50,000 pounds; they weigh 22,700 pounds empty.

The first C&TS passenger car, number 200, was constructed from boxcar 3339 in 1971, by volunteer workers. The original paint on number 200 was red with gold lettering and striping. The seats were placed length-wise in the center, facing outward. The steps and windows built for car 200 provided the prototype for other cars. Several other boxcars were rapidly converted before the start of the 1971 passenger season.

Only one caboose, 0503, was included in the sale of equipment to the Railroad Authorities. The caboose was built in 1880 by the D&RG, and rebuilt with modern couplers and air-brake equipment in 1923. Another caboose, 05635, was built from stock car 5635 in 1977. Caboose 0306 was built from boxcar 3060 in 1982. Privately built, it was sold to the Railroad Commission, and is available for charter. The beautifully appointed car holds 12 passengers and includes a wet bar and kitchen. Caboose 0579 was given to the C&TS in 1991.

Among the heaviest cars on the C&TS are the fourteen 6500-series steel frame flatcars, 41 ft 6 in long, that can carry as much as 107,700 pounds. They were rebuilt from standard gauge flatcars by the Rio Grande between 1940 and 1944. At one time they were equipped with canvas covers to carry new automobiles to Durango, and to other towns west of Durango on the Rio Grande Southern Railroad (photo, p. 85).

Seven of the 6500-series flatcars were converted into passenger coaches in the Antonito car shop in 1981-82. These coaches, with a steel framework and wooden sides, do not have clerestory roofs. (Clerestory roofs have small horizontal windows just below the the top of the roof line to let in light. On some coaches, these windows can be opened for ventilation.) These coaches are named for southern Colorado towns. Another grant was used to convert the remaining seven 6500-series flatcars to coaches during 1986-87. These were built with clerestory roofs, large windows that lower into the fiberglass sides of the coach and walk-over seats for 44 passengers. These cars are named for towns in New Mexico (photo, p. 72).

With the $550,000 appropriation approved by the U.S. Congress in 1992, the C&TS planned to build more coaches. The Commission located seats, standard gauge flatcars and trucks to build the new equipment. Some of the money was also used to restore engine 463, during in the winter of 1992.

One other steel passenger coach owned by the Railroad Commission is the *Hinman*. It was bought in Mexico, probably from the Nacionales de Mexico, by Thomas J. Hinman, who loaned it to the C&TS in 1971 and later donated it to the railroad. After being placed on U.S. narrow gauge freight trucks (Mexican narrow gauge trucks are higher than those used in the U.S.) it was moved to Chama. The *Hinman* is used mainly for movies; and has been repainted many times, for each new appearance.

In 2001 coach 510, the *Tres Piedras*, was converted into an extra-fare parlour car, the *Clarence Quinlan*, in honor of the Antonito resident and 1970 member of the Colorado state legislature. Mr. Quinlan was instrumental in passing the legislation to purchase the C&TS Railroad. Coach 511, formerly the *Santa Fe,* is now named the *Joseph C. Vigil*, in honor Joe Vigil who once served as C&TS General Manager and is now on the Board of Directors for the RGRPC. These coaches are painted tuscan red and have wicker seats for 24 passengers.

See p. 122-23 for a complete roster of all equipment.

Remodeled and repainted, the Joseph C Vigil parlour car ready for service. June 2001 (Earl Knoob)

Interior of the refurbished extra-fare parlour car Joseph C. Vigil. (Earl Knoob)

C&TS coach "Espanola," built in 1986 with a traditional clerestory roof.   *(Pat Barry)*

TRACK

The Cumbres & Toltec Scenic Railroad track is narrow gauge. It was built that way by the Denver & Rio Grande, whose officials knew that a narrow gauge road could be built and operated more cheaply than one built to standard gauge. "Narrow gauge" simply means that the inside surfaces of the rails (and the outer surfaces of the wheel flanges on the locomotives and cars) are less than 4 ft 8-½ in. apart. Exactly why a gauge of 4 ft 8-½ in. was adopted as standard in Britain and North America is not known, but perhaps coincidentally, this distance is the same as the distance between the wheels of Celtic and Roman chariots. Most narrow gauge railroads in the U.S., including the D&RG, were built with rails 3 ft apart, but others used 2 ft or 3-½ ft gauge track. The Colorado-New Mexico area formerly contained hundreds of miles of narrow gauge track, mostly of 3 ft gauge, although there were several notable 2 ft gauge lines and a few of 3-½ ft gauge.

Because the original narrow gauge engines and cars were smaller and lighter than standard gauge equipment, they could be operated safely on lighter rails and over less sturdily constructed bridges than could standard gauge equipment. Most narrow gauge equipment, being short, can operate around sharper curves than can standard gauge trains. Unfortunately, the light rail and sharp curves limit the speed of trains. Slow schedules and the expense of transferring freight to standard gauge cars brought about the demise of nearly all narrow gauge railroads in the Unites States.

The expense of transferring freight from one gauge to another caused the D&RG to convert to standard gauge most of the original narrow gauge main lines. As more of the track became standard gauge, the interchange point retreated from Denver southward to Pueblo, Salida, Walsenburg, and finally Alamosa in 1899. Standard gauge rails reached Antonito, Colorado, in 1901, but were operated mostly by narrow gauge engines on three-rail track, using special idler cars carrying additional couplers on each end to fit cars of both gauges. The interchange point between narrow gauge and standard gauge remained in Alamosa until 1966.

The original track over Cumbres was laid with very light 30 lb iron rail (rail weights are given in pounds per yard of rail length, so 30 lb rail weighs 30 pounds per yard). The source of this rail is not known, but it probably came from mills in the eastern U.S. or from England. The first rails rolled at the D&RG-controlled Colorado Coal and Iron Company in Pueblo were hauled over Cumbres in 1882 for use between Durango and Silverton. Rails weighing 40 and 45 pounds per yard made up most of the track from Alamosa to Durango by 1913. These rails were strong enough to support the small 2-8-0 and 4-6-0 engines then in common use. Heavier 2-8-2, K-27 engines had been in use westward from Salida to Gunnison since 1903, but could not be used on Cumbres at that time because of the light rail.

In 1913, 14-½ miles of track from Chama to Cumbres were relaid with used 65 lb steel rail. The 2-8-2 engines could then be used as helpers on the steep grade to Cumbres, although they had to be hauled unloaded to Chama before they could be placed in service. These engines were too heavy for the 40 lb rails when fully loaded. In 1922 and 1923, 70 lb rails were laid from Antonito to milepost 316 (about 1-½ miles east of Osier), and from Chama eastward for about 1-½ miles. In 1936, heavier 85 lb rails were laid from milepost 316 to the point 1-½ miles east of Chama.

The C&TS track is very steep from Chama to Cumbres, with a ruling grade of four percent, meaning that the track rises four feet for every 100 ft along the track. The grade is not a constant four percent, however, as shown by the profile, p. 73. From Antonito to Cumbres the grade is less steep, averaging about 0.8 percent, and in places attains a maximum of 1.42 percent. Some track is nearly level for short distances.

Railroad curves are measured in degrees, describing the angle marked at the center of the curve by two radial lines drawn from the ends of a 100 ft long chord to the curve. Maximum curvature on the C&TS is 20° between Big Horn wye and Lobato. Many sharp curves on both sides of Cumbres have additional rails spiked inside the running rails. These are guard rails designed to keep car wheels close to the running rails in case of derailment.

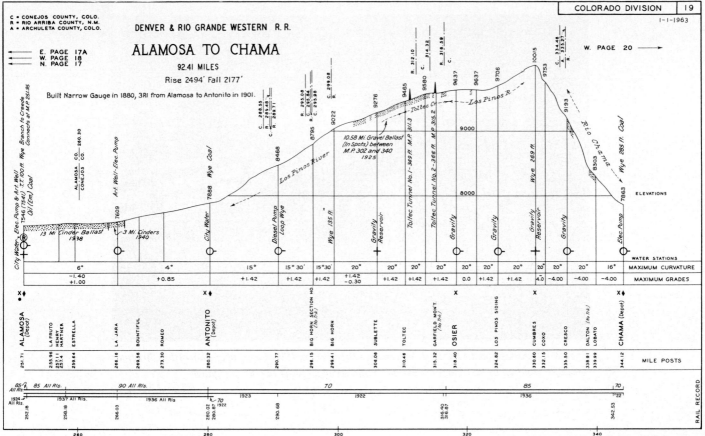

Profile of track between Alamosa, Colorado, and Chama, New Mexico. (Courtesy, Denver & Rio Grande Western Railroad)

Several times the Rio Grande considered standard gauging the Cumbres route. One of the most obvious indications of such intent was the track between Durango, Colorado, and Farmington, New Mexico, which was originally built to standard gauge, and was later converted to narrow gauge.

CASCADE AND LOBATO TRESTLES

In 1883, the original wooden Lobato trestle across the East Fork of Wolf Creek was replaced with the present iron deck-plate girder bridge, 100 ft high and 310 ft long. It has five 54 ft spans and one 40 ft span, on steel bents resting on masonry footings (photos, p. 49, 74).

The Cascade trestle is also a deck-plate girder bridge. It is 137 ft high and 408 ft long with seven 54 ft spans and one 30 ft span set on steel bents resting on masonry footings. Iron for both bridges was fabricated by the Keystone Bridge Company in 1881 (see pp. 38, 49 for new information about these bridges). The present bridge was not erected until 1889, however.

In an interesting turn of events, the deck-plate girders ordered in 1881 for the Cascade bridge were used at other locations on the D&RG system. Finally on October 24, 1888, J.E. Hubbard, B&B Superintendent at Pueblo, filled out the proper requisition form for two 54 ft iron deck girders and one 30 ft iron deck girder to be used for rebuilding the Cascade bridge. Notes on the requisition form state that: "In '81 an iron trestle with bents about eighty feet high and deck composed of girders 54 ft long and 30 ft long were purchased and deliv-

ered. In '86 the girders were taken away (probably in storage at Cañon City) and erected as common deck girders as follows: five 54 ft on 1st Division; two 54 ft and one 30 ft on 3rd Division. The five girders on the First Division are too light for the heavy engines and are ordered out; will return them to Cascade, but will have to purchase the three ordered above to complete." (ref. G).

The bridge builder's plate on the present-day Cascade Creek bridge, with a date of 1889, presumably was attached to one of the girders covered in Mr. Hubbard's requisition (ref. G).

According to other records unearthed by Jackson C. Thode, one 54 ft girder went to bridge 226A over Poncha Creek on Marshall Pass (the old 3rd Division) in 1888, and another 54 ft girder went to bridge 229A at mile 229.3 on the same line in October, 1886. Also, one 30 ft girder went to bridge 230A at mile 230.3 on Marshall Pass in 1885. The Bridge and Structure book states that the five 54 ft girders were returned to Cascade, after being used on the 1st Division just south of Denver, at Military Junction, and near Greenland, Colorado.

By 1886, the D&RG was in receivership. The company was concerned about competition from the standard gauge Colorado Midland Railroad being built from Colorado Springs to Leadville and Glenwood Springs. It was much more important to upgrade the Marshall Pass route than try and finance a permanent bridge on the remote San Juan Division.

Engine 487 crosses Lobato Trestle in light snow, December 16, 1990 during operation of the Christmas Train for children in the village of Chama. Santa seems to prefer the narrow gauge!

(Gerald M. Blea)

Engine 483 at the D&RGW depot in Antonito, Colorado with the last passenger train operated by the Rio Grande over Cumbres Pass in November 1968. This two-day special trip was for members of the National Park Service, the press, D&RGW officials, and others interested in preserving at least a portion of the narrow gauge between Antonito and Durango. The dual gauge (three rail) track ended a short distance west of the depot, on the right. The southbound standard gauge track on the left, originally the beginning of the narrow gauge branch to Santa Fe, New Mexico, ends at the perlite plant in the middle distance below San Antonio Peak on the skyline.

(Ernest W. Robart)

BUILDINGS AND FACILITIES

CHAMA

One concept upon which the purchase of the track and equipment by the Colorado and New Mexico Railroad Authorities was based was that it would become an operating museum of narrow gauge mountain railroading. The Chama terminal fits this concept well because all of the structures date from the period of the D&RGW mainline operation. Except for an unused sheet-metal covered warehouse that was removed to make room for a parking lot, and an addition to the engine house, Chama looks very much as it did during D&RGW ownership.

Because of its location between Alamosa and Durango, Chama was a busy place for many years. Freight trains normally required two days to travel between Alamosa and Durango in either direction, with a layover in Chama. Here, engines and crews were changed and helper engines were added to eastbound freights. As many as 400 engine servicings were done monthly during the oil boom of the 1950s. Several trains passed through Chama each day.

The original six-stall, wooden roundhouse at Chama was built in 1882, and burned in 1899 (p. 16, 76). The present brick roundhouse originally had nine stalls. Four stalls were removed by the D&RGW in 1936, and three more disappeared in the early 1950s, leaving only two stalls. Two new stalls were rebuilt by the C&TS in 1977. In 1991, the *Friends of the C&TS* spent two work sessions building a 14 ft by 64 ft storage annex on the west side of the roundhouse. East of the roundhouse was a large plant built in 1900 for dipping sheep in chemicals to kill ticks and other pests. The track which led to that plant is still in place. The original roundhouse had a 50 ft Keystone turntable; this was replaced by a 65 ft turntable in 1925 to handle larger helper engines. It was removed in 1940.

Another prominent feature of the Chama yards is the coal tipple. This structure was built in 1924, replacing a 60 ton coal chute built in 1902. It was originally painted a red color similar to that used on boxcars—the red paint can still be seen under the accumulation of coal dust. The tipple is probably the last operating coaling tower for steam locomotives left in the U.S. The water tank, built in 1897, may be the only operable double-spout tank left in the U.S.

A track scale, apparently obtained second-hand from Aspen, Colorado, was installed in 1889. It was replaced by the present track scale in 1929.

The original Chama depot, built in 1882, also burned in the 1899 fire. It was replaced by the existing depot the same year. The Chama depot was painted white with dark-green trim during the last years of the D&RGW ownership, as were other small buildings. The depot was damaged in 1932 when a former D&RGW employee drove his car through the wall. The brick oil house, office and storeroom were built in 1903. The original color schemes used in Chama are not known. The section house, now used as housing for *The Friends of the C&TS* volunteers is a classic example of rough-hewn solid log construction. An almost identical building stands at Sublette. Still standing near the tail of the wye, at the south end of the yards, are the stock pens which were built in 1888.

While visiting the Chama or Antonito yards, pick up a walking tour brochure published by the volunteer organization, *Friends of the C&TS Railroad.* Don't miss seeing the rotary snowplows and other work equipment (photos, p. 86-7), much of which has been or is being restored by the *Friends.* Other photos of Chama are on p. 15, 42, 70, 76.

ANTONITO

The original D&RG depot at Antonito was built in 1880 near the junction of the tracks to Santa Fe, New Mexico, and to Durango, Colorado. This wooden building was soon converted to a freight house, and a stone depot was built 116 ft north of the freight house, adjacent to the switch for the San Juan Extension. A three-room addition was built onto the stone depot in 1917. The building was owned by the D&RGW until 1992, when the railroad was absorbed into the Southern Pacific system.

Coal-loading facilities for the D&RG at Antonito originally consisted of a coal dock, built in 1888. A new coal chute was built in 1909. This chute was replaced by a functional, but less picturesque coal-loader in 1956. A one-stall engine house, long enough for two small engines, was built in 1883 directly across the track from the depot at Antonito, primarily to service engines on the Santa Fe branch of the D&RGW. This engine house was retired in 1927 and is not the present structure near the C&TS depot.

The buildings surrounding the C&TS depot have all been built since 1970. The small depot is now an office for the C&TS Railroad Commission. In May 1974, work began on the engine house, and by January 1975 engine 463, given to Antonito by Gene Autry, was safely stored inside. (The building was expanded with two more tracks by the end of the 1979 season.) Also during this period, a much-needed water tank was built—a great improvement over filling engine tenders with a garden hose! A Department of Commerce grant helped build the loop track, which was completed in August 1977. The large depot was completed in 1977. In addition to offices and ticket windows on the ground floor, the second floor has accommodations for train crews. Additional photos of Antonito are on p. 13, 25, 74, 76, 84.

This interesting old photograph of the original Chama roundhouse was taken before the building burned in the 1899 fire (p. 16). The hostlers, who posed for this photo, were about to get an 1878 Baldwin class 56 2-8-0 ready for work. This is probably engine 32, which was later sold to the Florence & Cripple Creek Railroad. All the equipment at this time still had link and pin couplers.   *(Earl G. Knoob collection)*

View north from the Antonito coal dock after 1909. This view shows one of the dual gauge stub turnouts. The large building in the center is the flour mill, and to its left is the Presbyterian church steeple.   *(W.D. Joyce collection)*

LAVA PUMPING STATION

Water for Lava Tank was brought up from the Rio de Los Pinos River by a pumping station along the river. In the 1891 D&RG Structures Book lists the water here as being "good and plenty!" Original structures at the pump station included a 23×27 ft frame house for the pump attendant and a pump house, both built in 1883. The original pump house was a 28×31 ft frame structure with an 8×30 ft coal bin, Cameron and Worthington water pumps, and two boilers, one of which was listed as a used locomotive boiler. To reach the water tank, 2,230 ft of 3 in iron pipe was laid (ref. A). A new pump house was built when a diesel-power plant replaced the original coal-fired boilers at the plant. At present, the water tank is not used.

BIG HORN

Along the north side of the track, on the inside of the lowest loop just west of milepost 296 was the Big Horn Section House (photo, p. 28). In 1891 there was a 16×28 ft frame section house with two frame additions, a 19×30 ft bunk house, a 9×13 ft coal house, and two 3×11×3 ft water boxes. By 1919, there was a well, with an underground storage tank, two bunk houses made from freight car bodies, and an additional 18×36 ft storage shed. All the structures were destroyed in 1952, except for the section house. It almost made it into the C&TS era, being retired in 1966 (ref. A,B).

SUBLETTE

The large frame building on the south side of the track is the original section house. Some years later a kitchen was added. The hand-hewn log structure is a bunk house built soon after the line was completed to this point. At one time there were two bunkhouses, one 19×30 ft and a second 16×22 ft in size. A phone booth once stood on the north side of the rail, directly opposite the bunk house. Also at Sublette is a metal tool house, installed in 1950, as well as several car body tool houses, and the old coal house that was moved from Allison, Colorado, in 1945 (ref. B). A shed for speeders was built from part of an old box car. During the summer of 1991, the *Friends of the C&TS Railroad* undertook major repairs to the section house. The south roof leaked badly, the old tar paper roofing was removed, new boards were added where needed and a new asphalt shingle roof was installed. The water tank was removed in 1937 and replaced with the present water standpipe (photos, p. 31, 61, 77, 83, 95, 100).

TOLTEC

Just west of Toltec Creek, in the open area on the east side of the track, was the site of the 1882 Toltec section house. The 1891 Bridge and Building record book also shows a 16×22 ft frame depot here. The section house, a 16×22 ft frame structure, was rebuilt with a 16×28 ft kitchen and a 12×18 ft, four-room addition. There was a 19×30 ft frame bunk house and an 8×12 ft coal house (ref. A). A standard 16×24 ft 1880 water tank was removed in 1925 with the coming of the larger K-27 type locomotives. The rest of these buildings were removed by 1938 (photo, p. 78).

OSIER

Original structures at Osier includes the red frame 16×24 ft 1880 depot (identical to the one listed at Toltec). It once had a platform. The section house was built in 1884 for $1,800.00 and is 16×52 ft with two additions, one 16×30 ft and the second, a six-room, 12×22 ft structure. There was an 1880 19×30 ft frame bunk house and a 10×15 ft coal house. To the west of the depot was a 50 ft Keystone turntable, covered by a snowshed, 60 ft in diameter. The turntable was retired in 1927 (ref. A). The water tank was built in 1880 for a cost of $600.00. Various improvements were made to the cattle pens in 1936. (Photos p. 38, 57, 79, 96, 115.)

LOS PINOS WATER TANK

In addition to the tank, railroad facilities in 1891 included a 10×12 ft watchman's house, a 16×28 ft section house with two additions, a frame 16×26 ft room and four additional rooms, 12×18 ft in size. In the 1930s, the section house was connected to a 9×26 ft trackside platform via a 3×56 ft walkway (ref B). Records indicate that the section house and bunk house were painted in 1936 and then torn down in 1938. There was a 16×31 ft bunk house, a 13×17 ft coal house and two coal platforms. Outside was the usual collection of outbuildings. The first coal house burned February 1, 1912, and was replaced with another one which lasted until 1929. Coal was needed for refueling the rotary snowplows, and for heating and cooking, as the section men and their families lived here. The tank is gravity fed from a well and reservoir located to the southwest, connected via 840 feet of pipe. The water was noted as being "good and plenty" in 1891 (ref. A). The water tank was built in 1880 for a cost of $600.00, and was rebuilt in 1986.

Taken from the coach window, the westbound <u>San Juan</u> *passenger train, powered by engine 488, pulls into Sublette in November 1950. This was the last full year of service for this train. The two bunk houses were still in use.*

(Collection of Earl G. Knoob)

78

The westbound <u>Colorado-New Mexico Express</u> has made a stop at Toltec, probably sometime after World War I. This is one of the few photographs known of Toltec.

(W.D. Joyce collection)

This rare photograph, looking north, shows the water tank and collection of buildings that once stood at Toltec, mile 313.44. The log bunkhouse appears to be the same construction as others on the line.

(Earl G. Knoob collection)

Osier, Colorado, looking south. This photo by George E. Mellen, must have been taken before 1888 as the 50 ft Keystone turntable had not been installed, and the trestle across Osier Creek is new. The track in the foreground has many hand-hewn ties. Traces of the old toll road are visible curving west through a row of snow fences below the depot and section house. The water tank is the original one built in 1880, which was later replaced. By 1884, the area east of the track was known as Jenkins Gardens where Mr. William Jenkins had a homestead. He was also the postmaster, tollgate keeper, saloon and restaurant owner.
(Colorado Historical Society)

CUMBRES

Structures at Cumbres in 1891 included a beautiful two-story, seven-room depot and platform, built in 1882; located east of the present depot, it was torn down by the Rio Grande in 1954. The present depot, also built in 1882, was actually the section foreman's house. It has had two additions, one 16×28 ft and a second, 12×22 ft. The station signal on the present depot-section house was built by volunteers in 1972 to duplicate a D&RGW design that was removed earlier by vandals. Also located nearby was a 16×30 ft frame bunk house and a small coal house.

Original water facilities consisted of a Haliday windmill on a 36 ft tower, a 16×30 ft frame pump house, and a standard water tank. The windmill was later replaced by a gasoline engine, and the old tank was replaced with the present cistern and water plug at an unknown date. The water tank was removed in 1937. Today, water comes from a spring above the lake north of the track. Pipe from the spring to the cistern was installed in the 1930s.

Facilities for servicing and turning engines at Cumbres included a 50 ft diameter gallows-frame turntable, installed in 1884, and covered by a 67 ft diameter turntable house that was added in 1887. The turntable probably was moved to Monarch, Colorado after 1910. There was also a 16×82 ft coal bin, a 7×10 ft sand house, and a 50 ft wooden ash pit.

Because of its strategic location, Cumbres was an important station throughout the history of Rio Grande operations. Helper engines were turned and serviced here, as they are now, for both eastbound and westbound trains. About 3,000 ft of sidings at Cumbres were used for inspection and storage of cars as eastbound trains were reassembled to continue their trips after being brought from Chama in several "cuts." An agent and a section foreman were stationed at Cumbres until the *San Juan* passenger train was abandoned. The section gang used the present section house at Cumbres until the mid-1960s. A car inspector, stationed at Cumbres, lived in a house that is still standing north of the depot-section house. This house, built about 1911, has been extensively repaired and repainted by the *Friends of the C&TS*. (Photos, p. 42, 80, 82-85, 94, 99, 100.)

CRESCO

During construction days, a 16×25 ft section house (with two additions) and a 16×30 ft bunk house were built on the south side of the track. An 1882 employees' timetable shows Cresco as "Siding No. 9." There was an 8×12 ft coal house, probably for the rotary snowplow trains. All of these structures were retired in 1938. The present water tank was built in 1893, and was rebuilt with a fiberglass liner in 1983. The siding is 1,702 ft long and has a capacity of 43 cars. In about 1909, an old 45 ft turntable was used as a bridge across a small stream; when it was retired is not known.

Photographer Davis climbed to the roof of the water tank on a cloudy, snowy day to capture this unusual view of Cumbres in 1909. On the left is the covered turntable and the original depot is to the right beyond two outfit cars on a siding. (Jackson C. Thode collection)

D&RG bridge and building carpenters are looking over the remains of the covered turntable being removed at Cumbres. This photograph was taken in 1916. Note the car inspector's house in the background.　　　　　　*(Jackson C. Thode collection)*

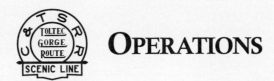

OPERATIONS

PASSENGER AND FREIGHT SERVICE

The San Juan Extension probably became the San Juan Division after completion of the line to Silverton in 1882. By 1887, the La Veta-Durango-Silverton branch was part of the Second Division of the D&RG Railway Company. On January 1, 1889, a general renumbering of the divisions took place, and the route became the Fourth Division. During the 1940s and 1950s, the name was again changed and it became part of the Pueblo Division.

A summary of operations by the Rio Grande is on p. 21.

Schedules were never particularly fast. In 1881, westbound passenger trains were scheduled to leave Antonito at 7:00 AM and to arrive in Chama at 1:00 PM. A freight train was scheduled to leave Antonito at 8:00 AM and to reach Chama at 4:00 PM.

Schedules in 1894 were a little faster; the passenger train left Antonito at 11:20 AM and arrived in Chama at 2:55 PM. In its later years, however, the *San Juan* left Antonito at 8:15 AM and arrived at Chama about noon. Your trip on the C&TS really isn't much slower than a ride on the *San Juan,* if lunch time is excluded. During snow blockades, however, D&RGW trains sometimes were weeks late.

The D&RGW operated the Cumbres Pass route as strictly as any other main line. In addition to a daily passenger train each way, there was at least one daily freight in each direction. Nor were these freights small affairs. Fifty- to seventy-car trains were common in the 1950s. Occasionally trains of more than 100 cars wormed their way across Cumbres Pass to Antonito. In 1955 about 12,000 carloads of freight were handled to and from the Chama-Durango-Farmington area. Two, three, and sometimes four engines were used on many eastbound trains.

Rio Grande freights running east from Chama required special operations. Two K-36 or K-37 engines could handle from 12 to 15 loaded cars up the four percent grade. Trains were cut into several parts at Chama, and each part was taken to Cumbres separately. The road engine was in front, with a helper at the rear. At Cumbres the cars were set out in the yards and the engines turned on the wye, so they could return to Chama for another "hill turn." When all the cuts were hauled to Cumbres, the train was reassembled. Westbound freights presented problems too. At Antonito a helper engine was placed in the middle of the train. If the train was very long or heavy, an additional engine was coupled ahead of the road engine, and perhaps a fourth added to the rear, ahead of the caboose.

Double-headed trains have their difficulties either eastbound or westbound. Weight restrictions require that at least five cars be placed between engines crossing the bridges at Lobato and Cascade Creek. That is why, if one is lucky enough to ride a double-headed C&TS train, a stop will be made at Lobato, and the helper will be cut off to cross the bridge light. The rest of the train then follows the helper engine across the bridge to the east side where the two engines are recoupled.

Freight traffic on the Fourth Division has included many items never envisioned by General Palmer and his company. Their goal was to reach the mining camps in the San Juans and carry supplies and mining equipment to the mines, and refined ores to eastern markets. Of course they planned on exploiting the known coal deposits located near the railroad, and probably realized there would be a growing market for lumber from the coniferous forests around Chama and westward toward Durango. In 1882 hauling long trains of oil from the San Juan Basin was unheard of. As the region became settled, large shipments of livestock and products needed for ranchers and farmers increased. By the 1940s, pinto beans and fruit from the Farmington, New Mexico area became important sources of revenue for the Rio Grande. Although not as glamorous as gold and silver ore concentrates, the lumber, oil, pipe, and agricultural products carried on the Division probably were much more profitable.

Interior of one of the D&RGW's deluxe parlor cars, rebuilt from a coach, for service on the San Juan *and the* Shavano *(which ran between Salida and Gunnison, Colorado.)*

(L.S. Robbins photo, Collection of Earl G. Knoob)

This rare photograph of an eastbound passenger train at Coxo probably was taken before 1883 when most Pullman car service across Cumbres Pass was switched to the Marshall Pass route to Salt Lake City. The last car on the right is one of the luxurious Pullman sleeping cars, Toltec, built June 1880. This car was among the first two Pullman coaches completed for the D&RG; the other was named the Zuni. There were ten sections and two toilets on the car, built by the Detroit Car Works of the Pullman Palace Car Company. A total of eighteen Pullman cars were built for the D&RG. Early in 1905, the Toltec, Antonito and Americano Pullman cars were sold to the Uintah Railway. When they were dismantled is not known. These is one of the few photographs that exists of the Toltec. The car was 42 ft 6 in long and fitted with Miller couplers. The helper engine is a diamond stack 2-8-0, and the road engine is a class T-12 4-6-0. (Earl G. Knoob collection)

In July 1947, the eastbound San Juan made its station stop at Cumbres. The rear parlor car, Durango, carries the drumhead from the long-abandoned Shavano passenger train.

(Colorado Historical Society)

The venerable K-28, 478, pulls the westbound <u>San Juan</u> into the double-reverse curves just west of Sublette in July 1947. At the rear is the new observation car <u>Silver Vista</u>, bound for service on the Durango-Silverton branch.   (Colorado Historical Society)

On May 25, 1991, the first train of the season pulls into Cumbres. Behind engines 489 and 487 is a railway post office car, carrying U.S. mail which was specially marked for the occasion. Three weeks earlier, rotary OY was busy clearing snow drifts at this location.
(Ray W. Osterwald)

Servicing 484 at Antonito, the evening of July 14, 1978. At this time, the engine house was only one year old.

(Ray W. Osterwald)

A Rocky Mountain Railroad Club eastbound extra makes a photo run-by at Cumbres. September 1, 1991.

(Martin R. Osterwald)

Flat cars loaded with new automobiles, in the D&RGW Durango yard, September 1951. Frank W. Osterwald)

Engine 493 has just switched some gondolas onto the house track (track closest to the depot) at Cumbres in the summer of 1967.

(Ray W. Osterwald)

MAINTENANCE-OF-WAY EQUIPMENT

Work equipment was (and still is) an important part of running a railroad. The C&TS is fortunate to have many interesting pieces of this type of equipment in the Chama yards. This is one more reason the C&TS is such an outstanding "living museum." Narrow gauge Jordan spreader, OU, is used for ballasting track, scraping back loose cuts, and plowing snow when coupled behind a flanger car. Air pressure actuates arms which move the large blades forward. The large tank is an air reservoir; the operator stands in the small shelter. Note arch-bar trucks, brake wheel placement, and end-sill detail.

(Ed Osterwald)

Narrow gauge derrick OP in the Alamosa yards, May 5, 1968. Note placement of grab irons, bracing on cab for A-frame, and supports on boom-tender flatcar (06063) for the derrick boom and cables. Compare this photo with the one on p. 100, after the derrick was restored by the <u>Friends of the C&TS.</u>

(Ed Osterwald)

Front quarter view of flanger OK at Chama in 1973, showing arch-bar trucks, shape of single flanger blade, hand-rail arrangement, brake cylinder on left end, and sheet-metal enclosure to protect the operating machinery. *(Carl R. Osterwald)*

Dual gauge idler car derailed in the Alamosa yards, June 11, 1967. Idler cars are short, heavy flatcars on standard gauge trucks, with both standard and narrow gauge couplers on each end. The short ladders were used by trainmen during switching operations. An idler car can be seen on the display track in the Antonito yards. *(Ed Osterwald)*

Flanger OL at Chama in 1973, showing the folding double blade. Flangers also have large chisels fitting inside the rails to clear away ice and hard-packed snow. The round target at the top of the flanger (resembling a switch stand) tells the locomotive engineer whether the chisels are up or down; the chisels must be raised when crossing switches. Blades and chisels are operated by air pressure from the locomotive. *(Carl R. Osterwald)*

GRAMPS OIL FIELD

In the extreme northeastern edge of the San Juan Basin, on land that was once part of the Tierra Amarilla Land Grant are several oil seeps which were first reported by geologist Arthur Lakes in 1901. One was along the Navajo River east of the Chromo anticline. Another oil spring was on the Price Ranch, about three miles north of the Hughes' Banded Peak Ranch. A few wells were drilled southeast of Pagosa Springs, on the Chromo and Azotea anticlines, and on the Monero dome, but no oil or gas in commercial quantities was found until the discovery of the Gramps field.

The Gramps oil field is in Archuleta County, Colorado about half way between Pagosa Springs and Chama, and six miles north of the state line. The field is on the Price anticline. It is believed that the oil accumulated against an east-west fault crossing a north-south anticlinal axis. Production is from the part of the structure that lies south of the fault. The oil probably accumulated in the lower part of the Mancos Formation and migrated less than five miles to the anticline.

On July 3, 1935, Lafayette M. Hughes started drilling the first well on his 54,000 acre ranch; it was a dry hole. Well No. 2 was spudded September 6, 1935 and completed as the discovery well December 3, 1935. Geological surveys and recommendations for drilling sites were made by the well-known geologist W.A. Waldschmidt. The producing wells in this 127 acre field, are 1,000 to 1,400 ft deep and are in the Dakota Formation. There are no flowing wells; all have to be pumped by electricity.

The Gramps oil field was named for Annie Clifton Hughes' grandfather, William E. Hughes, the father of Lafayette Hughes, who drilled the first well. Cumulative oil production from the Gramps field, through April, 1975 was 5,909,400 barrels of oil from 26 producing wells. Peak production was in 1942 when the family-owned company pumped 1,200-1,300 barrels of oil per day. The field is still in production, but oil is trucked from storage tanks on the property to a refinery at Bloomfield, New Mexico. Gradually the production has dropped to about 130 barrels of oil per day. At present, some wells produce more water than oil.

Because the Hughes family owned the land and oil company, they were able to build a 20,000 barrel storage tank at the site, as well as pumping facilities, a pipeline from the ranch to storage tanks in Chama, and arrange for the oil to be shipped on the narrow gauge to Alamosa before any outside organization knew about the discovery! During the summer of 1936 the company built the pipeline to Chama. In 1937 Hughes also built his own refinery in Alamosa. Some years later the refinery was sold to the Oriental Refining Co., which operated the plant until 1963, when it closed and was dismantled the following year. The D&RGW stopped hauling oil across Cumbres Pass in 1963 and the tank cars were scrapped.

A rather ingenious method was devised for transporting oil from the field to Chama. Oil was pumped from a storage tank through a 4 in pipeline encased in a box filled with sawdust (for insulation). The pipeline crossed the Continental Divide at an elevation of 8,709 ft, three miles from the ranch, after being pumped from the ranch, at an elevation of 7,876 ft. From the crest of the divide, oil flowed by gravity (except during the bitter cold winter when the oil congealed) to Chama. The route was along the Chamita River. At the Chama pumping station there was one 55,000 barrel and two 20,000 barrel storage tanks. Oil was then pumped from the storage tanks to the loading platform, and from there into waiting tank cars. The loading platform is still standing at the north end of the Chama yards (photo, p. 89).

A transfer depot was built in Alamosa in the spring of 1937.

The March 25, 1937 *Alamosa Daily Courier* reported:

> **The transfer depot, which is being built near the railroad shops, will accommodate twelve standard gauge cars and two narrow gauge cars. Eighteen men are employed in the building of the station.**
> **Tracks for the cars and pipes for the transfer of the oil are being installed. An elevated track is being constructed for the narrow gauge cars and a depressed track for the standard gauge so that the oil maybe transferred by gravity.**

When the Hughes company decided to lease some tank cars from the Union Tank Car Company (UTLX), the family reportedly asked the grandchildren how they thought the cars should be marked—"GRAMPS" was the logical choice. The number of narrow frame tank cars named for William E. Hughes is not known.

Employees working on a drill rig in 1936 at the Gramps oil field.
(L.S. Robbins photo. Earl G. Knoob collection)

OIL BOOM IN SAN JUAN BASIN

Oil and natural gas fields in the San Juan Basin south and west of Durango furnished the last rich source of revenue for the railroad. Before the boom started, the neglected, weedy Farmington Branch carried farm produce to market, but little else. By 1955, the population of Farmington had climbed from about 3,500 to more than 13,000 and the town was a bustling center for the oil business. That year the Farmington freight office handled the largest volume of business of any station on the entire D&RGW system! Doubleheaded freights ran west on the narrow gauge mainline every day, summer and winter. Long trains, with several dozen oil tank cars, were common during the 1930s and 1940s (photo, p. 90). The sidings east of Durango became choked with loads and empties. In addition to solid trains of pipe, large amounts of drilling mud, oil field machinery, and supplies were delivered to Durango and Farmington, and crude oil was shipped eastward.

To support this traffic, Alamosa transfer crews used three cranes and worked seven days a week to unload the 250 standard gauge cars that arrived each month from the east. Carmen were busy rebuilding and converting standard gauge flat cars for use on the narrow gauge, and boilermakers and machinists kept the engines healthy. New enginemen and trainmen were hired and began to learn how to run an 1880s railroad using steam engines at least 30 years old. This was even more unusual, as most mainline U.S. railroads no longer used steam engines, much less 1904 vintage wooden box cars.

During the 1950s, the 6500 series flat cars and open-ended gondolas, 30 ft in length, were in constant service hauling pipe and other supplies to the oil fields. When pipes were longer than 30 ft, they were placed on the car so the extra length extended equally beyond the ends of the car. Idler flat cars were converted from old box cars and stock cars. With long loads, the idler cars were coupled to each end of open-ended gondolas, thus allowing the long sections of pipe to be carried

safely around the crooked track between Antonito and Chama. In the late 1950s, more than 6,000 carloads of pipe were carried from Alamosa to Farmington, totaling more than 100,000 tons. Several types of gondola cars have been preserved and are on display in the Chama yards. A complete roster of equipment is on p. 122-3.

Loading dock for oil from the Gramps oil field. The vertical pipe (with valve) delivered oil from the storage tank west of the Chama yards to the tank cars. (Doris B. Osterwald / Friends of the C&TS RR)

Switching a train of pipe at the south end of the Chama yards in June 1953. The trainman standing beside the gondola is giving hand signal directions to the engineer.
(Frank W. Osterwald)

In the spring of 1936, engine 483 starts for Alamosa with a long train, including at least 23 tank cars filled with oil from the Gramps oil field. There are also at least 11 refrigerator cars in this train that is winding its way east on Tanglefoot Curve.

(L.S. Robbins photo. Earl Knoob collection)

Train load of oil field pipe in Alamosa yards ready to leave for Farmington, New Mexico in May 1968.

(Frank W. Osterwald)

NARROW GAUGE TANK CARS

The history of narrow gauge tank cars used by the Rio Grande is rather obscure, and very incomplete. Robert E. Sloan's article (1978) offers the most complete discussion available on this interesting type of railroad equipment.

The Rio Grande actually owned very few tank cars and these were used mainly for water or oil in work trains. The C&TS has two of these cars, the 0471 and 0472, that are still used during rotary snowplowing operations.

Tank cars were owned by the Union Tank Car Company (UTLX), Continental Oil Company (CONOCO, CONX), or the General American Transportation Corporation (CYCX, or TCX). These companies leased their cars to many railroads. It is believed that between 60 and 66 UTLX cars, built during 1907-08, were converted from standard gauge to narrow gauge for use on Colorado's slim gauge routes. Tank cars of both gauges carry 6,500 gallons of oil. Not all of the cars carried oil; many were used for water, molasses, or other liquids, such as chemicals.

There are two types of narrow gauge tank cars: frameless and narrow frame. Between 1924 and 1930 an unknown number of UTLX standard gauge cars were converted to narrow frame tank cars. These were used mainly on the Farmington Branch and across Cumbres Pass, but not all oil shipments from the San Juan Basin were shipped east to Denver. Some shipments left Durango on the Rio Grande Southern (RGS). At Ridgway, they rejoined D&RGW track to Montrose. There the oil was transferred to standard gauge tank cars for shipment to Salt Lake City, Utah.

The Rio Grande used at least three different sets of numbers on these long-abandoned narrow frame cars. The original numbers were in the 12,000 and 13,000 series. There may have been as many as 38 cars in this series. In 1946-47 the cars were renumbered depending upon whether the cars had or did not have heaters. Because the cars carried thick oils, they were fitted with steam pipes to warm or melt the contents of the tank, for easier transfer. These numbers were in the 88,000 series. A final renumbering occurred in February 1956 when the cars received numbers in the 11,000 series. See p. 101 for more on this historic acquisition, and p. 123 for the equipment roster, which includes these cars. Between February 27 and March 3, 1992, six narrow frame tank cars returned to familiar territory, thanks to the *Friends of the C&TS* and many individuals and organizations.

GRAMPS tank cars in Antonito yards in June 1953. The GRAMPS herald was white; reporting marks were yellow. These cars had no underframes. The oil shipped in these cars came from the Gramps oil field northeast of Chama, New Mexico.

(Frank W. Osterwald)

WINTER PROBLEMS

(Monte Ballough)

The challenges the Rio Grande faced in keeping the railroad open across Cumbres Pass through the long winter months were incredible. Again, General Palmer and his associates, who made the decision to build across Cumbres Pass, never dreamed the route would present such monumental problems.

The line was only three years old when fierce winter storms inundated most of the Colorado mountains. The winter of 1884 offered a prelude of things to come. Along with the rest of the narrow gauge system, the line was shut down for weeks at a time. The winters of 1886, 1891 1905, 1906 and 1909 were also severe. In 1886 the line between Antonito and Silverton was shut down for four weeks. Another blockade in 1891 lasted 51 days. In January 1906, a passenger train was stranded on Cumbres Pass for four days by high winds and blowing snow and when the train finally reached Durango, the sides of the coaches were still coated with ice. The same year, another train was marooned on Cumbres Pass for 10 days. A relief train finally reached the snow-covered train with its 50 hungry and exhausted passengers. In 1909 Cumbres Pass was closed on January 24, but opened two days later, only to be blocked again in three days. Such blockades continued through the rest of the winter.

Between 1884 and 1908 more than 13,000 ft of snowsheds were built on the Cumbres Pass route in an attempt to keep blowing snow off the track and enable the trains to keep moving. This effort was less than successful and by the 1920s all the snowsheds had been removed by the Rio Grande except the covered wye at Cumbres. A complete list of snowsheds and their locations is on p. 124.

Until the invention of a successful rotary snow plow in the 1880s, the only way the Rio Grande had to open the line was with a string of small engines (with diamond stacks) to which a huge wedge plow was bolted to the front of the lead engine. A rotary snow plow is not self-propelled. It consists of a steam boiler jammed into a large wooden box. The wheel at the front of the plow is driven by steam from a boiler connected to flywheels inside the plow body. A chute at the top of the wheel housing directs the plowed snow to either side of the track. The wheel is a combination cutter and blower fan. The fan forces the snow out the chute at the top of the wheel housing. If the spinning wheel encounters hard-packed ice, rocks, or tree limbs, it is stopped immediately.

Rotary OM was the 24th snow-throwing machine built by the Cooke Locomotive Works in Paterson, New Jersey, using a design developed by Orange Jull, a talented mechanic and inventor. The gabled roof over the tender and the cab roof, and side extensions on the OM were added by the D&RGW to keep snow out of the coal and off the fireman. The OM has always been assigned to Chama. Rotary OY also was built by Cooke Locomotive Works in 1923 at a cost of $38,336.26, and is somewhat larger.

Operation of a rotary snow plow requires at least three crew members: a pilot (qualified locomotive engineer) to coordinate forward movement of the plow and its locomotives, a wheel-man (also a qualified locomotive engineer) to control the direction of the snow deflector, and a fireman, in addition to the locomotive crews. Also in the consist for snowplowing operations is an auxiliary water car (originally a tender from an engine, but later a modified tank car), a tool car, and one or more outfit cars (for crew members), and a caboose. Until an auxiliary water car was added, the snow plow train could carry only enough fuel and water for three hours of continuous plowing through deep snow. That is why supplies of coal were kept at Cresco, Cumbres, Los Pinos, Osier, and Sublette in the early days. When the snow train became stuck, the crews often had to shovel snow into the tenders of the rotary and the engines to keep them "alive."

The C&TS is fortunate to own two of the former D&RGW rotary snow plows and three flangers. The OM is being restored and the OY is occasionally used to open the line before the start of the summer season. It is an unforgettable sight to watch the plow cut through snowdrifts and toss snow off the track in huge, graceful plumes. The whistle on the rotary has a shrill, piercing sound that is so different from that of the engine whistles.

One other snow-fighting machine is a flanger (photos, p. 87). This is a small flatcar on which two folding blades stick out on each side to move the snow away from the sides of the track. Flangers also have large chisels that fit inside the rails to clear away ice and hard-packed snow. The blades and chisels are operated by air pressure from the locomotive, and are always raised when crossing roads or switches. When either or both of these mechanical devices fail—the section crews are called to shovel the snow from the track and at switches.

The upper end of Los Pinos Creek is one of the worst places for snowdrifts and blockades. The following account, related to the author in 1971 by D&RGW engineer Ben Greathouse, is one example of problems the railroad faced during a typical winter.

"I was on an eastbound passenger train and we got stuck about milepost 322, there below Los Pinos, at the old Los Pinos siding. We were doubleheading, and I was firing the helper engine. We had come in from Chama on a freight train, and a fellow by the name of Donaldson was the engineer. We came out of Cumbres in this blizzard, and we remarked that there would be no 41 tonight!" (Number 41 was the regular west-bound freight train and was scheduled to leave Antonito at 12:15 AM.)

After some maneuvering, the train finally got moving and the passenger train reached Antonito many hours late, after having met the westbound freight at Lava.

"We couldn't understand why they had headed the 41 west in this storm. Well, they got (the freight) as far as Los Pinos and had to give up their train. They got the meat car and the caboose and made it to Chama and left the rest of the train on the mainline at old Los Pinos."

Greathouse lived in Alamosa, and the next morning he was called to help the westbound passenger train.

"We got up on the hill, and it got deeper and deeper, and we got stuck, right in there at old Los Pinos siding. We stayed there until they came for us because the main line was blocked with cars, and we couldn't back up!"

Another experience Ben Greathouse related was a incident of a work train attempting to open the line at Windy Point.

"We had two engines, both headed east, the flanger, and a caboose. They asked me in Chama if I could make it to Alamosa, and I said we could, if we can just get going. The fact of the matter was that a traveling engineer was running the other engine and that's what stuck us. He was out of Durango, and had never held a regular job as an engineer. He had never worked on this hill; and only worked out of Durango. I was in the lead engine, the 487, and we got stuck up there below Windy Point. We'd been through there with the rotary and we were trying to get the trainmaster to go in with a bulldozer and push all the snow on the lower side, down and over Windy Point because it was right up against our running gear."

After plowing the track from Coxo siding, the train headed east toward Windy Point when the flanger went off the track and the train was stuck.

"Finally the head brakeman and the traveling engineer walked up to Cumbres and got the section crew. The section men came down, and finally got the flanger (back on track). The traveling engineer crawled in my window because that was the only way to get in the engine. The snow was just closed right up against

the valve gear, and high. He handed me the orders that said if we couldn't get out within an hour to kill my engine, leave it there, take the other engine and caboose and go back to Chama."

Greathouse replied, "How in hell do they think we are going to get back to Chama? We can't get down to Coxo, let alone get through it."

The blizzard continued and the traveling engineer returned to his locomotive. Later he returned to say, "Well it don't look like we're going to get out of here. We better go back to Chama."

Ben looked at the engineer with dismay and replied, "Jimmy, how do you expect to get back to Chama? You gonna walk? You can't back that caboose up through the snow. Further-more, I'm not leaving this engine, and I'm not killing it."

He replied, "But that's your orders!"

Ben answered, "I don't give a damn about my orders. I'm in charge of this engine, not the dispatcher. She's mine. I signed for her in Chama. If I kill this engine she's gonna freeze up and bust everything because I can't get down to drain it. You go ahead, I'll be here, but I'm not killing this engine. If we could get out of here I could be in Cumbres in five minutes if someone gets hold of that throttle back there."

He said, "You think so?"

"Yes, if that throttle on that rear engine is opened up. Jimmy, I pulled you all the way up here (I knew he could run it because he'd already been told!)."

By this time the section crew had the flanger back on track after picking ice out from the ball of the rail. The train then backed down to the big loop at milepost 332.

"We opened them up (both engines) and went right on up to Cumbres."

The OM ("Old Maude" to railroaders), has just arrived in Antonito after plowing the line from Chama. There are only three sturdy 2-8-0s in this photo; the D&RGW sometimes was forced to used up to seven of these engines to push a rotary through the deep snow drifts.

(Jackson C. Thode collection)

This great action photograph was taken by Monte Ballough in 1908 or 1909. The rotary is working to capacity with snow nearly up to the top of the hood. Taken at Windy Point, the plow is being pushed <u>down</u> the four-percent grade.   *(Jackson C. Thode collection)*

View looking west at Cumbres depot and covered wye. The two-story depot is more than half buried by the deep winter snows. The order board (signal) on the depot was installed in 1888. This photo was taken about 1910 by C.R. Lively, the Cumbres agent-operator.   *(W.D. Joyce collection)*

The D&RGW ran a rotary snow plow train across Cumbres Pass for the last time on March 5-6, 1962. In this view, work has started on the first of the heavy drifts east of Sublette, near milepost 298. The OY was pushed by engines 483, 487 and 488. A work train with 5 or 6 cars followed the rotary. (Jackson C. Thode)

In this view, taken from the tender of engine 483, the sky has darkened as the OY tackles a drift near Los Pinos. The winter of 1962-63 was the last year of continuous operation across Cumbres Pass by the D&RGW.

(V.H. Immroth photo, collection of Jackson C. Thode)

The rotary outfit tied up for the night of March 5, 1962 at Osier. The next morning, Vern Immroth, editor for the D&RGW company magazine, The Green Light, *found engine 488 running light just east of Osier in frigid early morning temperatures.*
(Jackson C. Thode collection)

In February 1957, one of the worst storms ever to hit Cumbres Pass raged for days. Two trains and several light engines were stranded, and Joe Dalla, on the 491, was actually "lost" near Los Pinos as the engine was completely buried in snow. Here, in an operation covered by the national press, the U.S. Army has just returned to Chama from Coxo after rescuing several marooned railroaders.
(Ray Jones)

1991 ROTARY SNOWPLOW OPERATIONS

Heavy snows during 1990-91 required the service of the OY to open the line prior to the start of the operating season. Just west of Cresco, near milepost 334, the OY found some of the first deep snow. May 4, 1991. (Ray W. Osterwald)

The OY works on a deep drift on Windy Point, May 4, 1991 at the same location photographed by Monte Ballough many years ago (p. 94). This special rotary snow plow was followed by a passenger train chartered by the <u>Friends of the C&TS</u>. The event was covered by the news media and made the CBS Evening News a few days later. (Gerald M. Blea)

FRIENDS OF THE C&TS RAILROAD

Volunteers have been an important part of the C&TS since the railroad began in 1970. During those first years the citizens of Chama and Antonito have contributed thousands of dollars in time, material and labor to aid in the preservation and restoration of this historic railroad. In 1970 additional volunteers banded together to form two organizations to aid the C&TS during those first years. The Society for the Preservation of the Narrow Gauge, Inc. and the Narrow Gauge Railroad Association, Inc. both worked tirelessly painting equipment, laying track, building the wye at Antonito and also serving as attendants for the fold-down steps on the first coaches built from boxcars.

The Colorado Historical Society, the Historical Society of New Mexico, the Railroad Club of New Mexico, the Rocky Mountain Railroad Club and four chapters of the National Railway Historical Society also volunteered countless hours to help preserve and promote the C&TS as a living museum of railroad history.

In 1988 the *Friends of the C&TS Railroad* was formally incorporated as an outgrowth of the two previous volunteer groups. The stated goals of this volunteer non-profit organization are to preserve and restore to operating condition some of the unique railroad equipment, preserve sites of historic interest and promote public knowledge and interest in the railroad.

The *Friends* coordinate their volunteer activities with the Railroad Commission. They should be commended for stepping forward in 2000 and offering to help run the railroad as a non-profit operation. They raised over $300,000 for a new corporation, the Rio Grande Railroad Preservation Corporation (RGRPC) which was formed as a separate company from the *Friends*. However, several members of the new Board of Directors of the RGRPC are also members of the *Friends* organization (see p. 22).

The organization has grown from several hundred members in 1988 to more than 1,700 in 2000 with more than 250 volunteers working during one or more of the six work sessions— and donating more than 15,000 hours of volunteer labor. Each summer, members with diverse backgrounds and many with little or no actual railroading experience gather in Chama or Antonito to work on the multitude of projects laid out for the summer. All is not work for this group, however. Special moonlight excursions, riding behind a special freight consist, or sponsoring a special train to follow the rotary snowplow at work in the early spring are a few of the bonuses available to members. The *C&TS Dispatch* is published quarterly and contains a wealth of information about the railroad, its equipment and history.

In 1963 the D&RGW began to scrap much of the narrow gauge equipment used on the Fourth Division and the last remaining tank cars were sold to Floyd W. Reed of La Jara for scrap. In 1965 Reed sold sixteen tank cars to the White Pass & Yukon Railroad where they were used until the line shut down in 1982. It was reopened in 1988 with passenger service from Skagway, Alaska to the top of the pass at Fraser, British Columbia. At Fraser, passengers either return to Skagway or go on to Whitehorse by bus. After the WP&Y agreed to sell their eight remaining tank cars for $7,500 per car, delivered to Vancouver, British Columbia, the *Friends* began their first major fund-raising drive to return the cars to Colorado.

The Colorado Railroad Museum at Golden, Colorado decided to purchase two of the cars, and helped with this effort. The Union Tank Car Company, Burlington Northern, Union Pacific, and Southern Pacific/Denver & Rio Grande Western railroads all donated money or free transportation to move the cars from Vancouver to Alamosa. On February 27, 1992 the six cars arrived in Alamosa on a cold snowy morning. Two days later a press conference and formal dedication ceremonies were held in front of the former D&RGW depot in Alamosa.

During the 1991 work sessions the Sublette section house was re-roofed and in subsequent years all the buildings at this site were repaired and by 1997 painting was complete with what some call "abandonment green" color, referring to earlier years when the Rio Grande, if they painted the buildings at all, used whatever paint was handy.

Because the former operator, the Cumbres & Toltec Scenic Railroad, Inc. did not maintain the locomotives, repair and repaint equipment or do any track work in 1999, several large grants and additional appropriations from both states resulted in a massive rebuilding program. Track maintenance had been largely ignored for several years. Tie plates used to hold the rails more firmly in place on the ties were installed at a number of sites. With generous donations from the members of the *Friends*, roundhouse crews worked all winter repairing the locomotives for the 2000 season. Before opening day in May, 2000, the *Friends* painted and re-lettered passenger coaches, cleaned the yards, and planted flowers around the depot in Chama During the winter of 2000-01 shop crews working for the RGRPC completed major repairs on four of the six engines owned by the C&TS Railroad. Two coaches were rebuilt into extra-fare Parlour cars (see page 71).

This interesting photo was taken when the second snowshed covering the wye at Cumbres was being built by D&RG construction crews after the turntable, located in the west leg of the wye, was removed in 1916 (see photos, p. 80).
(Unknown photographer, collection of A.L. Stevenson, Grand Junction, Colo. Copy courtesy, Jackson C. Thode)

What goes around, comes around! Eighty four years after the above photograph was taken, volunteers of the <u>Friends of the C&TS Railroad</u> were found hard at work erecting the outermost bay. It was assembled on the ground and then hoisted into place in August 1991. Much more work will be needed to return the snow shed to its former appearance.   *(Bill Lock)*

Derrick OP after restoration. Compare this photo with the one on p. 86. In August 1990, this car was part of the consist of a special <u>Friends</u> train run for the volunteers.   *(Bill Lock)*

After all the carpentry work was completed, the paint crew went to work on the car inspector s house at Cumbres. This photo was taken during the August 1991 work session.   *(Bill Lock)*

Restoration of the car inspector s house at Cumbres was completed in 1996. A new roof, chimney repairs, and paint greatly improved the appearance of this former home at the top of Cumbres Pass.   *(Tom Cardin)*

During the 1996 work session the Cumbres section house received badly needed structural repairs and a new roof. Work continues on this historic building.

Major rebuilding of flatcar 06051 during this work session in 1998. Ray Blizzard (left) checks the end sill while Dave Sands guides and Tony Kassen (right) position the beam using a "come along."

During 1999, volunteers worked in the Antonito yards on the sills for flatcar 6708.   (All photos courtesy Tom Cardin)

Plans for the 2001 work sessions include continued work on flatcar 06051 and idler flatcar 6708, caboose 0579, restoring the stock pens at the Chama wye, more work on the Osier and Cumbres sections houses, paint mileposts, complete painting of refrigerator car 55 and 163, along with more landscaping, tree trimming and weed control work. The list goes on and on. Hats off to this talented and dedicated group of volunteers.

For information on this volunteer organization, contact:

Friends of the C&TS Scenic Railroad, Inc.
6005 Osuna Road NE
Albuquerque, NM 87109
phone: 505-991-2444
fax: 505-881-2333

MOVIES FILMED ALONG THE C&TS

In 1968, while the states of New Mexico and Colorado were considering the purchase of what is now the C&TS Railroad, the movie *"The Good Guys and the Bad Guys"* was filmed at many locations between Durango and Antonito using D&RGW engine 483. Many wonderful scenes of the train chugging along at various locations were made by photographers who obviously loved trains. Engine 483 was resplendent in a gold, black and red paint job. Much to the disgust of some railfans, even the counter-weights were an unforgettable bright red color. *"The Good Guys and the Bad Guys,"* was directed by Burt Kennedy and starred Robert Mitchum, George Kennedy, David Carradine, Martin Balsam, Lois Nettleton, Tina Louise and Douglas Fowley. This western comedy-drama involves an aging gangster (Kennedy) who has been abandoned by his outlaw gang for being "over-the-hill," so to speak. The marshall (Mitchum) is determined to track down his life-long foe, Kennedy.

The first movie filmed along the C&TS was *"Shootout,"* a Universal Picture made during the fall of 1970; the movie was released the following June. It starred Gregory Peck, with Pat Quinn, Robert F. Lyons, Susan Tyrrell, Jeff Corey, James Gregory, Rita Gam, and Dawn Lyn in the supporting cast. This western is about a bank robber (Gregory Peck), recently released from prison who seeks out the person who betrayed him. Several scenes were filmed at Lobato, where a small depot, Weed City, and a strange-looking water tank were built. Margaret Palmer's Volume 9 of the *Chama Valley Tattler* has some interesting sidelights about the actors living in Chama during the filming of this and other movies.

During the spring of 1972, Universal Studio returned to the area to film *"Showdown,"* featuring Dean Martin, Rock Hudson, Susan Clark, Donald Moffat, John McLiam, and Ed Begley Jr. Scenes were filmed at Tierra Amarilla, Ghost Ranch and in Chama. Many local residents worked on the sets and served as extras. Marie Donaldson, who lived in Chama at that time, worked in the wardroom and related many interesting stories of working on the costumes for the crew. During the filming, Dean Martin's horse died; he walked off the set for two weeks, completely stopping all production. *"Showdown"* was the last movie George Seaton directed. It is the story of two friends, Dean Martin and Rock Hudson, both of whom are in love with Susan Clark. They go their separate ways until Hudson, now a sheriff, is forced to hunt down Martin, now a robber.

In 1972, an independent movie company filmed *"El Savaje"* using the railroad, but this film was never released.

The popular, four-star movie (according to Leonard Maltin, 1991) *"Bite the Bullet"* was filmed along the C&TS during May 1974. This Columbia film was released in June 1975. Directed by Richard Brooks, it starred Gene Hackman, Candice Bergen, James Colburn, Ben Johnson, Ian Bannen, Jan-Michael Vincent, Robert Donner, Paul Stewart, Dabney Coleman and Sally Kirkland. Engine 483, the *Hinman* and several other coaches also had starring roles. Many wonderful scenes were filmed in the Chama yards, depot and roundhouse, on the flats west of Antonito, and at Mud Tunnel. The covered wye at Cumbres Pass was still standing and was used as one of the sets. The photography is outstanding. This grand adventure is the story of a grueling 700 mile race sponsored by a newspaper in 1906. Most of the diverse group of characters are intent on winning a horseback race and a $2,000 prize. Sometimes it seems the race is between the train and the contestants on horseback! Before the film ends, the finalists develop a great deal of respect for each other.

Also in 1974, *"The Fortune"* was filmed in the area by Columbia Pictures. Warren Beatty, Jack Nicholson, Stockard Channing, Scatman Crothers, Florence Stanley, and Richard B. Shull starred in this wacky Laurel and Hardy-like comedy about two bumblers (Beatty and Nicholson) who plan to marry and then murder a dizzy heiress to get her money.

In 1975, *"Missouri Breaks"* was filmed in Chama as well as in Montana. It was released the following year. Marlon Brando, Jack Nicholson, Kathleen Lloyd, Randy Quaid, Fredric Forrest, and Harry Dean Stanton had parts in this movie that never received much praise. There were a number of scenes using the C&TS, and the Hinman coach was even shipped to Montana for some of the filming. The story is about the confrontation between a horse thief and a hired gun.

"Butch and Sundance: The Early Years" was filmed in 1978. This 2-½ star movie featured William Katt, Tom Berenger, Jeff Corey, John Schuck, Michael C. Gwynne, Brian Dennehy, Jill Eikenberry, Peter Weller and Arthur Hill. This movie was a "prequel" to *"Butch Cassidy and the Sundance Kid."* The story had little substance, but the photography, locations and performances of the actors made up for a weak plot.

During the spring of 1980, the *"Legend of the Lone Ranger"* was filmed in the area. It was released in 1981 and never received good reviews. The cast included Klinton Spilsbury, Michael Horse, Jason Robards Jr., Richard Farnsworth, Christopher Lloyd, Matt Clark, Juanin Clay, John Hart, and John Bennett Perry. It is the story of how the Lone Ranger first met his Indian companion Tonto. The voice of the Lone Ranger was dubbed-in. Merle Haggard provided the narration. This movie left much to be desired.

In October 1980, the *"Ballad of Gregorio Cortez"* was filmed in the area and also featured the train in several scenes. This movie, directed by Robert M. Young, was originally produced for PBS' American Playhouse series. It was released to movie theaters in 1982. Edward James Olmos, James Gammon, Tom Bower, Bruce McGill, Brion James, Alan Vint, Rosana DeSoto, Pepe Serna, William Sanderson, and Barry Corbin were members of the cast. This true story relates an incident in 1901 when a young Mexican killed an American sheriff and then managed to elude a 600-man posse for nearly two weeks.

A made for TV movie, *"Where the Hell's That Gold,"* was filmed along the C&TS in early June 1988 and released the same year. The movie was written, produced and directed by Burt Kennedy. Stars in this western include Willy Nelson, Jack Elam, Delta Burke, Gerald McRaney, Alfonso Arau, Michael Wren, and Gregory Sierra. Nelson and Elam, old Civil War buddies, attempt to recover gold Nelson had stolen earlier and hidden somewhere in Mexico. Interwoven with the story is a "madam" (Delta Burke) and her five "ladies" who conduct their business in a railroad coach (the Hinman). The story is weak, but the photography is excellent. Unforgettable scenes include the burning (accidental) of Ferguson's trestle at mile 285.87, and also scenes at Mud Tunnel, Big Horn and other sites. Engine 484 was used for this movie, as was the Hinman coach, which was painted a bright red color.

"Indiana Jones and the Last Crusade" is the third of the Indiana Jones spectaculars directed by Steven Spielberg. Harrison Ford plays the son of his famous archaeologist father, Sean Connery. Others in the the cast include Denholm Elliott, Alison Doody, John Rhys-Davies, Julian Glover, River Phoenix, Michael Byrne, and Alex Hyde-White. Portions of the movie were filmed along the C&TS in September 1988. The movie was released in May 1989. There are many great scenes, including the wild chase of the circus train. Other scenes were filmed in Antonito, Chama, Mud Tunnel, and Weed City. Engine 484 also starred in this movie in a gaudy red and black paint job. Photography is excellent. The movie won an Oscar for sound effects and editing.

During the cold month of January 1991, Desperado Productions of Tucson, Arizona, filmed *"Brotherhood of the Gun"* in Chama. The TV movie starred engine 487, an RPO car, the Hinman coach, a flatcar and a "caboose. Part of the story involved two brothers who robbed a U.S. Army train. In one scene the door of the RPO car is blown off so the robbers could get the loot. There were many problems in filming because of the three feet of snow along the track between Chama and Lobo Crossing. As a precaution, C&TS officials insisted that another engine be in the train as back-up power, so diesel engine 19 was camouflaged to look like a caboose. 487 was disguised for this production with a fake balloon stack and a kerosene headlight that was painted a strange blue color.

In addition to the movies filmed in the area, many commercials, a Japanese network film, several documentaries, and even a music video have been made that have featured the trains, buildings, or spectacular locations along the C&TS. The following is a partial list of those productions:

Year Filmed	Title	Remarks
1973	Texas Rangers Hall of Fame	Documentary, narrated by James Arness
1973	Grande Canadian Liquor	Commercial
1973	San Diego Hall of Science	Travelogue
1974	*The Big Blue Marble*	PBS TV children's series
1975	John Deere Snowmobiles	Commercial
1975	*...And Some Rain*	TV special, based on a poem
1978	Miller High Life Beer	Commercial
1979	*Paradise Trails*	PBS TV
1984	*History of the English Language*	Japanese Fuji Network
1987	*Long Arm*	TV pilot film
1988	Italian TV commercial	Commercial
1990	Colorado National Bank	Commercial
1990	*Heartbreak Station*	Music video by Cinderella rock group
1993	*Wyatt Earp*	Movie, starring Kevin Costner

Engine 484 all dolled up for action in "Butch and Sundance: The Early Years," filmed in 1978 in Chama. (Clif Palmer)

Several scenes in the movie "Where the Hell's That Gold" were filmed near Big Horn wye. The train crew, from left to right are Orlando Gallegos, section hand, Henry Gallegos, conductor, actor Jack Elam, Marvin Casias, engineer, Leslie Salazar, fireman, and Gerald Blea, brakeman. Salazar was the only member of the crew who had a speaking part. He announced the boiler was out of water. Blea was a soldier in the Mexican army and was in a scene where they dropped off the Hinman coach at Big Horn siding.

(Gerald M. Blea photo)

In September 1988, during the filming of "Indiana Jones and the Last Crusade," the train crew had many interesting experiences watching the filming. This scene is near mile 281.7. (Gerald M. Blea)

The Hinman coach, as it looked in "Bite the Bullet." The car was used for the officials promoting the race, sponsored by the Western Press Newspaper. In this photo, workers are putting the finishing touches on the car. May 1974. (Clif Palmer)

In 1975, the Hinman coach was used in the movie "Missouri Breaks." In this scene, movie floodlights are in the background between an outfit car and the Chama depot, which had become the Cheyenne depot. (Clif Palmer)

The Hinman coach was again used in the movie, "Brotherhood of the Gun," filmed for the most part between Chama and Lobo Crossing. Movie crews are getting ready to film a scene of the robbers blowing off the door of the RPO car. This action movie was filmed in January 1991. (Gerald M. Blea)

NATURE

LIFE ZONES

Life zones may be defined as communities of plants, animals, and birds that live in specific elevational zones. These zones contain distinctive assemblages of plants and animals that have achieved a balance between local climate and elevation. Climate is determined by both elevation and latitude. As one climbs a mountain, for every 1,000 ft rise in elevation, the average temperature drops 3°F. Put another way, climbing 2,000 feet in elevation is equivalent to traveling northward 720 miles at sea level. The montane zone in Colorado contains plants that are found at sea level at 50° to 60° north latitude. Thus desert plants do not grow in the high mountains, nor do the tiny alpine zone wildflowers live in the dry climate of the plains or desert. Some plants that bloom in the San Luis Valley in June will bloom at Toltec Gorge in July or August, however. Animals also thrive at a particular climate and elevation. Gila monsters are never found in the subalpine or alpine zones, for example.

In southern Colorado and northern New Mexico there are five life zones from the plains to the alpine tundra. The *plains* (4,000 and 5,500 ft), the *pinyon-juniper* (5,500 ft to 8,000 ft), *montane* (8,000 ft to 10,000 ft), *subalpine* (10,000 ft to treeline), and the *alpine* life zone, above treeline.

Life zones do not have sharp boundaries, but overlap and merge into each other. Many plants are found in two or more zones. Many factors affect a plant or animal community in addition to climate and elevation. The type of soil, slope conditions, topography, moisture, humidity, wind, and temperature also affect this balance. Commonly, the north-facing slope of a valley supports a different ecosystem from that found on an opposite south-facing slope. Changes from one zone to another are easier to observe in the mountains than they are on the plains. This is because you can quickly go from one zone to another by going up or down in elevation.

The route of the C&TS traverses the foothills and montane zones and reaches the subalpine zone at Cumbres Pass. Some of the more common trees, shrubs, flowers, birds, and mammals found along the track are listed below.

PINYON-JUNIPER ZONE PLANTS, ANIMALS, BIRDS

5,500 to 8,000 ft (1,650 to 2,400 m)

TREES:

Pinyon and juniper trees are the dominant species found on the hills and in the basins between mountain ranges. At slightly higher elevations, scrub oaks are common, as are big-tooth maple and box elder; river willows and cottonwoods are common along water courses. Ponderosa pine, Douglas fir, Rocky Mountain juniper, and aspen occur at the higher elevations and extend into the montane zone.

SHRUBS:

Mountain mahogany, rabbitbrush, squawbush, big sagebrush, serviceberry, chokecherry, apache plume, snowberry, barberry, and buffalo currant.

FLOWERS:

Whitish blossoms: Yucca, mariposa lily, clematis, prickly poppy, foothills daisy, white sweet clover, milk vetch, horsemint, white aster, fleabane, wild onion, Rocky Mountain loco, miner's candlestick, baby aster, and Easter daisy.

Yellowish blossoms: Sweet clover, dandelion, stickweed, prickly pear cactus, oyster plant, snakeweed, goldenrod, bee plant, sunflower, golden smoke, gumweed, mullein, ragwort, sulfur flower, coneflower, and Oregon holly grape.

Pink or reddish blossoms: Buckwheat, cranesbill, loco, globemallow, cactus, pink phlox, milkweed, gilia, penstemon, and paintbrush.

Blue or purplish blossoms: Spiderwort, bee plant, milk vetch, flax, verbena, daisy, scorpionweed, tansy aster, and purple oyster plant.

ANIMALS:

Mule deer, antelope, coyote, mountain lion, cottontail rabbit, jackrabbit, golden-mantled ground squirrel, pine squirrel, 13-lined ground squirrel, least chipmunk, northern pocket gopher, striped skunk, prairie dog, fox, porcupine, badger, muskrat, bat, Rocky Mountain toad, bullfrog, horned lizard, fence lizard, bullsnake, garter snake. and prairie rattlesnake.

BIRDS:

Golden eagle, bald eagle, mourning dove, band-tailed pigeon, marsh hawk, Cooper's hawk, western red-tailed hawk, magpie, raven, crow, red-winged blackbird, western meadowlark, grackle, pheasant, quail, Steller's jay, pygmy nuthatch, bank swallow, black-headed grosbeak, evening grosbeak, gray-headed junco, house finch, hummingbird, and Lewis' woodpecker.

Montane Zone Plants, Animals, Birds

8,000 to 10,000 ft (2,400 to 3,000 m) elevation

Trees:

Thick stands of aspen, Douglas fir, lodgepole pine, white fir, limber pine, white pine, blue spruce, willow, and birch. Fewer ponderosa pine, juniper, cottonwood, and scrub oak. Engelmann spruce occurs at the higher elevations, along with some subalpine fir at Cumbres and La Manga Passes.

Shrubs:

Chokecherry, ninebark, red-berried elder, mountain mahogany, squaw currant, gooseberry, apache plume, rabbitbrush, sagebrush, serviceberry, rose, raspberry.

Flowers:

Whitish blossoms: Yucca, Canada violet, stickweed, scorpionweed, candytuft, white cranesbill, pussytoes, strawberry, gilia, phlox, wand lily, mariposa lily, miner's candlestick, yarrow, milk vetch, Rocky Mountain loco, cornhusk lily or false hellebore, thistle, buckwheat, aster, fleabane, and monument plant.

Yellowish blossoms: Oregon holly grape, draba, sage, bahia, buttercup, ox-eye daisy, golden banner, wallflower, golden smoke, puccoon, ragwort, stonecrop, cinquefoil, paintbrush, sulfur flower, sunflower, golden aster, goldenrod, butterweed, gumweed, sneezeweed, mullein, oyster plant, marsh marigold, and subalpine buttercup.

Pink or reddish blossoms: Scarlet gilia, red beardtongue, cactus, pussytoes, vetch, bearberry, locoweed, globemallow, paintbrush, cranesbill, horsemint, lousewort, fireweed, Wright's buckwheat, and scarlet penstemon.

Blue or purplish blossoms: Iris, larkspur, bull thistle, flax, chiming bell, fleabane, penstemon, lupine, loco, beard-tongue, harebell, Jacob's ladder, monkshood, aster, daisy, gentian, spiked verbena, tansy aster, and blue columbine (Colorado's state flower).

Animals:

Mule deer, elk, coyote, bobcat, mountain lion, black bear, red fox, porcupine, Colorado chipmunk, golden-mantled ground squirrel, pine squirrel, tufted ear squirrel, Richardson's ground squirrel, muskrat, beaver, badger, otter, deer mouse, pack rat, long-tailed weasel, marten, and snowshoe rabbit.

Birds:

Mountain bluebird, mountain chickadee, Steller's jay, raven, Cooper's hawk, blue grouse, bald eagle, red-breasted nuthatch, house wren, tree swallow, cliff swallow, olive-sided flycatcher, Clark's nutcracker, warbling vireo, ruby-crowned kinglet, white-crowned sparrow, western tanager, pine siskin, and downy woodpecker.

Mule deer.   *(National Park Service)*

Rocky Mountain iris
Iris missouriensis

Fireweed
Epilobium angustifolium

Colorado's blue columbine
Aquilegia caerulea

Mountain Harebell
Campanula rotundifolia

Wild geranium
Geranium caespitosum

DETAILS AND USES OF SELECTED PLANTS

Big sagebrush or wormwood, *Artemisia tridentata,* is common in the San Luis Valley and is an important plant in the west. It is a valuable food for antelope, elk, and mule deer because of its high fat content. Sagebrush provides good ground cover for many small animals and birds. Indians and pioneers pounded the dried seeds into a meal called "pinole." Tea, made from dried sagebrush leaves, was used as a remedy for colds, sore eyes, and as a hair tonic. Indians rubbed themselves with sagebrush leaves and sat or stood in sagebrush smoke to purify themselves before important ceremonies. Early settlers knew the land was good for farming if the sagebrush grew tall and lush.

Two other shrubs that are common along the track between Antonito and Big Horn are rabbitbrush and mountain mahogany. Rabbitbrush, or chamisa, *Chrysothamnus nauseosus,* is as common as sagebrush, and most often grows on disturbed, overgrazed or neglected soils. The 2 to 4 ft, silver-gray, bushy shrub is topped with bunches of small, golden-yellow flower heads from July through September. The heavily scented plants contain rubber. A yellow dye can be produced from the flowers, and a green dye from the inner bark.

Mountain mahogany, or buckbrush, *Cercocarpus montanus,* belongs to the Rose family. It is found throughout the west at elevations between 4,500 and 9,000 ft. It blooms in the early spring, bearing yellowish or dull-white flowers. It is a favorite browse plant for deer and elk. A reddish-brown dye can be made from the stout, dark-brown branches. The seeds are attached to beautiful silvery-white, spiral-shaped plumes, which contract and expand with moisture changes, and act as corkscrews to bury the seeds in the ground. Indians used mountain mahogany boughs on the floors of their tepees to keep out lice and bedbugs.

At Tanglefoot Curve and around Cumbres Pass, a large (1 to 6 ft tall) coarse, leafy-stemmed plant with bright yellow-green pleated leaves, that appear to be partly rolled up is cornhusk lily, or false hellebore, *Veratrum tenuipetalum.* It thrives in marshes and wet meadows. This plant contains several alkaloids used medicinally to slow the heartbeat and lower blood pressure. It can be fatal if taken in large doses. When cooked, the plant is rich in starch and was a valuable food for Indians. Cornhusk lily is related to taro, an equally important food of the Polynesians. Roasted roots were ground into a flour. The seeds are poisonous, but the poison decreases as the plant matures. After a frost and the plant becomes dried, it is apparently harmless to animals.

Near Cresco, Colorado, the conspicuous 3 to 5 ft tall spiked plant with lance-shaped, bright green leaves up to 1 ft long is *Frasera speciosa,* monument plant, green gentian, or elkweed. This is a biennial plant that blooms in early summer. It has pale-greenish-white flowers, spotted with purple, that grow outward from the axils of the upper leaves. It stands throughout the winter as a dried, brownish-colored stalk, similar to dried mullein. Most members of the gentian family have been used for medicines. The fleshy roots can be eaten raw, roasted, or boiled. Elk, deer and cattle like to browse on the young leaves.

Another spiked plant (up to 6 ft tall) that is common in Wolf Creek Valley is mullein, *Verbascum thapsus,* a member of the Figwort family. Mullein is a biennial, forming a rosette of soft, woolly, light-green leaves the first year; the flowering stalk, with small, bright yellow, 5-lobed flowers develops the second season. The dead flower stalks may stand for several years. Small birds love to retrieve the seeds from the dead stalks. The plant was introduced from Europe and grows throughout temperate North America. The leaves have been used for medicinal purposes. They contain chemicals used in lotions to soften the skin and in medicines to soothe inflamed tissues. Elk will eat the dead leaves and stems when other preferred foods are not available.

Fireweed, *Epilobium angustifolium,* is one of the most beautiful and distinctive plants found in the mountains in August. The four-petaled, pink or reddish-purple blossoms form a symmetrical unbranched stem from 1 to 5 ft tall. Fireweed grows on moist, rich soil, or on man-disturbed ground. It is one of the first plants to reappear after a forest fire, thus the name. The young leaves are excellent in salads and dried leaves can be used for a tea. The plant is valuable forage for deer, elk, bear, and cattle.

Rocky Mountain iris, *Iris missouriensis,* is common during the early summer at the west side of Cascade Trestle and in the moist meadows at Tanglefoot Curve. This lovely species has variegated violet-blue flowers about 2 to 3 in long on stems up to 2 ft tall. The roots contain a poison, irisin, which is a violent emetic and cathartic. Some Indian tribes poisoned arrowheads by dipping them in a concoction of iris roots and animal bile. It has been reported that many warriors, only slightly wounded by such poisoned arrowheads, died within 3 to 7 days.

COLUMNAR SECTION

Era	Period	Epoch	Symbol used on geologic maps	Formation Name & Age where known.	Description of Formation
CENOZOIC	QUATERNARY	Pleistocene to Holocene	Qal	Alluvium, alluvial fans, terrace gravels	Sand, silt & gravel deposited by streams.
			Ql	Landslides	Poorly-sorted, mostly angular rock debris derived from bedrock deposits and moved downslope by gravity.
		Pleistocene	Qg	Glacial deposits	Poorly-sorted material deposited by glaciers or by postglacial fluvial activity.
			Qa	and Stream alluvium less than 3 million years old	Isolated bodies of gravel, boulders, sand, and silt.
	TERTIARY	Pliocene	Ths	Servilleta Formation 3.6 - 4.5 million years	Thin flows of porphyritic tholeiitic basalt, with small olivine phenocrysts.
			Thc	Cisneros Basalt 4.7 - 5.3 million years	Fine-grained silicic alkali-olivine basalt. Caps mesas as erosional remants of formerly extensive lava flows.
		Oligocene to Pliocene	Tlp	Los Pinos Formation 5 - 25 million years	Volcaniclastic conglomerates, sandstones, and mud-flows derived from erosion of volcanic centers in eastern San Juan Mtns.
		Oligocene	Tmp	Masonic Park Tuff 28.2 million years	Ash-flow tuff erupted from Mt. Hope caldera. Quartz latite in composition.
			Ttm	Treasure Mountain Tuff 28.8 - 29.8 million years	Composite sequence of three ash-flow sheets with locally interbedded ash-fall tuffs from Platoro caldera.
			Tc	Conejos Formation (vent facies) 31.1 - 34.7 million years	Chaotic lava flows and flow breccias of andesite, rhyodacite, and quartz latite erupted from several volcanic centers.
			~~ Unconformity ~~~~~~		
		Eocene	Tbb	Blanco Basin Formation More than 35 million years old	Red to brown arkrose, mudstone, sandstone, and conglomerate.
MESOZOIC	CRETACEOUS		K	Mancos Shale	Dark-gray marine shale.
			K	Niobrara Formation	Evenly-bedded limestones with minor layers of light gray limy shale.
			Kd	Dakota Formation	Two or three massive sandstone layers separated by thinly-bedded gray marine shale.
	JURASSIC		Jm	Morrison Formation 135 million years	Variegated claystone and mudstone with interbedded sandstone.
			~~ Unconformity ~~~~~~		
PROTEROZOIC	PRECAMBRIAN		P€	Ancient crystalline igneous & metamorphic rocks 1450 - 1700 million years	Foliated gneiss, schist, and amphibolite intruded by granite and pegmatite.

Adapted from Lipman, P. W. 1975.

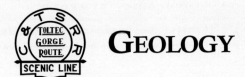

GEOLOGY

SUMMARY OF GEOLOGIC HISTORY

PROTEROZOIC ERA

Precambrian metamorphic rocks, as much as 1,700 million years old, are visible at Toltec Gorge. These ancient rocks were originally layers of sedimentary and volcanic rocks that were changed by high heat and pressure. About 1,450 million years ago, the metatmorphic rocks were invaded by younger Precambrian granites and pegmatites.

PALEOZOIC ERA

Throughout Paleozoic time, the old Precambrian crystalline rocks in this mountain mass remained above sea level as part of the Brazos Uplift.

MESOZOIC ERA

The first sedimentary material deposited in the area during Mesozoic time was the Jurassic Morrison Formation (135 million years old), comprising wide-spread continental sandstones and variegated shales derived from an old landmass where Precambrian and Paleozoic rocks cropped out. During Morrison time, dinosaurs flourished and roamed over vast, swampy floodplains. The Morrison contains many uranium deposits at many places in New Mexico, Colorado, and Utah. Erosion of the landmass was rapid and beginning about 110 million years ago the Dakota Sandstone was deposited on the Morrison as a non-marine coastal-plain sandstone. In late Cretaceous time, seas covered the Precambrian landmass. The Niobrara Formation and the Mancos Shale (95 million years old) were deposited as marine calcareous mudstones and shales in these seas. These Jurassic and Cretaceous sedimentary rocks are visible at several places in the cliffs along Wolf Creek and the Rio Chama east of Chama. The littoral and deltaic sandstones of the Mesa Verde Group intertongue with the upper Mancos Shale, and contain many thick beds of bituminous coal in western New Mexico, western Colorado, eastern Utah and northwestern Arizona.

CENOZOIC ERA—TERTIARY PERIOD

After the close of the Mesozoic era, a vast mountain-building episode ensued, and the Rocky Mountains were uplifted from the Cretaceous seas. With this **orogeny** during the early part of the Tertiary Period—termed the Laramide Revolution—faulting was very common and many of the structures along the C&TS route were formed. Previously horizontal sedimentary rocks (Morrison, Dakota, Niobrara, and Mancos) were up-warped, as were the Precambrian rocks of the Brazos Uplift, a north-south mountain range between the Chama Basin and the western San Luis Valley. Vast amounts of debris were eroded from the uplifted mountains and redeposited as Lower Tertiary sedimentary rocks along the flanks of this range. The Eocene Blanco Basin Formation, estimated to be at least 35 million years old, was formed in this manner. It rests with pronounced **angular unconformity** upon the upturned Morrison Formation in the Chama valley.

Following the deposition of the Blanco Basin, perhaps the most fascinating sequence of geologic events in the San Juans commenced. During the Oligocene Epoch, volcanism began throughout what is now the San Juan Mountains. This mountainous region is an erosional remnant of an extensive volcanic field which formed upon a dissected domal structure produced by Laramide tectonism. The first eruptions, from numerous volcanos, began about 35 million years ago. These volcanos erupted rocks of intermediate chemical compositions, mostly **andesites, rhyodacites and quartz latites.** In the southeastern part of the San Juan mountains, these early intermediate rocks comprise the Conejos Formation. Much of the C&TS track crosses lavas and breccias of the Conejos.

About 30 million years ago, volcanic activity changed. **Ash-flow tuffs,** more silicic in chemical composition than the Conejos rocks, were erupted explosively, eventually covering many of the older volcanics. Two important ash-flow sheets along the C&TS route, the Treasure Mountain and Masonic Park tuffs, were derived from large **calderas** 25 to 50 miles northwest of the railroad.

Numerous ash-flow sheets are recognized throughout the San Juan Mountains. However, the activity that formed these rocks ceased about 23 million years ago, and was succeeded by relatively quiet eruptions of **alkali basalt** and **rhyolite** volcanic rocks. These quiet eruptions stopped about 4 million years ago.

The beginning of basalt-rhyolite volcanism almost coincided with the subsidence of the Rio Grande Depression, a large **rift** zone that extends from northern Mexico into central Colorado. The local expression of the rift is the San Luis Valley, a down-dropped fault block surrounded by mountainous highlands on the east and west. The Sangre de Cristo Mountains form a prominent fault scarp, rising abruptly along the eastern side of the San Luis Valley. The nature and size of this vast structural feature will become apparent as the train heads westward from Antonito.

CENOZOIC ERA—QUATERNARY PERIOD

Other features visible on the trip are the effects of glacial ice on the landscape. The Great Ice Ages probably began about 3 million years ago. Glaciers were cradled in the high valleys of the San Juans. The ice gradually moved downward to carve and sculpture the mountains into the U-shaped valleys we see today. After the ice melted about 11,000 years ago, the landscape was further altered by numerous **landslides** and **talus** slopes, many of which are still active today.

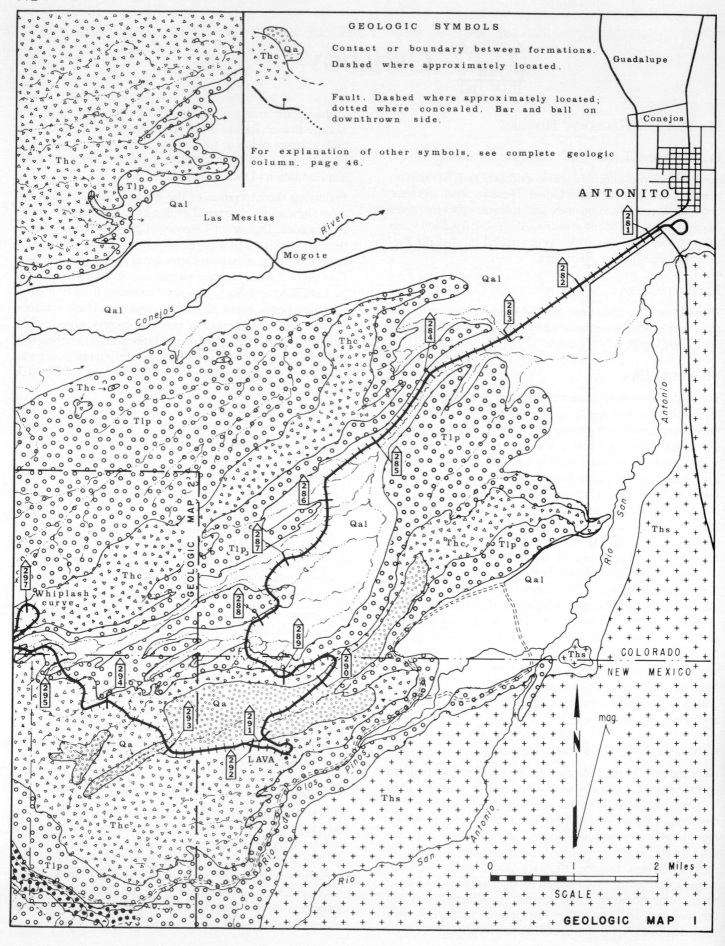

GEOLOGIC SYMBOLS

Contact or boundary between formations.
Dashed where approximately located.

Fault. Dashed where approximately located;
dotted where concealed. Bar and ball on
downthrown side.

For explanation of other symbols, see complete geologic
column, page 46.

GEOLOGIC MAP I

MILE BY MILE GEOLOGIC GUIDE

The Cumbres & Toltec Scenic Railroad traverses the southeastern flank of the San Juan Mountains, passing many fascinating geologic features. For this reason, a separate guide to the geology along the narrow gauge is included. The text is keyed to accompanying geologic maps and to mileposts set along the track. Directions in brackets [ ] are for the eastbound trip. Terms in **bold face** type are defined in the glossary, page 121. Geologic formations are mappable units of rocks that can be traced from one locality to another. A complete geologic column is on p. 110.

Mile
280.70 ANTONITO, COLORADO.
elev 7,888 ft (2,404 m)

Eastern terminus of the Cumbres & Toltec Scenic Railroad. From Antonito to about mile 288.30 the track is built on recent deposits of **alluvium.** At many places along the sides of the San Luis Valley, large amounts of such loose material were deposited as spreading, gently-sloping, fan-shaped masses called **alluvial fans.** One such fan, deposited by the Conejos River, is west of Antonito.

Milepost
287 LAVA-CAPPED MESAS.

As the train winds through this tributary valley of Rio San Antonio, the mesas visible on either side of the track dip gently eastward and are capped by hard alkali basalt, called the Cisneros Basalt (Thc), about 4.7 to 5.3 million years old. The track gradually climbs onto a mesa [descends from a mesa] where the Cisneros will be at track level.

Mile
288.30 LOS PINOS FORMATION.

From here to mile 289.60 small railroad cuts are in the Los Pinos Formation (Tlp). The Los Pinos is composed of sandstones, gravels, conglomerates, and other **clastic** materials which resulted from weathering and erosion of nearby volcanic highlands, followed by redeposition of the debris at lower elevations. This Formation was first studied and described along Rio de los Pinos, south of Lava water tank, milepost 292, hence the name. The clastic material spread outward as an apron around major volcanic centers. Some **basalt** flows and **tuffs** also are interlayered within the formation.

In this vicinity, the Los Pinos Formation is about 600 ft (180 m) thick and is about 25 millions years old. It is the most continuous and widespread of the Tertiary volcaniclastic formations in the eastern San Juan Mountains, extending for many miles along the mountain front.

Mile
285.55 LEAVE COLORADO.

This is the first [last] of eleven crossings of the Colorado-New Mexico state boundary.

Milepost
289 OUTCROPS OF BASALT.

At track level are outcrops of basalt that probably are the Jarita Member of the Los Pinos Formation. It is not shown on the geologic map because it is not continuous. Along the top of the mesa, the capping Cisneros Basalt can be observed easily in railroad cuts.

Milepost
290 STREAM ALLUVIUM.

From mile 289.70 to about milepost 292, the track is on locally derived, well-rounded gravels, cobbles, boulders, and some fine-grained loose material (Qa) deposited on the Cisneros lava cap.

To the southeast is San Antonio Peak, elev 10,935 ft (3,333 m), a large dome-shaped **shield volcano.** The volcanic rocks within the Rio Grande **rift** zone, including those of San Antonio Peak, are younger than the Cisneros Basalt, and also differ chemically.

Mile
291.55 LAVA TANK.
elev 8,506 ft (2,593 m)

A long railroad cut in the Cisneros Basalt is west of the water tank. The rock is fine-grained, dark brown to gray, and often contains large crystals of green **olivine,** and whitish **plagioclase feldspar.** Many cavities in the rock resulted from the escape of steam and gas during cooling. The peak visible across the Conejos Valley to the north is Los Mogotes, elev 9,818 ft (2,993 m), a volcano from which the Cisneros lavas poured onto the surface, in places covering the Los Pinos Formation. The Cisneros represents the last (or youngest) known eruption in the San Juan volcanic field.

Between Lava Tank and milepost 296, the track winds across a fairly flat mesa capped by the Cisneros Basalt, crosses the Los Pinos Formation several times. and locally crosses **alluvium** deposits (Qa).

To the southeast, across the Rio de los Pinos Valley, the layered volcanics exposed in the north-facing cliffs are the Servilleta Formation, deposited between 3.6 to 4.5 million years ago, and probably are younger than the rocks on San Antonio Peak. The Formation is composed of beds of sand and gravel intertongued with **olivine tholeiite** basalt flows that accumulated in the subsiding Rio Grande Depression. These lavas were generated in a different manner from those in the San Juan Mountains.

Milepost
296 BIG HORN SECTION HOUSE SITE.

Track crosses the alluvium-filled valley and climbs [descends] the south side of a mesa along outcrops of the Los Pinos Formation. Near the top of the mesa are basalts of the Cisneros Formation. Three levels of track are visible.

Milepost
297 WHIPLASH CURVE.

The milepost is at the northern end of the curve. From here is a great view to the north of the Conejos River Valley and Los Mogotes volcano, about six miles away.

Milepost
298 VIEW OF BIGHORN PEAK.

To the southeast is a nice view of Bighorn Peak, elev 9,442 ft (2,878 m), which is capped by a resistant layer of the Jarita Basalt Member of the Los Pinos Formation.

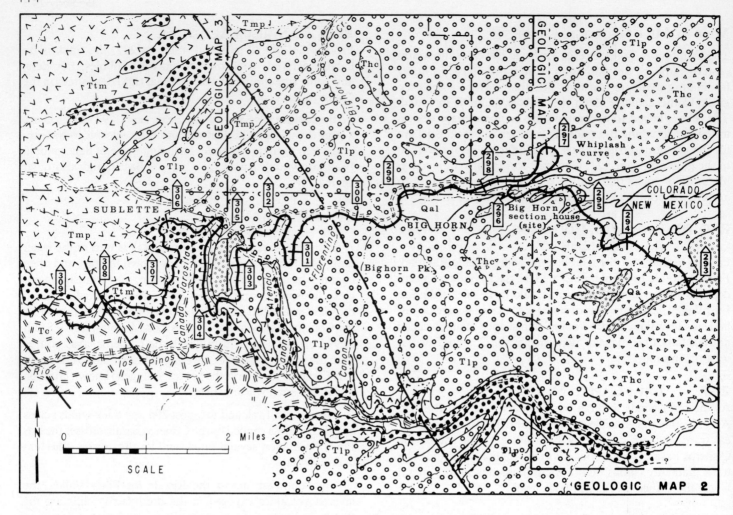

Mile
299.41 Big Horn Wye and Siding.
elev 9,022 ft (2,750 m)

From here to mile 303.70, railroad cuts expose soft, light-gray, cross-bedded tuffaceous sandstones and conglomerates of the Los Pinos Formation. Many gravels, cobbles, and boulders are visible in these cuts. These fragments were smoothed and well-rounded during transport by streams. At mile 303.50, a large deposit of this material was excavated for use as railroad track ballast.

At mile 300.30, a northwest-trending **fault** crosses the track, but displacement of beds in the Los Pinos Formation is hard to see at this point.

Mile
303.70 Masonic Park Tuff.

Between mile 303.70 and mile 305.50 railroad cuts expose the Masonic Park Tuff, (Tmp) **welded ash-flow tuff** composed of fine-grained material that was blown out of a volcano and consolidated by heat about 28 million years ago (photo, p. 116). This is the only location where the formation is at track level. Material in the Masonic Park Tuff probably came from the Mt. Hope **caldera** located a few miles northwest of the Summitville, Colorado mining district. The purplish-gray or pinkish-gray, fine-grained tuff weathers into platy or slabby pieces of rock that are visible on the hillsides above Sublette where the formation is from 50 to 100 ft (15 to 30 m) thick.

Mile
306.06 Sublette, New Mexico.
elev 9,276 ft (2,827 m)

Along the track is the contact between the Masonic Park Tuff (Tmp) and the Treasure Mountain Tuff (Ttm), another widespread volcanic formation. The Treasure Mountain Tuff is mostly a non-welded ash-fall tuff with some dark-colored welded tuffs, and interlayered water-carried beds of buff to gray tuffaceous standstones and conglomerates. Large boulders fill old stream channels in some places.

The Treasure Mountain Tuff is as much as 250 ft (76 m) thick along the north side of the Rio de los Pinos. The ash-flow and ash-fall tuffs were erupted from the Platoro caldera located about 25 mi (40 km) northwest of Sublette. The Treasure Mountain and Masonic Park Tuffs were deposited during a violent type of volcanic activity that started in the San Juans about 30 million years ago and lasted until about 23 million years ago. Along the C&TS route, the Treasure Mountain was deposited on a very irregular upper surface of the older Conejos Formation.

South of Sublette, dense vegetation makes it almost impossible to see outcrops of the Treasure Mountain tuff along the track, but between milepost 307 and mile 308.10 are several railroad cuts in this unit.

Phantom Curve in the early 1880s. This W.H. Jackson photo shows the dramatic spires, pedestal rocks, and weird shapes of the chaotic breccias and conglomerates of the Conejos Formation. The group is standing near the site of the 1948 derailment (p. 33).   *(Colorado Historical Society)*

View northeast of Osier Mountain on the skyline, capped with Cisneros Basalt. The rounded slopes below Osier Mountain are landslide deposits. The train is passing outcrops of the Conejos Formation near mile 317.20, on the first public excursion for the new C&TS Railroad, October 4, 1970. This trip was for members of the press and officials of the states of Colorado and New Mexico. This excursion was exactly 90 years after the first excursion on the San Juan Extension, (p. 20). The old road in the foreground led southward to the Tierra Amarilla Land Grant.   *(Doris B. Osterwald)*

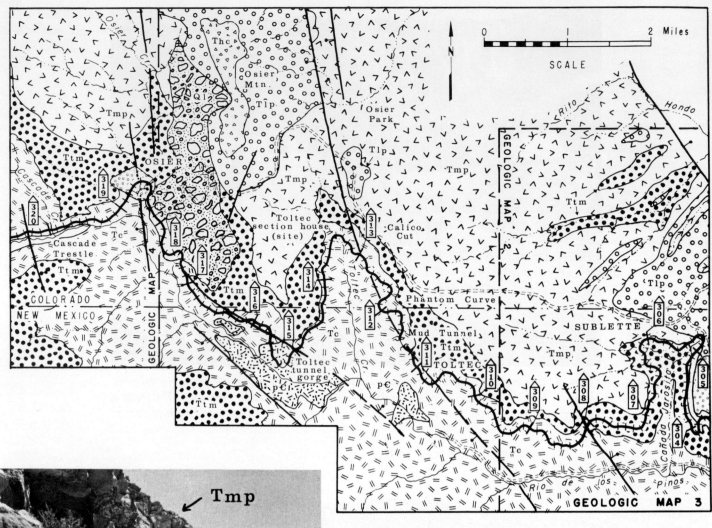

Railroad cut at mile 303.90 showing the contact between the Masonic Park Tuff (Tmp) at the top, and the Treasure Mountain Tuff (Ttm) below.

(Doris B. Osterwald)

Mile
308.10 CROSS FAULT.

A small northwest-trending fault brings the Conejos Formation upward to track level. This formation was first described along the Conejos River, three miles downstream from Platoro, Colorado. The spectacular spires, pinnacles, pedestals, and jumbled masses of brightly colored rocks visible from here to Coxo, mile 332.20, are all in the Conejos Formation—a very photogenic rock type.

The Conejos Formation, one of the oldest volcanic sequences in the San Juan volcanic field, began forming from numerous volcanoes as early as 34 million years ago and stopped erupting about 30 million years ago. During that time, great quantities of intermediate composition lava flows, flow **breccias,** and explosive **tuff breccias** were erupted. Those rocks are interlayered with conglomerates and tuffaceous sandstones derived from erosion of volcanic centers in southern Colorado. These eruptions were more passive than the explosive types that formed the younger Treasure Mountain and Masonic Park tuffs. Rock types in the Conejos include alkali **andesite, rhyodacite,** and mafic **quartz latite.** The Conejos rocks were deposited upon an eroded upland surface. The formation varies in thickness along the route of the C&TS railroad, from 1,000 ft (300 m) west and northwest of Toltec Gorge, to about 4,000 ft (1,200 m) thick elsewhere in the eastern San Juans.

Between mile 308.10 and milepost 309, the train passes tall cliffs and spires left from erosion of the Conejos breccias. Large angular fragments of igneous rock are easy to see in the rusty red to pink cliffs.

Mile
310.30 EAST SWITCH, TOLTEC SIDING.
elev 9,465 ft (2,885 m)
The rocks at track level locally appear to have been burned by heat from younger (overlying) lava flows. There is also much alteration of the Conejos rocks along a fault that trends northwest on the east side of Toltec Creek Valley.

Milepost
311 WEST SWITCH, TOLTEC SIDING.
Toltec Creek Valley follows a large fault (see Geologic Map 3) that parallels the railroad track for several miles. Because of this fault, the Conejos Formation breccias were chemically changed by weathering, alteration, circulating ground waters, and other processes, and are now a soft mud that flows easily when wet. These mudflows caused many problems for the D&RGW in past years. During periods of heavy rain, this unstable material slips and flows onto the track.

Mile
311.30 MUD TUNNEL.
The 342 ft (104 m) tunnel had to be lined because the soft, weathered Conejos Formation is very unstable.

Mile
312.10 ENTER COLORADO.

Milepost
312 VOLCANIC SPIRES.
to
313
This is one of the most spectacular sections of track along the C&TS route and has been photographed from nearly every conceivable angle. The chaotic breccias and conglomerates that form the weird shapes, pedestal rocks, and jumbled outcrops are the result of alteration by hot waters and by weathering of the hard and soft breccias. The wide variety of colors are due to chemical changes in the rocks. A deep cut near milepost 312 is a good place to see these Conejos breccias (photo, p. 115).

Mile
313.20 CALICO CUT.
This cut shows the results of faulting and hydrothermal alteration of the Conejos breccias. The colors range from red to orange to purple to tan. Many mud slides have occurred along this section of track.

Mile
313.44 CROSS TOLTEC CREEK.
elev 9,574 ft (2,918 m)

Milepost
314 GEOLOGIC CONTACT.
The contact (boundary) between the Conejos Formation and the Treasure Mountain Tuff is on the cliff above the track between milepost 314 and the telephone box east of Rock Tunnel. Some loose rocks from the Treasure Mountain Tuff also are scattered on the hillsides and along the track; this is a good opportunity to compare the two types of rock. To the east and northeast, the Conejos outcrops of Phantom Curve and

Calico Cut form dramatic gashes on the slopes of Toltec Creek canyon. High above the track on the skyline, outcrops of Masonic Park Tuff cap the mesa. Below the Masonic Park is the Treasure Mountain Tuff, which in turn rests upon the Conejos Formation.

Mile
314.25 PEDESTAL ROCKS.
On the east side of the track are two erosional remnants of the Conejos Formation that resemble two people looking intently at each other. In the valley below are thick ledges of the Conejos.

Mile
314.32 ENTER NEW MEXICO.

Mile
315.20 ROCK TUNNEL AND TOLTEC GORGE.
elev 9,631 ft (2,936 m)
At milepost 315, the track crosses a fault contact between ancient Precambrian crystalline rocks (pC) and the Tertiary Conejos Formation (Tc). Many outcrops of these crystalline **metamorphic** and **igneous** rocks are visible along the track, inside the tunnel, and in Toltec Gorge. The metamorphic rocks are about 1,700 million years old, and were intruded by igneous rocks that are a mere 1,450 million years old.

These crystalline igneous and metamorphic rocks were exposed by erosion following mountain uplift at the end of the Cretaceous Period, about 70 million years ago. At that time, this entire region was a broad northwest-trending highland about 300 miles (483 km) long. Large-scale faulting accompanied the uplift and continued into the Tertiary Period, bringing the crystalline rocks into contact with much younger volcanic rocks. Some of these faults are shown on the geologic maps.

The rocks along the track and downward into Toltec Gorge are metamorphic **gneiss, schist,** and **amphibolite** that were intruded by younger **granite** and **pegmatite.**

Mile
315.60 GEOLOGIC CONTACT.
The contact of the Precambrian with the Conejos Formation is at track level. From the tunnel to mile 316.40 are nice views of jagged Precambrian rocks in the Rio de los Pinos canyon. Toltec Gorge is a very narrow, deep, V-shaped canyon because the stream had a difficult time eroding the harder, more resistant crystalline rocks.

Milepost
317 CUTS IN CONEJOS FORMATION.
West of this milepost are several deep railroad cuts in breccias and flows of the Conejos Formation and near milepost 318 is a small outcrop of Treasure Mountain Tuff.

Mile
318.40 OSIER, COLORADO.
elev 9,637 ft (2,937 m)
The grass-covered hillside to the north is a large **landslide** (Ql) that came from the west side of Osier Mountain and along Osier Creek. The top of Osier Mountain, elev 10,736 ft (3,272 m), is capped with the Cisneros Basalt; below is the Los Pinos Formation, but most of this unit is covered by landslides near Osier. Westward from Osier to Cumbres Pass, the Conejos Formation contains successively less breccia (photo p. 115).

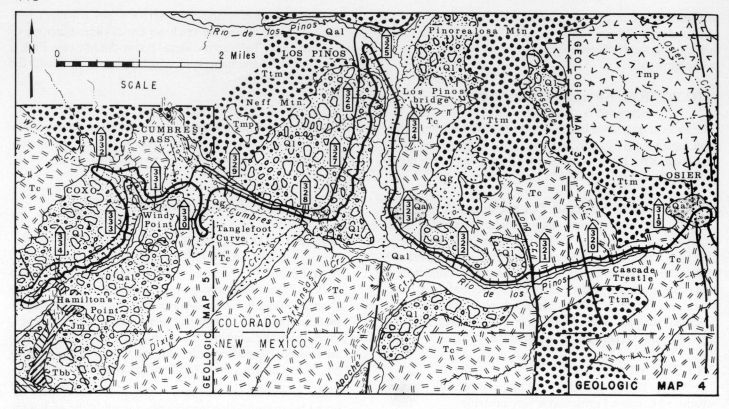

An earthquake was felt by residents of Osier and Cumbres in March 1884. Apparently the snow was shifted about, but no damage was noted. In May 1966, another quake occurred at Dulce, New Mexico, west of Chama. Earthquakes that can actually be felt, however, are uncommon in this area.

Mile
319.95 CASCADE TRESTLE.
Conejos Formation breccias crop out in the railroad cuts along this section of track. Across the Rio de los Pinos are steep slopes partly covered with large, angular-shaped rock fragments that were broken from ledges high on the hillside, and gradually slid down into the valley to form large piles of loose, broken rock at the base of the hills. This loose material is called **talus.**

Milepost
321 PUMICE OUTCROPS.
At track level are some outcrops of light-buff to tan-colored **pumice**, and ash-fall tuffs that are part of the Conejos Formation.

In the bottom of the valley are several nearly flat alluvial terraces along the stream. The Rio de Los Pinos has cut a new channel through the alluvium, part of which came from glacial debris and landslide deposits.

West of the milepost, outcrops along the track are reddish-colored Conejos breccias. It is easy to see large, irregular, angular blocks and pieces of volcanic igneous rocks cemented in fine-grained material.

Mile
322.95 LOS PINOS PHONE BOOTH.
To the west, across the valley where the track is at a higher level, is a large landslide. The rounded, hummocky, irregular

slopes are characteristic expressions of the downward and outward motion of landslides.

On the western skyline is Neff Mountain, elev 10,888 ft (3,319 m). The cap rock is Masonic Park Tuff; the slopes below are Treasure Mountain Tuff, most of which are covered by extensive landslides.

Mile
324.52 CROSS RIO DE LOS PINOS.
From the north end of the bridge to mile 325.20 is a straight section of track built on alluvium. The Cumbres Pass fault trends north-northeast through this valley, north to La Manga Pass, across the Conejos River, and continues northward where it intersects another large fault that is part of the Platoro caldera. Most of the obvious traces of the fault in this valley are covered by alluvium and glacial debris, so it is shown on Geologic Map 4, as a dotted line.

Mile
325.50 LOS PINOS WATER TANK.
elev 9,710 ft (2,960 m)

Milepost
327 LANDSLIDE DEBRIS.
Track is built on landslide debris. Between milepost 327 and milepost 329 are several large blocks of the Conejos that appear to be actual outcrops, but may be large, loose blocks broken from outcrops high on the mountain and moved downward by landslides.

Milepost
329 CROSS CUMBRES CREEK.
This portion of the track is on unstable glacial debris.

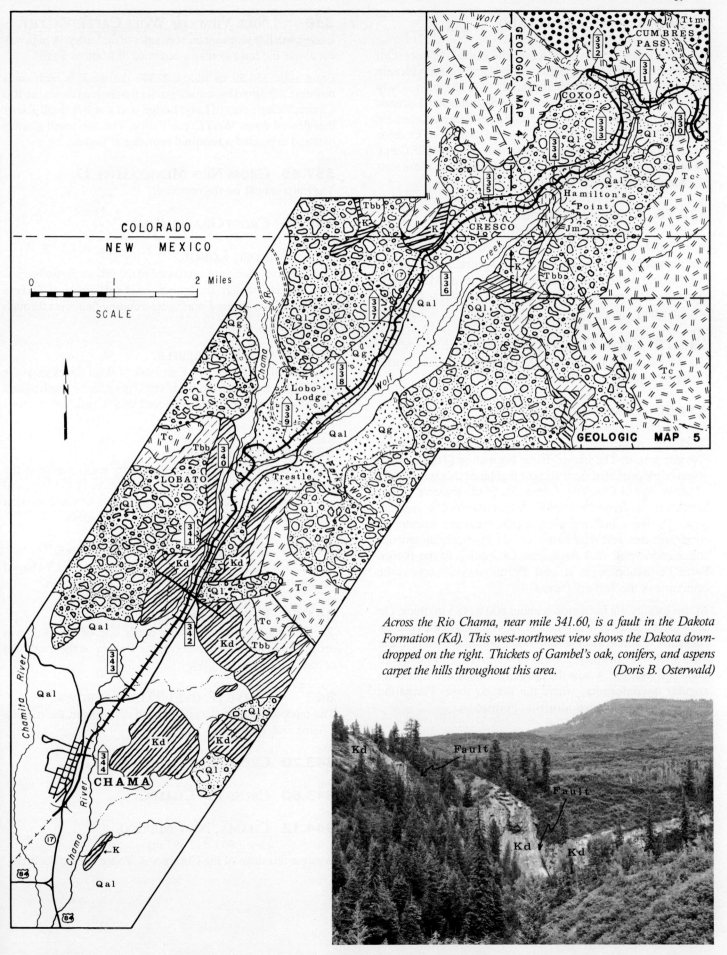

COLORADO
NEW MEXICO

0   1   2 Miles

SCALE

N

GEOLOGIC MAP 4

CUMBRES PASS

COXO

Hamilton's Point

CRESCO

GEOLOGIC MAP 5

Lobo Lodge

Trestle

LOBATO

CHAMA

Across the Rio Chama, near mile 341.60, is a fault in the Dakota Formation (Kd). This west-northwest view shows the Dakota down-dropped on the right. Thickets of Gambel's oak, conifers, and aspens carpet the hills throughout this area.   (Doris B. Osterwald)

Fault

Fault

Kd

Kd

Kd

Mile
330.60 CUMBRES, COLORADO.
elev 10,015 ft (3,053 m)

West of the station, the track leaves the glacial deposits (Qg) and returns to the chaotic, highly colored and altered **volcanic breccias** of the Conejos Formation (Tc). As the train slowly rounds Windy Point, mile. 331.09, and descends into [ascends from] Wolf Creek Valley, many tall spires and pinnacles are visible along the track. Another colorful display of Conejos rocks is on the high slopes to the west across Wolf Creek Valley. The rocks in all these outcrops are similar to those seen at Phantom Curves and Calico Cut.

Mile
332.20 COXO, COLORADO.
elev 9,753 ft (2,973 m)

From Coxo to Lobato Trestle, the track is on glacial and landslide debris, except for a half-mile section at Hamilton's Point where **sedimentary** rocks are at track level. Many large, loose blocks from the Conejos Formation are visible throughout the valley.

Mile
332.75 CROSS COLORADO HWY 17.

Good views to the northeast of Windy Point and the colorful Conejos breccias.

Mile
334.50 HAMILTON'S POINT.

Along the track and in the cliffs across the steep canyon of Wolf Creek are sedimentary rocks, that are not derived from any volcanic source. The Blanco Basin Formation (Tbb), is composed of rocks eroded from ancient highlands that were uplifted at the end of Cretaceous time. All of the material in this formation was derived from older sedimentary or Precambrian rocks. The white, buff, red, pink, or yellow-colored sandstones, conglomerates, and shales also contain Precambrian igneous and metamorphic rock fragments. Deposition of the Blanco Basin Formation began at least 35 million years ago at the beginning of the Tertiary Period.

At this locality the formation is about 600 ft (183 m) thick. On the wide, outside curve at mile 334.50, outcrops of the Dakota, Niobrara, Mancos, and the Morrison Formations are visible at track level. The Morrison consists of red, green, and variegated shale and siltstone. Across the canyon is a good example of an **angular unconformity,** where the Blanco Basin Formation overlies the steeply tilted Morrison Formation.

Mile
335.10 CRESCO, COLORADO.
elev 9,193 ft (2,802 m)

This siding and water tank are built on landslide debris.

Mile
335.60 CROSS COLO.–NEW MEX. STATE BOUNDARY.

This is the last [first] crossing of the state line before reaching Chama.

Milepost
336 NICE VIEWS OF WOLF CREEK VALLEY.

Large landslide scars are on both sides of the valley. A highway cut above the track contains outcrops of Mancos Shale.

From mile 336.20 to milepost 340 the track is built on a **moraine** deposited by a small glacier that moved down the Rio Chama Valley north of Lobo Lodge, and another small glacier that flowed down Wolf Creek Valley. The two small glaciers met and deposited a **terminal moraine** at Lobato.

Mile
337.45 CROSS NEW MEXICO HWY 17.

The track is built on the moraine.

Mile
336.65 CROSS GRAVEL ROAD.

Milepost
339 LOBO LODGE.

The cliffs to the west are composed of the Blanco Basin Formation, beneath which are brown, resistant ledges of Dakota Sandstone. An inferred northwest-trending fault cuts through this area.

Mile
339.75 LOBATO TRESTLE.

Due west of the trestle, the East Fork of Wolf Creek joins the Rio Chama flowing from the north. This is as far south as any glacial ice moved as it slowly carved Wolf Creek Valley into a U-shape.

Mile
339.99 LOBATO SIDING.

Across the Rio Chama, the sedimentary rocks visible in the ledges are brown to tan Dakota Formation at the top, and below, are variegated shales and siltstones of the Morrison Formation. The sediments dip gently to the south.

Mile
340.50 ENTER [LEAVE] "THE NARROWS."

Wolf Creek Valley at this point is more narrow and V-shaped because the small glaciers did not move this far south.

Mile
341.60 FAULT IN DAKOTA FORMATION.

The Dakota Formation on the north side of the fault was dropped downward in relation to the Dakota on the south side of the fault (photo, p. 119).

Milepost
342 LEAVE [ENTER] "THE NARROWS."

The track is built on glacial outwash debris from the melting Chama and Wolf Creek glaciers.

Mile
343.20 CROSS NEW MEXICO HWY 17.

Mile
343.60 CROSS RIO CHAMA.

Mile
344.12 CHAMA, NEW MEXICO.
elev 7,863 ft (2,397 m)

Western terminus of the Cumbres & Toltec Scenic Railroad.

GLOSSARY OF GEOLOGIC TERMS

alkali basalt. Basalts which contain olivine, as well as feldspathoids and sodic pyroxenes as accessory minerals.

alkali feldspar. Feldspars that contain potash and sodium but little calcium. Common varieties are microline, orthoclase, albite, and sanidine.

alluvium. Loose sand, clay, silt, and gravel carried from the mountains by water and deposited along stream valleys.

alluvial fan. A flat to gently sloping mass of loose rock debris, shaped like an open fan, deposited by streams at places where the streams issue from a narrow mountain valley onto a broad plain or valley.

amphibolite. A very dark-colored foliated metamorphic rock composed mostly of the amphibole group of minerals (hornblende is common) and little or no quartz. Most have a layered or foliated structure.

andesite. A dark-colored, fine-grained extrusive igneous rock with 52 to 60 percent silica, of intermediate chemical composition between basalt and rhyolite.

angular unconformity. A break in the geologic record, indicated by missing rock units, in which one rock unit is overlain by another that is not next in the normal sequence of deposition. "Angular" implies that a time of folding took place after the first unit was deposited. The first rock unit then is more steeply tilted than the second rock unit.

ash-flow tuff. See welded tuff.

basalt. Dark- to medium-colored mafic volcanic (igneous) rock containing calcium-rich feldspar and pyroxene in a glassy or fine-grained matrix.

breccia. A coarse-grained rock composed of broken, angular fragments cemented by finer-grained material.

caldera. A large bowl-shaped depression, more or less circular in shape, that results from the collapse of the vent area of a volcano. This is caused by the rapid extrusion of large amounts of volcanic ash, dust and lava.

clastic. Refers to fragments broken from pre-existing rocks or minerals that have been transported some distance from their point of origin and redeposited.

extrusive. An igneous rock that erupted onto the surface of the earth.

fault. A break or fracture in a rock or surface along which movement and displacement have occurred.

foliation. See schist.

gneiss. A foliated metamorphic rock in which layers of quartz and feldspar alternate with layers of foliated mica and hornblende. Foliation is not as pronounced as in a schist.

granite. A coarse-grained igneous rock with 20 to 60 percent quartz, 35 to 90 percent feldspar, and traces of mica, homblende, magnetite and other minerals.

igneous. Rocks solidified from molten or partly molten material called magma.

intrusive rock. An igneous rock that formed by crystallization from magma, prior to reaching the surface of the earth.

landslide. A general term for a number of mass movement landforms and processes involving the moderately rapid to rapid downslope transport by gravity.

magma. See igneous.

metamorphic. Rocks that were changed from one form to another in the solid state by heat, pressure, and chemical changes, resulting from deep burial or closeness to igneous intrusions.

moraine. A mound or ridge of unsorted, unstratified glacial debris deposited by the direct action of slowly moving ice.

olivine. A gray-green, olive-green, or brown silicate mineral containing magnesium and iron. It is common in mafic or low-silica igneous rocks such as gabbro. basalt, peridotite, or dunite.

orogeny. The process by which mountain ranges are formed, or the time during which major mountain systems are formed.

outwash. A broad, flat, or gently sloping alluvial sheet of sedimentary material deposited by streams flowing in front of, or beyond, the end moraine of a glacier.

pegmatite. A light-colored, coarse-grained, igneous rock with large, interlocking crystals of feldspar, quartz, and micas. Many pegmatites contain rare or unusual minerals of economic value.

phenocryst. A large prominent mineral in an igneous rock surrounded by a finer-grained groundmass.

plagioclase feldspar. A light-colored silicate mineral containing sodium, calcium and aluminum. One of the commonest rock-forming minerals.

pumice. A light-weight, light-colored, glassy, volcanic igneous rock having the composition of rhyolite, containing a large percentage of bubbles formed by escaping gases. Most pumice will float in water.

quartz latite. An extrusive igneous rock of intermediate composition. It contains quartz, plagioclase, biotite, and/or hornblende as phenocryst minerals, with alkali feldspar and quartz in the glassy groundmass.

rhyodacite. Extrusive volcanic (igneous) rocks of intermediate composition between basalt and rhyolite, containing large crystals (phenocrysts) of quartz, plagioclase feldspar, and either biotite or hornblende in a fine-grained or glassy matrix composed of alkali feldspar and quartz.

rhyolite. Light-colored extrusive volcanic (igneous) rocks containing large crystals (phenocrysts) of quartz and alkali feldspar in a glassy to very fine-grained matrix. Most rhyolites show flow textures.

rift. A major flaw in the Earth's crust, caused by large forces that thin the crust by slowly pulling apart a strip, thus allowing the strip to sag. Rifts contain many faults caused by local forces that break the rocks and drop blocks downward into the sagging strip.

schist. A metamorphic rock that readily splits into thin, parallel layers or slabs because of its elongated and parallel minerals. The resulting structure is called foliation.

sedimentary. Rocks formed by the deposition, consolidation, and cementation of loose sediment, accumulated in layers from the disintegration and decomposition of pre-existing rocks.

shield volcano. A volcano with a broad, low cone containing a central vent, usually located near the top. The lava that flows out of the vent is usually basaltic and therefore very fluid, allowing it to flow for long distances before congealing.

talus. An accumulated heap of rock fragments derived from, and lying at the base of a cliff or very steep slope.

terminal or end moraine. A curving or crescent-shaped ridge of rock debris deposited across a valley by a glacier, that marks the farthest advance of the ice.

tholeiitic basalt. Basalt which generally has no olivine crystals.

till. An unsorted mixture of sand, clay, gravel, cobbles, and boulders mixed with finely ground-up rock debris deposited beside, in front of, and underneath a glacier. It is derived from debris carried in the ice.

tuff. A pyroclastic volcanic rock formed by the lithification of ash (ie., fragments less than 4 mm. in diameter). Tuff may also contain larger rock fragments blown from a volcano.

tuff breccia. A volcanic rock in which large rock fragments are set in a fine-grained tuffaceous matrix.

volcanic breccia. A lithified rock with angular volcanic rock fragments larger than 64 mm set in a matrix of fine-grained volcanic material. The fragments have sharp edges and unworn corners.

welded tuff. A pyroclastic volcanic rock formed by compaction of hot, glassy and lithic material following an explosive "glowing avalanche" type eruption.

EQUIPMENT ROSTER

LOCOMOTIVES

Number	463	483[1], 484, 487, 488, 489	492[1], 494[1], 495[1] 497	15[3], 19
Class	K-27	K-36	K-37[2]	DE B+B 22 (diesel–electric)
Wheel arrangement	2-8-2	2-8-2	2-8-2	B+B
D&RGW motive power class	125	189	—	—
Year built	1903	1925	1928-30	1943
Builder	Baldwin	Baldwin	D&RGW	General Electric
Service	passenger	passenger	passenger	switcher
Diameter of cylinders	17	20	20	2 180HP V-8 diesel engines
Stroke of cylinders	22	24	24	—
Operating boiler pressure	200 psi	195 psi	200 psi	—
Superheater	yes	yes	yes	—
Total heating surface	1,526 sq ft	2,118 sq ft	2,159 sq ft	—
Diameter of Drivers	40"	44"	44"	36"
Weight of locomotive	140,250 lb	187,100 lb	187,250 lb	47 tons
Weight on drivers	108,300 lb	143,850 lb	148,280 lb	
Tractive effort	27,000 lb	36,200 lb	37,100 lb	22,000 lb
Weight of loaded tender	83,000 lb	99,500 lb	120,000 lb	—
Tender, water capacity	4,100 gal.	5,000 gal	6,000 gal	—
Tender, coal capacity	8.5 tons	9.5 tons	9 tons	—
Total weight, engine and tender	223,550 lb	286,600 lb	307,250 lb	—

[1]not in service, 1994
[3]Leased from Georgetown Loop RR
[2]K-37 class rebuilt from standard gauge class C-41 2-8-0's, originally built in 1902 by Baldwin

BOXCARS—NARROW GAUGE

Lettering	No.	Year built	Last used	Remarks
D&RGW	3014	1904	10-90	
C&TS	3016	"	?	
C&TS	3073	"	9-91	
D&RGW	3090	"	10-89	
D&RGW	3125	"	10-90	
D&RGW	3231	"	9-90	
D&RGW	3254	"	'72 ?	
C&TS	3331	"	9-91	
D&RGW	3422	"	9-89	
C&TS	3484	"	?	
D&RGW	3524	"	?	Antonito display
D&RGW	3570	"	10-90	silica sand car
D&RGW	3585	"	?	
D&RGW	3592	"	9-90	
D&RGW	3669	"	10-90	

BOXCARS—STANDARD GAUGE

Lettering	No.	Year built	Last used	Remarks
D&RGW	X-5082	1916	1981	original No. 66306
D&RGW	X-5086	"	"	original No. 66977

used as freight cars until 1959; converted to maintenance-of-way tool-material cars until 1981; renumbered. X-5082 and X-5086 at this time; sat in Alamosa yards until 1990 when they were given to the *Friends of the C&TS*.

BOX-OUTFIT CARS

Lettering	No.	Year built	Last used	Remarks
C&TS	04258	1890 ?	10-90	sleeper-outfit
D&RGW	04407	"	9-91	sleeper-outfit, rotary OY?
D&RGW	04426	"	8-85	cable car
D&RG(W)	04444	"	8-88	block car
D&RGW	04549	"	"	tool car
D&RGW	04904	"	?	water service car
D&RGW	04982	"	10-90	section foreman outfit

FLAT-BOTTOM GONDOLAS

Lettering	No.	Year built	Last used	Remarks
D&RGW	1000	1902	'78 ?	
D&RGW	1039	"	9-90	
D&RGW	1149	1902	9-87	
D&RGW	1456	"	9-87	
D&RGW	1667	1903, '04	9-87	

FLAT-BOTTOM GONDOLAS CONT.

Lettering	No.	Year built	Last used	Remarks
D&RGW	1059	"	?	
D&RGW	1082	"	?	
D&RGW	1145	1902	9-91	open-ended
D&RGW	1159	"	?	
D&RGW	1232	"	?	
D&RGW	1246	"	9-91	open-ended
D&RGW	1268	"	8-88	
D&RGW	1343	"	?	
D&RGW	1357	"	?	observation car
D&RGW	1534	1903, '04	?	
D&RGW	1557	1903, '04	9-91	observation car
D&RGW	1610	"	?	open-ended
D&RGW	1648	"	9-91	observation car
D&RGW	1733	"	?	
D&RGW	1746	"	'85	observation car
D&RGW	1839	"	?	
D&RGW	9213	1898, '04	?	open-ended
D&RGW	9249	1898, '02	?	"
D&RG	9378	1898, '02	9-90	wooden draft gear
D&RGW	9558	1898, '02	?	open-ended
D&RGW	9613	1953	'85	"
D&RGW	9615	1953	'89	"

DROP-BOTTOM GONDOLAS

Lettering	No.	Year built	Last used	Remarks
C&TS	700	1904	'83	Chama display
D&RGW	724	"	6-91	
D&RGW	727	"	6-91	
D&RGW	728	"	9-91	
C&TS	731	"	9-91	ballast service
C&TS	756	"	6-88	ballast service
D&RGW	769	"	6-91	
D&RGW	774	"	?	
D&RGW	783	"	6-91	
C&TS	787	"	6-91	ballast service
D&RGW	790	"	?	
D&RGW	791	"	?	
D&RGW	798	"	6-89	

DROP-BOTTOM GONDOLAS CONT.

Lettering	No.	Year built	Last used	Remarks
D&RGW	801	"	'78 ?	Antonito display
D&RGW	811	"	?	
C&TS	848	"	6-91	ballast service
D&RGW	859	"	6-91	

HOPPER CARS

| C&TS | 1307, 1311 | | | 35 ft, 50 ton; purchased from |

Butte, Anaconda, & Pacific Railroad, 1990; converted to narrow gauge

REFRIGERATORS

Lettering	No.	Year built	Last used	Remarks
D&RGW	55	1904	?	30 ft car; being restored
D&RGW	157	1924, '26	9-91	40 ft car
D&RGW	163	"	9-91	40 ft car
D&RGW	166	"	'78 ?	40 ft car; Antonito display
C&TS	169	"	9-91	40 ft car

STOCK CARS

Lettering	No.	Year built	Last used	Remarks
D&RGW	5549	1904		
D&RGW	5553	"	?	double-deck (sheep)
D&RGW	5600	"	?	"
D&RGW	5633	"	?	"
D&RGW	5674	"	?	"
D&RGW	5691	"	9-90	single-deck (cattle)
D&RGW	5706	"	9-90	single-deck; metal roof
D&RGW	5747	"	?	single-deck; Antonito display
D&RGW	5841	"	?	double-deck

WOODEN FLATCARS

Lettering	No.	Year built	Last used	Remarks
D&RGW	1001	1902	?	
D&RGW	1033	"	'78	
D&RGW	1515	1903, '04	'85	
D&RGW	1567	"	?	
D&RGW	6314	1926	9-91	40 ft car
D&RGW	9533	1898, '02	?	
D&RGW	9557	"	9-89	
D&RGW	9569	"	?	

STEEL FLATCARS

Lettering	No.	Year built	Last used	Remarks
D&RGW	6601	1955	10-90	
D&RGW	6613	"	9-89	
D&RGW	6627	"	?	
D&RGW	6649	"	?	

WOODEN FLATCARS, STEEL REINFORCED

Lettering	No.	Year built	Last used	Remarks
D&RGW	6200	1918	'78	
D&RGW	6214	"	5-88	

IDLER FLATCARS

Lettering	No.	Year built	Last used	Remarks
C&TS	6708	1955	9-91	
D&RGW	6746	1957	10-90	
D&RGW	6755	"	9-91	
D&RGW	010793	?	?	std. gauge; Antonito display

CABOOSES

C&TS	0503	1880		rebuilt 1923
C&TS	0579	1880 ?		short; given to C&TS, 1991
C&TS	05635			built from stock car 5635, 1976
C&TS	0306			parlor-caboose car built from boxcar 3060, 1982

MAINTENANCE-OF-WAY EQUIPMENT

Lettering	No.	Year built	Last used	Remarks
D&RGW	OB	1891	?	pile driver
D&RGW	OJ	1888	?	flanger
C&TS	OK	1888	10-90	flanger
D&RGW	OL	1888	5-73	flanger
D&RGW	OM	1889	2-76	rotary snowplow
D&RGW	OP	1911	'90	construction derrick
D&RGW	OU	1924	11-83	Jordan ditcher
C&TS	OY	1923	5-91	rotary snowplow
D&RGW	053	?	'81	rotary OM cook car
C&TS	54	?	5-91	used as outfit car by D&RGW
C&TS	65	?	5-91	used as outfit car by D&RGW
C&TS	0452	?	'78 ?	tourist-outfit car

MAINTENANCE-OF-WAY EQUIPMENT CONT.

Lettering	No.	Year built	Last used	Remarks
D&RGW	252	1889	?	tourist-sleeper, orig. D&RG no. 470
D&RGW	0292	1881	?	coach, orig. D&RG no. 68
D&RGW	W462	?	?	water car (tender of K-27 462)
D&RGW	0471	1908	10-90	rotary OM water war
D&RGW	0472	1908	10-90	rotary OY water car
D&RGW	06008	?	?	pile driver OB idler flat
D&RGW	06051	?	8-85	rail and tie car
D&RGW	06063	1911	7-90	derrick OP idler flat
D&RGW	06092	?	8-85	wheel and tie car
D&RGW	09410	?	?	coal outfit; tender tank on flatcar

EX-UTLX NARROW-FRAME TANK CARS

Built standard gauge 1908; rebuilt narrow gauge, 1927-30

Lettering	Present no.	Original no.	1946 no.	1956 no.
WP&Y	50	13084	88112	11024
WP&Y	51	12739	88113	11025
WP&Y	62	12962	88101	11013
WP&Y	63	13168	88103	11015
WP&Y	64	12918	88100	11012
WP&Y	65	12757	88106	11018

C&TS PASSENGER CARS

No.	Name	Old D&RG no.	Orig. year built	Rebuilt by C&TS	Type	Capacity
200		3339	1904	1971	coach	32
201		3742	"	"	"	"
202		3537	"	"	"	"
203		3719	"	"	"	"
204		3643	"	"	"	"
205		3475	"	"	"	"
206		3278	"	"	"	"
207		3414	"	"	"	"
208		3064	"	"	"	"
209		3605	"	1972	"	"
210		3156	"	"	"	"
211		3469	"	1973	"	"
212		3316	"	"	"	"
213		3476	"	"	"	"
214		3161	"	"	"	"
248		3071	"	1972	rest/coach	22
249		3244	"	"	"	"
250		3527	"	"	"	"
251		3405	"	"	"	"
500	Alamosa	6521	1940, '44	1982-'83	coach	48
501	Antonito	6510	"	"	"	44
502	Monte Vista	6542	"	"	"	"
503	Del Norte	6516	"	"	"	"
504	San Luis	6540	"	"	"	48
505	La Jara	6537	"	"	rest/coach	
506	Conejos	6533	"	"	handicap/rest	
510	Quinlan	6566	"	2001	parlour	24
511	Santa Fe	6501	"	"	"	"
512	Chama	6512	"	1986-'87	coach	48
513	Taos	6518	"	"	"	"
514	Ojo Caliente	6538	"	"	"	"
515	Española	6541	"	"	rest/coach	
516	Dulce	6543	"	"	handicap/rest	
517	Big Horn	AX4629	1957	1996-'97	rest/coach	40
520	Cumbres	AX4609	?	1993	coach	44
521	Osier	AX4628	?	"	"	"
522	Sublette	AX4606	?	"	"	"
523	Los Pinos	AX4619	1957	1996-'97	"	"
450		3591	1904	1973	snack	
451		3533	"	1980	snack	
401		3686	"	1973	*Friends* car	
301		6205	1918	1970	observation car	
1204		1204	1902	1985	observation car	
Hinman coach			1920 ?			

SNOWSHEDS ON CUMBRES PASS

Shed No.	Location	Built	Length	Clear height	Clear width	Notes
317A	317.11	1884	435'	17'	14' 6"	Retired AFE 457
319A	319.46	1894	359'	16' 6"	14'	Retired AFE 3402
321A	321.02	1908	374'			50' blown down by gale 11-11-11
323A	323.12	1900	287'			Destroyed by fire 9-12-20
323B	323.19	?	310'			Retired AFE 3403
326A	326.09	1895	385'	18'	14' 9"	Retired AFE 2893
326B	326.13	1887	450'	16' 6"	15' 6"	Destroyed by fire 11-10-21
326C	326.50	?	393'			180' destroyed by fire 11-24-22; balance retired AFE 2268, 1925
327A	327.08	1884	821'	16'	14'	Retirement not known; snow fence built, 1921
327B	327.68	1890	818'	17'	14' 6"	Retired and replaced by snow fence, 1924
328A	328.80	1890	487'	17'	14' 6 "	Destroyed by fire 9-4-21
329A	329.26	1890	232'	16' 9"	14' 6"	Destroyed by fire 9-18-20
329B	329.73	1908	314'			Retired and replaced by snow fence, 1924
329C	329.85	1884	472'	16'	14'	Destroyed by fire 9-13-21
330A	330.48	?	526'			Rebuilt 1916; rebuilt again 1991
330B	330.78	?	214'			Destroyed by fire 9-30-21
331A	331.28	1884	348'			Destroyed by fire 6-20-20
331B	331.36	?	152'			Rebuilt 10-31-15 after fire; retired, 1925
331C	331.43	?	181'			Destroyed by fire 5-3-21
332A	332.12	?	306'			Burned prior to 10-12-98 and rebuilt; rebuilt again 1915; retired, 1938?
332B	332.55	?	395'			Destroyed by fire 8-6-19
332C	332.66	?	97'			Destroyed by fire 6-14-22
332D	332.74	?	121'			Retired and replaced with snow fence, 1924
332E	332.78	?	121'			Destroyed by fire 4-29-21

Adapted from list compiled by Jackson C. Thode from D&RGW Building Records of the 4th Division.

AFE: Authority for Expenditure.

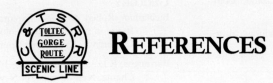

REFERENCES

HISTORY

Adams, Robert, 1974, The Architecture and Art of Early Hispanic Colorado: Colorado Association University Press, in cooperation with The State Historical Society of Colorado, 238 p.

Bauer, W.H., Ozment, J.L., and Willard, J.H., 1975, Colorado Postal History: The Post Offices: The Creede News Inc., 248 p.

Brayer, Herbert O., 1949, William Blackmore, The Spanish-Mexican Land Grants of New Mexico and Colorado, 1863-1878: v. 1, Bradford-Robinson Printing Co., Denver, Colo., 381 p.

Buchanan, Robert H., 1971, The San Luis Valley—A Land of Paradox: *in* New Mexico Geological Society Guidebook, 22nd Field Conference, San Luis Basin, Colo., p. 243-245.

Catholic Church, Conejos, Colorado, 1934, Articles on the parish churches in the Southern San Luis Valley: Antonito, Colo.

Crofutt, George A., 1885, Crofutt's Grip-Sack Guide of Colorado: CUBAR Reprint 1966, Golden, Colo., 264 p.

Daggett, Eleanor, 1973, Chama, New Mexico: Nature Trek Publication, Albuquerque, N. Mex., 22 p.

Dane, Carle H., 1960, Early Explorations of Rio Arriba County, N. Mex. and Adjacent Parts of Southern Colorado: *in* New Mexico Geological Society Guidebook, 11th Field Conference, p. 113-127.

Flower, Judson Harold, Jr., 1966, Mormon Colonization in the San Luis Valley, 1878-1900: M.A. Thesis, Brigham Young Univ., 118 p.

Hill, C.C. 1949, Wagon Roads in Colo., 1858-1876: M.A. Thesis, University of Colorado, 78 p.

Ingersoll, Ernest, 1885, The Crest of the Continent: R.R. Donnelley & Sons, Chicago, Ill., 344 p.

Lavender, David, 1954, Bent's Fort: Doubleday & Co., Garden City, N.Y., 450 p.

Maltin, Leonard, 1991, Movie and Video Guide, 1992: Signet Books, published by Penguin Books, USA, New York, N.Y., 1487 p.

Palmer, Margaret, 1989, The Gramps Oil Field: *in* Chama Valley Tattler, v. 7, Chama, N. Mex., 20 p.

_____, 1991, Movie Making in the Chama Valley: *in* Chama Valley Tattler, v. 9, Chama, N. Mex., 20 p.

Pearce, T.M., editor, 1965, New Mexico Place Names, A Geographical Dictionary: University of New Mexico, Albuquerque, N. Mex., 187 p.

Rivers, Art, 1973, Introducing Chama Country: La Chispa Promotions, Chama. N. Mex., 40 p.

Sarah Platt Decker Chapter, N.S.D.A.R., 1942, 1946, 1952, 1961, Pioneers of the San Juan Country: v. 1 and 2, Outwest Printing Co.,Colorado Springs, Colo., v. 3, Durango Printing Co., v. 4, Big Mountain Press, Denver, Colo.

Sprague, Marshall, 1964, The Great Gates, the Story of the Rocky Mountain Passes: Little Brown & Co., Boston, Mass., 468 p.

State of Colorado Archives, Certificates of Incorporation for Toll and Wagon Roads in Colorado.

Stauter, Patrick C., 1958, 100 Years in Colorado's Oldest Parish: Ye Olde Print Shoppe, Alamosa, Colo., 40 p.

The San Luis Valley Historian: San Luis Valley Historical Society, Inc., Alamosa, Colo., v. 1, no. 1. Jan. 1969, 15 p.

The San Luis Valley Historian: San Luis Valley Historical Society, Inc., Alamosa, Colo.. v. 1, no. 2, April 1969, 32 p.

The San Luis Valley Historian: San Luis Valley Historical Society, Inc., Alamosa, Colo., v. 1, no. 3, July 1969, 36 p.

Ubbelohde, Carl, 1965, A Colorado History: Pruett Press, Inc., Boulder, Colo., 339 p.

U.S. Army Engineers, 1876, Annual Report of the Chief of Engineers: (Ruffner Report) Washington, D.C.

U.S. Army Engineers, 1878, Annual Report of the Chief of Engineers: (Ruffner Report) Washington, D.C.

Valdez, Luis, and Steiner, Stan, editors, 1972, Aztlan, An Anthology of Mexican American Literature: Vintage Books, 410 p.

W.P.A. Writer's Program, 1948, Colorado, A Guide to the Highest State: Nastings House, New York, N.Y. 511 p.

Westermeier, Clifford p., 1970, Colorado's First Portrait: University of New Mexico Press, Albuquerque, N. Mex., 206 p.

Wheeler, G.M., 1889, Geographical Report: U.S. Geographical Surveys West of the 100th Meridian: v. 1, Washington, D.C.

Wilson, Dorothy D., 1971, They Came to Hunt, Early Man in the San Luis Valley: *in* New Mexico Geological Society Guidebook, 22nd Field Conference, San Luis Basin, Colo., p. 203-207.

RAILROADS

Anonymous, 1962, Old standard and narrow gauge house cars: *in* Model Railroader Magazine, v. 29, no. 4.

_____, 1980, Locomotives of the Rio Grande: Colorado Railroad Museum, Golden, Colo., 96 p.

Athearn, Robert G., 1958, The Independence of the Denver & Rio Grande: *in* Utah Historical Quarterly, v. XXVI, Jan. 1958.

_____, 1962, Rebel of the Rockies: Yale University Press, New Haven, Conn., 395 p.

Best, Gerald M., 1968, Mexican Narrow Gauge: Howell-North Books. Berkeley. Calif., 180 p.

Beebe, Lucius, 1947, Mixed Train Daily: E.P. Dutton Co., New York. N.Y., 368 p.

Beebe, Lucius, 1958, Narrow Gauge in the Rockies: Howell-North Books, Berkeley, Calif., 224 p.

Beebe, Lucius, 1962, Rio Grande, Mainline of the Rockies: Howell-North Books, Berkeley, Calif., 380 p.

Brayer, Herbert O., 1949, William Blackmore, Early Financing of the Denver & Rio Grande Railway and Ancillary Land Companies, 1871-1878: v. 2, Bradford-Robinson Printing Co., Denver, Colo., 333 p.

C&TS Dispatch, newsletter published by the Friends of the C&TS Railroad, 1988-1992.

Carstens, Hal, 1991, Slim Gauge Cars: Carstens Publications, Inc., Newton, N.J., 100 p.

Chappell, Gordon, 1967, Farewell to Cumbres: *in* Colo. Railroad Museum, Rail Annual, 1967, p. 1-27.

_____, 1969, To Santa Fe by Narrow Gauge: *in* Colorado Rail Annual, 1969, Colorado Railroad Museum, p. 3-47.

_____, 1971, Logging Along the Denver & Rio Grande: Colorado Railroad Museum, Golden. Colo., 190 p.

D&RG Timetables for 1890, 1915, reprinted by Colorado Railroad Museum, Golden, Colo.

D&RG Employee's Timetables:
No. 10, July 23, 1882
No. 102, July 20, 1919
No. 124, February 2, 1947
No. 164, March 7, 1954

D&RGW References:
A. Bridges, Building and Other Structures, D&RG, Jan. 1, 1891.
B. Right-of-Way and Track Map of the D&RG, Fourth Division. Chief Engineer's Office, June 30, 1919, corrected to December 31, 1936.
C. Engineering Department Report of Chief Engineer J.A. McMurtrie to Gen. W.J. Palmer, April 1, 1881.
D. The Denver Tribune, August, 1881.
E. Construction and Filing Map Records, Office of Chief Engineer, November 1, 1937 with revisions of January 1, 1949 and March 1, 1954.
F. Condensed Profile of the D&RGW System. Office of Chief Engineer, January 1, 1934.
G. Personal communication from Jackson C. Thode, March 23, 1976.
H. Snowsheds on the Fourth Division. Compiled by Jackson C. Thode.

Day, Jerry, B., 1989, Narrow Gauge Pictorial, v. 7, Denver & Rio Grande Western Work Equipment—A to OZ, 224 p.

Dorman, Richard L. 1988, Chama/Cumbres with a Little Chili: R.D. Publications, Santa Fe, N. Mex., 206 p.

Everett. George G., 1966, The Cavalcade of Railroads in Colo. from 1871 to 1965: Golden Bell Press, Denver, Colo., 235 p.

Gjevre, John A., 1971, Chili Line, the Narrow Gauge to Santa Fe: Rio Grande Sun Press, Espanola, N. Mex., 100 p.

Hauck, Cornelius W., and Richardson, Robert W., 1963, Steam in the Rockies, A Steam Locomotive Roster of the Denver & Rio Grande: Colorado Railroad Museum, Golden, Colo., 35 p.

Iron Horse News, compiled and edited by Robert W. Richardson for the Colorado Railroad Museum, Golden, Colo., 1954-1991.

Le Massena, Robert A., 1974, Rio Grande to the Pacific, Sundance Ltd., Denver, Colo., 416 p.

Lind, Richard F., 1963, Narrow Gauge Country, Boulder, Colo., 120 p.

Maxwell, John W., Scale drawings of D&RGW equipment, Wheat Ridge, Colo.

Myrick, David F., 1970, New Mexico's Railroads—An Historical Survey: Colorado Railroad Museum, Golden, Colo., 197 p.

Ormes, Robert M., 1963, Railroads and the Rockies: Sage Books, Denver, Colo., 406 p.

Savery, Merle, 1977, The Celts: in National Geographic Society, v. 151, no. 5, p. 582-631.

Sloan, Robert E., 1978, Colorado Narrow Gauge Tank Cars: in Narrow Gauge Gazette, July/August, p. 29-34.

Thode, Jackson C., 1970, A Century of Passenger Trains: in The 1970 Denver Westerners Brand Book, Johnson Publishing Co., Boulder, Colo., p. 83-253.

Wilson, Spencer, and Glover, Vernon J., 1980, The Cumbres & Toltec Scenic Railroad, The Historic Preservation Study: University of New Mexico Press, Albuquerque, N. Mex., 170 p.

GEOLOGY

Bieberman, Robert A., 1960, Exploration for Oil and Gas in the Chama Basin: in New Mexico Geological Society Guidebook, 11th Field Conference, Rio Chama Country, p. 110-112.

Burroughs, R.L., and Butler, A.P., 1971, Rail Log Antonito, Colorado to Chama, New Mexico: in New Mexico Geological Society Guidebook, 22nd Field Conference, San Luis Basin, Colo., p. 49-66.

Butler, Arthur P., 1971, Tertiary Volcanic Stratigraphy of the Eastern Tusas Mountains, Southwest of the San Luis Valley, Colorado—New Mexico: in New Mexico Geological Society Guidebook, 22nd Field Conference, San Luis Basin, Colo., p. 289-300.

Chronic, John, and Chronic. Halka, 1972, Prairie Peak and Plateau, A Guide to the Geology of Colorado: Bulletin 32, Colorado Geological Survey, Denver, Colo., 126 p.

Geologic Atlas of the Rocky Mountain Region, 1972: Rocky Mountain Association of Geologists, 331 p.

Bates, R.L., and Jackson, J.A., editors, 1987, Glossary of Geology: 3d Ed., American Geological Institute, Alexandria, Virg., 788 p.

James, H.L., 1971, Road Log No. 4, Chama, New Mexico to Antonito, Colorado via Highway 17: in New Mexico Geological Society Guidebook, 22nd Field Conference, San Luis Basin, Colo., p. 82-87.

Lipman, Peter W., 1969, Alkali and Tholeiitic Basaltic Volcanism Related to the Rio Grande Depression. Southern Colorado and Northern New Mexico: Geological Society of America Bulletin, v. 80, no.7, p. 1343-1353.

_____, Steven, Thomas A., and Mehnert, Harald H., 1970, Volcanic History of The San Juan Mountains, Colorado, as indicated by Potassium-Argon Dating: Geological Society of America Bulletin, v. 81, no. 8, p. 2329-2351.

_____, 1975, Evolution of the Platoro Caldera complex and related rocks, Southeastern San Juan Mountains, Colo.: U.S. Geological Survey Professional Paper 852, 128 p.

Lochman-Balk, C., and Bruning, J.E., 1971, Lexicon of Stratigraphic Names: in New Mexico Geological Society Guidebook, 22nd Field Conference, San Luis Basin. Colo., p. 101-111.

Hansen, W.R., editor, 1991, Suggestions to Authors of the Reports of the United States Geological Survey: 7th edition, U.S. Government Printing Office, 289 p.

Ryder, Robert T., 1985, Oil and Gas Potential of the Chama-Southern San Juan Mountains Wilderness Study Area, Colorado: U.S. Geological Survey Bulletin 1524 D, p. 79-121.

Smith, Clay T., and Muehlberger, William R., 1960, Road Log from Taos to Chama to Cumbres Pass and return to Chama: in New Mexico Geological Society Guidebook, 11th Field Conference, p. 11-23.

Stokes, V.L., and Varnes, D.J., 1955, Glossary of Selected Geologic Terms: Colorado Scientific Society Proceedings, v. 16, 165 p.

Waldschmidt, W.A., 1946, Gramp's [oil] Field, Archuleta County, Colorado: American Association of Petroleum Geologists Bulletin, v. 30, no. 4, p. 561-580.

NATURE

Arnberger, Leslie P., 1968, Flowers of the Southwest Mountains: Southwest Monuments Assoc., Globe, Ariz., 112 p.

Baerg, Harry J., 1955, How to Know the Western Trees: Wm. C. Brown Co., Dubuque, Iowa, 170 p.

Craighead, John J., Craighead. Frank C., Jr., and Davis, Ray T., 1963, A Field Guide to Rocky Mountain Wildflowers: Houghton Mifflin Co., Boston, Mass., 277 p.

Custer, George A., 1874, My Life on the Plains: University of Nebraska Press, Lincoln, Neb. (reprinted in 1962), 626 p,

Dixon, Hobart N., 1971, Flora of the San Luis Valley: in New Mexico Geological Society Guidebook, 22nd Field Conference, San Luis Basin, Colo., p. 133-135.

Dodge, Natt N., 1967, 100 Roadside Wildflowers of Southwest Uplands: Southwest Monuments Association, Globe, Ariz., 32 p.

Hale, Mason E., 1969, How to Know the Lichens: Wm. C. Brown Co., Dubuque, Iowa, 226 p.

Harrington, H.D., 1964, Manual of the Plants of Colorado: Sage Books, Chicago, Ill., 666 p.

Jefferson County Schools, Activity File of Outdoor Education Laboratory Schools, 1976.

Keen, Veryl F., 1971, Fauna of the San Luis Valley: in New Mexico Geological Society Guidebook, 22nd Field Conference, San Luis Basin, Colo., p. 137-139.

Kirk, Donald R., 1970, Wild Edible Plants of the Western United States: Naturegraph Publishers, Healdsburg, Calif.,

Miller, David H., 1963, Custer's Fall: Bantam Books, New York, N.Y., 204 p.

Nelson, Ruth Ashton, 1970, Plants of Rocky Mountain National Park: Rocky Mountain Nature Association & National Park Service, 168 p.

Patraw, Pauline M., 1964, Flowers of the Southwest Mesas: Southwestern Monuments Assoc., Globe, Ariz., 112 p.

Pesman, Walter M., 1967, Meet the Natives: 7th edition, Denver Botanic Gardens, Smith-Brooks Printing Co., Denver, Colo., 219 p.

Peterson, Roger Tory, 1961, A Field Guide to Western Birds: 2nd Ed., Houghton Mifflin Co., Boston, Mass., 309 p.

Sweet, Muriel, 1962, Common Edible and Useful Plants of the West: Naturegraph Co., Healdsburg, Calif., 64 p.

Weber, William A., 1967, Rocky Mountain Flora: University of Colorado Press, Boulder, Colo. 437 p.

NEWSPAPERS AND MAGAZINES

Alamosa Expositor

Alamosa Independent Journal

San Luis Valley Courier—Alamosa

Valley Courier—Alamosa

Antonito Ledger

Antonito Ledger News

Colorado Springs Daily Gazette

Colorado Springs Weekly Gazette

Denver & Rio Grande Western Magazine, v. 2, no. 7, May 1926.

Durango Semi-Weekly Herald

The Green Light, D&RGW Employees Magazine, 1940 to present.

Silverton La Plata Miner

Silverton Standard and the Miner

Pagosa Springs News

Pueblo Daily Chieftan

Pueblo Weekly Colorado Chieftan

Rio Grande Sun Historical Edition, 1962. Espanola, N. Mex.

Santa Fe Daily New Mexican

Santa Fe Weekly New Mexican

SOURCES FOR GUIDE MAPS

Base maps were prepared from U.S. Geological Survey topographic maps.

The geologic maps were compiled from the following maps and supplemented with personal field work:

Tweto, Ogden, 1979, Geologic Map of Colorado: U.S. Geological Survey.

Burroughs, R.L., and Butler, A.P., 1971. Maps with Rail Log from Antonito, Colo., to Chama, New Mexico: in New Mexico Geological Society Guidebook, 22nd Field Conference, San Luis Basin, Colo., p. 43-67.

Dane, Carle H., and Bachman, George O., 1965, Geologic Map of New Mexico: U.S. Geological Survey.

Lipman, Peter W., 1975, Geologic Map of the Lower Conejos River Canyon Area, Southeastern San Juan Mountains. Colo.: U.S. Geological Survey Map I-901.

Smith, Clay T., and Muehlberger, William R., 1960, Geologic Map of the Rio Chama Country: in New Mexico Geological Society Guidebook, 11th Field Conference, Rio Chama Country.

Steven, T.A., Lipman, P.W., Hail, W.J., Barker, Fred, and Luedke, R.G., 1974, Geologic Map of the Durango Quadrangle, Southwestern Colo.: U.S. Geological Survey Map I-764.

U.S. Bureau of Land Management records on early surveys, southern Colorado and northern New Mexico.

128

ABOUT THE AUTHOR

As a Colorado native, Doris B. Osterwald was introduced, at an early age, to the infinite variety of natural features of the West, and to its fascinating history. These interests led her to study geology. While working on a MA degree at the University of Wyoming, she met her future husband, also a geologist, Dr. Frank W. Osterwald. The couple coauthored Bulletin 45, *Wyoming Mineral Resources* for the Geological Survey of Wyoming in 1952.

Doris and Frank shared many related avocations, including Frank's life-long interest in railroading. Their family enjoyed decades of last runs and special excursion railroading events. On a family outing to ride the Durango-Silverton narrow gauge in 1964, Doris recognized the need for a guidebook combining the railroad history with an explanation of the scenery, geology, and natural history of the route. Ten months later *Cinders & Smoke, a Mile by Mile Guide® for the Durango to Silverton Narrow Gauge Trip* was published.

Cinders & Smoke was followed in 1972 by *Narrow Gauge to Cumbres, a Pictorial History of the Cumbres & Toltec Scenic Railroad* (now out of print), and in 1976, *Ticket to Toltec, a Mile by Mile Guide® for the Cumbres & Toltec Scenic Railroad*. In 1989 she completed *Rocky Mountain Splendor, a Mile by Mile Guide® for Rocky Mountain National Park*. *High Line to Leadville, a Mile by Mile Guide® for the Leadville, Colorado & Southern Railroad*, Colorado's newest tourist railroad was published in 1991. Both *Rocky Mountain Splendor* and *High Line to Leadville* received an award for excellence from the Colorado Connoisseur magazine.

In 1994, *Beyond the Third Rail with Monte Ballough and His Camera* was published. Ballough's photographs document life in the San Juan Mountains of Colorado between 1898 and 1922. The book features D&RG and RGS photos in a portfolio of railroading history, Indian portraits, San Juan scenics, Indian ruins, and the towns of Rico, Dunton, Chama, and Durango.

Rails Thru The Gorge, a Mile by Mile Guide® for the Royal Gorge Route, was published in 2003.

Doris has degrees in geology from the University of Denver and the University of Wyoming. Along with other professional positions, she taught geology in the the Jefferson County [Colorado] Outdoor Education Program at the Mt. Evans and Windy Peak Camps. She is a member of the Colorado Authors' League, National Association of American Pen Women, the Denver Women's Press Club, Colorado Scientific Society, Rocky Mountain Railroad Club, National Railway Historical Society, and the Denver Posse of Westerners.

East Portal Toltec Tunnel

Your Personal Guide
for America's Longest and Highest
Narrow Gauge Steam Railroad

Entering "The Narrows"

9 780931 788277

01095

ISBN 0-931788-27-7

Student Study Guide

for use with

Human Adjustment

John W. Santrock

Prepared by
Kathleen Field and Terry Pettijohn